SPELLBOUND

From Ancient Gods to Modern Merlins
A Time Tour of Myth and Magic

DOMINIC ALEXANDER

Reader's
Digest

The Reader's Digest Association, Inc.
Pleasantville, New York/Montreal

A READER'S DIGEST BOOK

This edition published by The Reader's Digest Association, Inc., by arrangement with Amber Books Ltd

Editorial and design by
Amber Books Ltd
Bradley's Close
74–77 White Lion Street
London N1 9PF

FOR AMBER BOOKS
Project Editor: James Bennett
Design: Neil Rigby
Picture Research: Lisa Wren

FOR READER'S DIGEST
Project Editor: Kimberly Ruderman
Project Copy Editor: Vicki Fischer
Project Designer: George McKeon
Executive Editor, Trade Publishing: Dolores York
Senior Design Director: Elizabeth Tunnicliffe
Editorial Director: Christopher Cavanaugh
Director, Trade Publishing: Christopher T. Reggio
Vice President & Publisher, Trade Publishing: Harold Clarke

Library of Congress Cataloging in Publication Data

Alexander, Dominic.
    Spellbound, from ancient gods to modern Merlins : a time tour of myth and magic /
Dominic Alexander.
      p. cm.
    Includes index.
    ISBN 0-7621-0379-5
    1. Magic--History. I. Title.

BF1589 .A54 2002
133.4'3'09--dc21

                                                        2002018979

Address any comments about *Spellbound* to:
        The Reader's Digest Association, Inc.
        Adult Trade Publishing
        Reader's Digest Road
        Pleasantville, NY 10570-7000

For more Reader's Digest products and information, visit our online store at **rd.com**

Printed in Italy

1 3 5 7 9 10 8 6 4 2

Contents

introduction

The late Douglas Adams, author of *The Hitchhiker's Guide to the Galaxy*, had a favourite joke. A man who did not understand how televisions work was convinced that there must be lots of little men running around inside, doing all the work. An engineer kindly explained it all to him in terms of receivers, amplifiers, cathode-ray tubes and the electromagnetic spectrum. At the end of the explanation, the man nodded, apparently enlightened, and then said: 'But I expect there are just a few little men in there, aren't there?'

Was he confused, misguided or plain stupid? If so, he's not alone. Western Europe may have enjoyed the Age of Enlightenment over 200 years ago, but at the start of the twenty-first century, with the human genome mapped and the age of quantum computing fast approaching, science still has to compete for our vote with religion and magic. And, like political parties, all three have always enjoyed a more complex relationship behind the scenes than their manifestos would suggest.

Alchemy, for instance, is broadly understood as a magical process by which base metals are turned into gold. Roger Bacon was a thirteenth-century English philosopher and scientist, but he was suspected of sorcery because his experiments in physics and chemistry involved alchemy. Even Sir Isaac Newton, the father of modern science, practised alchemy. In fact, early scientists, who hoped to use astrology and alchemy to understand the true nature of matter, can, in a way, be compared to today's theoretical physicists. Alchemy also fostered the development of chemistry. Meanwhile,

In a society where technological marvels are commonplace, Hollywood movies such as Harry Potter and the Philosopher's Stone *allow mankind to indulge in its ancient fascination with magic and witchcraft.*

Renaissance magicians, anxious to keep their magic secret, contributed to science – and espionage – through their interest in cryptography and mathematics.

To many people, astrology probably means a half-curious, half-dismissive glance at their star sign in the paper, but the astrological system familiar today was, in fact, developed by Greek astronomers, and its study did lead to a new understanding of the solar system.

At the heart of astrology is the concept of a magical relationship between separate physical entities – between human beings and planets millions of miles away. It's an idea that finds logical extension in sympathetic magic – the belief that similarity between one thing and another forges a connection between them. The theologian Thomas Aquinas believed that certain herbs and minerals had 'magical' qualities that could be used for healing, and monks of the Middle Ages practised sympathetic magic by means of charms involving plant materials. Lungwort, for instance, was regarded as a cure for consumption (tuberculosis) because its leaves were thought to resemble tubercular lungs. Nothing much has changed today. Take a quick stroll along the main street of your town today and you'll soon find at least one shop stocked to the ceiling with herbal remedies and alternative therapies that orthodox medicine largely – though not entirely – dismisses. A few minutes browsing the Internet should put you in contact with your local homeopath, who purports to cure 'like with like'.

The ancient Egyptians, among others, believed in demons. Plato rationalized this belief by equating a person's good demon with his soul, and everyone is familiar with the image of someone torn between the conflicting counsels of an angel and a little devil. While the ancient Egyptians wore amulets to stave off disease and misfortune, Christianity invested the bones of holy men with similar powers, and New Age healing is awash with protective crystals.

The ancient art of necromancy involved seeking out a man or woman said to have a 'familiar' spirit, who would help summon a dead person to divulge secrets hidden from the living. Today, mediums and Tarot-card readers do much the same.

Just as Egyptian hieroglyphics were believed to have power in their actual form, numerology claims to reveal your destiny from the numerical value of the letters of your name. Certain numbers, such as seven and four, have long been regarded as being innately powerful. But the mystical

Magic is intricately bound up with the rise of civilizations, politics, power, history and culture.

conviction that numbers contained the keys to all mysteries also led to the revival of mathematics.

But in the realm of magic, nothing has exercised such a grip on the human imagination as witchcraft. The great European witch-hunt craze, which lasted from approximately 1450 to 1750, resulted in 40,000–50,000 executions. The madness that seized Salem, Massachusetts, in 1692 led to 24 deaths and gave the world an enduring metaphor for baseless and vindictive persecution. Witch-hunting was still taking place in modern Nigeria as late as 1978, and ritualistic murders for supernatural purposes – though small in number – have been reported in Europe even as this book goes to press. And, on a lighter note, did witches really fly on broomsticks? Or, upstaging Aldous Huxley, Timothy Leary et al. by a few hundred years, was it – in a cultural echo of Amazonian and Indian shamanism – a flight of the spirit induced by psychotropic drugs?

Magic is intricately bound up with the rise of civilizations, politics, power, history and culture. Its story is a densely tangled composite of myths, distortions, truths, half-truths and outright lies. *Spellbound* unties the knots and sifts the facts from the fantasy to provide a fascinating account that will horrify and appall, charm and amuse, inform and delight. If you've ever wondered where the expressions 'hair of the dog' and 'you'll pull through' originate, or what 'abracadabra' has to do with the Great Plague, or if you're even mildly curious about the role of Irish fairies in the building trade, read on and you'll find out, about these and all the other 'little men in there'.

Among the most famous witches of Western literature are the three who appear in Shakespeare's Macbeth. *The witches predict Macbeth's bloody rise to become king of Scotland.*

magic and civilization

Intriguing tales of magic and sorcery have been passed down through the ages, undoubtedly embroidered, embellished and edited. Such tales, so much a part of our human heritage, are inextricably linked with the development of civilization. Yet given that these tales are so deeply entrenched in practically every culture throughout the world, magic was rarely seen as a thing apart from the natural way of the world. In fact, in ancient times magic and religion were practically indistinguishable.

A GREY AREA

Magic and religion continually overlapped in ancient times. The gods were believed to be able and willing – or worse, unwilling – to intervene in the day-to-day affairs of the ordinary people who turned to them in all matters. Most misfortunes – disease, famine, enemy attacks – were attributed to hostile supernatural forces, usually incorporating malevolent gods, and people appealed to their protector gods to guard them against such forces. These appeals were considered – at any rate by those doing the appealing – to be a religious act. Magic, on the other hand, was considered to be an attempt to manipulate or control supernatural spirits specifically for personal gain. Clearly in ancient times there was a very fine line between magic and religion.

MAGIC VERSUS RELIGION

The biblical story of Balaam illustrates the dilemma of identifying precisely what was magic and what was religion. As hordes of Israelites began descending on Palestine from Egypt, Balak, the panic-stricken king of Moab, decided he needed supernatural assistance and hastily sent for the most powerful magician-priest he knew: Balaam from nearby Mesopotamia. Ordered by the king to curse the Israelites and halt their invasion, Balaam climbed the highest mountain in the region and performed a special rite: he prepared seven altars upon which he sacrificed seven oxen and seven rams to the Baal (the Baals were local gods who traditionally lived in 'high places', such as mountains). This performance should have persuaded the Baal to curse and destroy the Israelites, but meanwhile, the God of Israel intervened and forced Balaam to bless the Israelites instead. Three times King Balak urged Balaam to curse the Israelites, and three times God intervened and made Balaam give them his blessing. Here lies the dilemma: while the authors of the Bible regarded Balaam as no more than a magician for appealing to supernatural gods rather than to their own 'true' God, other ancient peoples considered him a priest, one who practised their own form of religion.

The authors of the Bible dismissed the 'religions' of both Babylon (a city in ancient Mesopotamia, some 88 km [55 miles] south of Baghdad) and ancient Egypt as mere magic and trickery. In an ancient battle of the giants, Moses himself took on the so-called 'sorcerers of Egypt', in a 'magic duel' instigated by the pharaoh. In the contest Moses orders Aaron to fling down a staff that will – by the power of the God of the Israelites – transform into a serpent at the pharaoh's feet. The Egyptian sorcerers do likewise, relying on the powers of their own gods.

Behind this myth lies the reality that surviving staffs from this period are often carved in the shape of a cobra. The contest of magic continued after this first demonstration, and at the climax, Moses led the people of Israel out of Egypt, commanding the Red Sea to part with his staff.

An eighteenth-century Hebrew service book shows Egyptians drowning in the Red Sea after the Israelites safely pass through the parted waters.

Three times King Balak urged Balaam to curse the Israelites, and three times God intervened and made Balaam give them his blessing.

On his way to serve King Balak, Balaam is confronted by an angel of God commanding him to speak only according to God's will.

A GRUESOME READING

Many of the magical practices described in the Bible originated in the early Mesopotamian civilizations. In the Sumerian civilization, which flourished in southern Mesopotamia around the third millennium BC, each city was ruled by a king who adopted the role of 'tenant farmer' for his own powerful patron, his city-god. Ongoing battles for land and water between the rival kings of Sumeria meant that the kings regularly sought help and advice from their city-god. It was crucial, therefore, for each king to appease him in all sorts of ways.

Animal sacrifice was one of the central rites of appeasement. It had a dual purpose: to gain the city-god's favour, and to try to predict the future. Since it was the custom to conduct sacred rites in 'high places', as close to the heavens as possible, the Sumerians built ziggurats (early pyramids) and, on top of these, constructed shrines to the gods. The sacrifices were carried out there, after which the officiating priest – or magician – inspected the animal's entrails to see if the blood, gristle and bile revealed any omens of the future. Apparently the most useful organ to 'read' was the liver. Indeed, many clay models of animal livers dating back to this period have been discovered.

SEARCHING FOR OMENS IN CURIOUS PLACES

Liver reading, or hepatoscopy, survived into the religious practices of the Babylonian empire in the early second millennium BC. It spread to Palestine and to the Hittites of Anatolia (Turkey) and was also practised in ancient Greece and Rome. But there were plenty of other, less grisly ways of divining the will of a deity, such as rhabdomancy (water divining) or the study of trees.

Trees were considered to be sacred symbols linking the earth and sky, and thus the rustling of leaves in the wind, the budding of twigs and even the shadows cast by trees could all be studied for omens. The Bible even hints that tree observance was practised in ancient Israel, and various prophets were associated with trees, notably the prophetess Deborah, who 'dwelled under a palm tree'.

SECRETS OF THE DEAD

Necromancy – the summoning of dead spirits – is one of history's most enduring magic practices. In ancient times, all manner of strange superstitious beliefs surrounded death and the dead. It was a commonplace and firmly held belief that those who had 'gone beyond' had knowledge of all sorts of sinister secrets denied to the living. Naturally some of the secrets would have involved future predictions, and the curious living were eager to find out what lay in store for them. To contact the dead, people would seek out a man or woman reputed to have a 'familiar spirit'. With the help of this spirit, a dead person could be summoned and asked questions.

To protect themselves from harmful magic, Egyptians wore amulets like this symbolic heart, which was meant to defend a person's soul.

Necromancy had a fearful reputation even in ancient times, and was a magic of last resort. One of the most famous ancient figures to have resorted to this dangerous art was the Israelite king, Saul. Saul, living at the end of the second millennium BC, had already outlawed magic which relied on 'familiar spirits', but soon he was desperate for precisely that magic. Saul was at war with the Philistines, and was fearful that he would lose. His own seers could not bring him any advice from God, so breaking his own law, he went to the 'witch of Endor'. This woman had a demonic familiar spirit which gave her the power to raise the ghost of the great prophet Samuel. Samuel appeared to King Saul, but was angry at being summoned from the underworld, and foretold the king's defeat and doom. This story was a warning against the use of dangerous magic. Necromancy offended God, and could not bring anything but misery.

The witch of Endor, imagined by a nineteenth-century artist, summoning Samuel while Saul falls to his knees before the great prophet.

GODS IN THE HEAVENS

Perhaps in the long term the most fruitful form of divination was the study of the heavens themselves. Indeed, genuine astronomical knowledge developed out of this practice. The movements of the heavenly bodies were associated with the gods, and the ancient Mesopotamian civilizations in particular were noted for the development of early astronomy and mathematical systems. During this period, forms of knowledge that today seem semi-scientific, but were in fact part of the complex of religion and divinatory magic, were limited to the priestly caste, since only they could read or write.

The earliest astronomical text dates from the old Babylonian

A painting from an Egyptian mummy case, showing the god Ptah. These paintings were probably an integral part of the magic needed to guide the deceased to rebirth in the afterlife.

kingdom, between 1900 and 1600 BC. The Babylonians identified seven heavenly bodies – the Sun, the moon, and five visible planets that provided the basis for their version of astronomy. They believed that future events could be predicted by studying the movement of the 'gods in the heavens'. Each planet was identified with a Babylonian deity; for example, Venus was the goddess Ishtar. Even at this early date many of the general characteristics later attributed to the planets were already in place: Mercury was associated with intellectual ability, Mars with aggression and Venus with love.

BEJEWELLED AMULETS AND PROTECTIVE SHELLS

The astrological system of the Babylonians was taken up by other ancient civilizations, and at the end of the first millennium BC, the ancient Greeks developed it further into the form that passed on to later Western civilizations – and which still exists today. The overwhelming abundance of information concerning magic in the ancient world is associated with the worship of the dominant gods of the kings and the elite priestly caste. Most ordinary people also probably practised forms of magic and divination, but information about their lives at this time is sketchy at best. Ancient archaeological records do at least provide a few hints about ordinary people's participation in magic. There is evidence that people wore protective amulets to stave off disease and misfortune, ranging from exotic, jewelled creations, obviously owned by the upper classes, to simple pieces made from shells.

MAGIC AND RELIGION IN ANCIENT EGYPT

It is particularly difficult to distinguish between magic and religion in ancient Egypt since priests were defined as specialists who conducted magical ceremonies and sought to appease one or more gods, rather than teachers and legislators of morality.

As in Sumeria and Palestine, each ancient Egyptian city existed under the protection of its own city-god. The god Ptah was worshipped at Memphis, Horus at Edfu, Amun at Thebes, and Osiris at Busiris. Gradually the cities were united into larger kingdoms, the Upper Kingdom being northern Egypt, and the Lower Kingdom around the southern stretch of the River Nile. Ancient Egypt's most notable rulers were the pyramid builders of the Old Kingdom (2900–2200 BC), who united the Upper and Lower kingdoms, making Egypt the most powerful state then in existence. The pyramids, and later the royal tombs, preserved in stone many religious inscriptions, known as 'the pyramid texts', dating from the twenty-fourth to the twenty-second centuries BC. These ancient records of mythology set the pattern for subsequent writings.

DIVINE WORDS

No standard ancient Egyptian collection of national myths has ever been discovered, so it is through the fragments of the pyramid texts and later funereal writings that information about life in ancient Egypt has been revealed. The funereal writings were ritual instructions to assist the kings in their passage from this life to the 'other world', where they would assume their place among the gods in heaven. Originally found only in royal tombs, such writings gradually began to appear in the tombs of high officials of the Egyptian state. By the seventeenth century BC the *Book of the Dead* appeared on royal shrouds and funeral equipment, and soon afterwards passages from this 'book' written on papyrus were buried in the tombs of priestly families. The writings contained parts of the diverse system of mythology relating to the reckoning of the soul after death and onwards through the afterlife. Hieroglyphics – the system of writing used for these texts – themselves were regarded as having power in their actual form. The word 'hieroglyph' means 'divine word'.

GETTING IN TOUCH WITH THE 'FIRST TIME'

The mythical narratives contained in the funereal texts were essentially spells to help the soul of a dead king pass easily though the underworld. Yet the

(*continued on page 20*)

> The funereal writings were ritual instructions to assist the kings in their passage from this life to the 'other world' where they would assume their place among the gods in Heaven.

Was Egypt the 'mother of magicians'?

Illustrating Egypt's great reputation in the ancient world is the Greek legend of Solon, a great Greek ruler of the sixth century BC, who travelled to Egypt to meet with Egyptian priests. They insulted him, however, scoffing at Greek ignorance and dismissing his country's youthful civilization as 'ignorant' compared to that of Egypt.

The great pyramid at Giza was already so old in the second century BC that some believed it to be the work of ancient magicians.

In describing Egypt as the 'mother of magicians' in the early third century AD, the Christian church father Clement of Alexandria was simply following the long-standing tradition of attributing the origins of magic and esoteric wisdom to this most ancient and widely admired of cultures. Indeed, the very building of the pyramids of Egypt is surrounded by myths of magic and sorcery.

Egyptian records provide some genuine historical figures associated with the building of the pyramids, but once the sophisticated architectural knowledge employed to build the structures had been lost, later traditions inevitably associated them with magic. For example, Imhotep, the architect who built the Step pyramid at Saqqara in the twenty-seventh century BC, was described as a magician by the second century BC. He was reputed to have achieved the building of the pyramid through his ability to read ancient magical texts. Another legend has him tutored in magic by the god Thoth. It is understandable, however, that 'modern' Egyptians of the second century BC might well be preoccupied with fanciful myths of obscure texts dating back 3,000 years or more.

Egyptians were fascinated with the idea of secret texts and were quick to label anyone in the past who achieved anything remarkable a magician. Prince Khaemwaset (1279–1213 BC) was a high priest of Memphis as well as a keen architect and restorer of Egypt's already ancient tombs and pyramids. Yet in a cycle of stories dating between the second century BC and the second century AD, the prince was portrayed as a magician who had a vast knowledge of the esoteric. The legend tells how the magician-prince discovered the hiding place of the god Thoth's most secret book of spells. But when he tried to steal the book, he incurred the wrath of the god, who accused him of being too unworthy to receive such powerful knowledge. The prince seems to have escaped any punishment from the god, and the moral of the story was that there were limits to the magical knowledge that even the greatest and wisest of humans should have. The dangers encountered in the search for magical knowledge became proverbial in many stories of this time. The original story of the Sorcerer's Apprentice, about a fictional magician who studied at Memphis, was told by the Roman writer Lucian. Today this story is known through charming and comical scenes in the Disney movie *Fantasia*, but in the ancient world the story was a dark warning of the dangers of uncontrolled magic.

Some aspects of Egyptian magic mythology survive even to this day. Sets of obscure symbols and designs and the modern perception of a magician as a kindly bearded old man equipped with a wand, derives ultimately from the Greek and Roman perceptions of Egyptian magic that have passed down through the ages.

An Egyptian image of the god Osiris, who was murdered by his brother Seth and resurrected by his wife Isis. Osiris was a major god of the underworld.

Heka, the Egyptian concept of a magical energy spread through creation, may be compared to the mystical 'Force' which forms part of the mythology of the Star Wars *universe, and is mastered by the Jedi knights. (Courtesy Lucasfilm)*

texts also contained spells designed to cure mundane ailments, such as headaches. The power of the spells enshrined in the funereal texts relied on the officiating priest's ability to access the creative power of the 'First Time' – this was the period of mythical history when the gods created the world.

MAGIC POWERS FOR NEARLY ALL

Many religions believe that one creator god made the universe by imposing order on primordial chaos. It followed that this god, being the original source of power, was also the ultimate source of magic. One of the Egyptian words for magic, heka, was also the name of the entity who was sometimes identified as the creator god. Heka was not just a god, but was also an energy spread through much of the universe. (You could compare it to the Jedi 'Force' in the movie *Star Wars*.) As a result, all supernatural spirits and beings also had innate heka, and could therefore perform magic. Heka was the creative force which fuelled magic, but associated with heka was akhu, which translates as sorcery or spells. Akhu was the knowledge and power to use the magical, creative force of heka. Neither heka nor akhu was considered inherently good or evil in itself, but both could be used to perform acts of good or evil. Even so, reports of magic being used to harm others are extremely rare in the records of ancient Egypt before the period of Roman rule in 30 BC.

It was not just the gods and goddesses of ancient Egypt who had this magical power. Kings also possessed heka, as did those who were physically different, such as dwarfs. Hardly surprisingly, the dead were particularly associated with akhu, since in the underworld they could gain the knowledge to use magic. But the catalogue of those possessing these supernatural qualities does not end there. Beyond figures with intrinsic magical powers, others, particularly priests, could also access magic through ceremonies and spells.

MYTHS TO HELP MAGIC

Priests could not access magical power on their own since they were only ordinary men with no magical power in their nature. They needed to call upon the magic that resided in the gods themselves, and they did this by telling mythological stories. Just as the written word had power in itself, written stories telling of the gods' magical deeds could recreate their magic.

The goddess Isis was one of the most popular deities in ancient Egypt, and like all the gods, her magic could be accessed by mere mortals. Her great magical power was demonstrated when she brought

The gods Seth and Horus are pictured here pouring 'life' over the pharaoh Seti I (c.1310 BC). Seth was often characterized as a violent and unpredictable god, but he was not necessarily seen as malevolent.

She then put a spell on the clay snake to make it come to life at the right time. When Ra walked by the place where she had hidden the snake, it came to life and bit him.

her husband, Osiris, back from the dead. The god Seth, a bringer of chaos, had murdered Osiris and dismembered his body. As in so many Egyptian myths, the story exists in several different versions, but the general theme is that Isis used her akhu to prevent or reverse the decay of her dead husband's body. In one version of the story, Isis sewed his dismembered body back together. Thereafter Osiris was identified with death and the underworld. Because Isis had healed Osiris, the goddess was regularly invoked in healing spells. She was also regarded as the goddess most sympathetic to the plight of the poor and powerless in Egyptian society.

As in many ancient mythologies, the Egyptian gods appear like a petty and squabbling family, each god jealous of the others and likely to cause harm and violence on a whim. Isis was no different from the other gods, and many stories show her cunning and resourcefulness in pursuing her plans. Isis was determined to have the most magical power of all the gods, and she was reputed to know the names and identities of millions of gods and spirits. Even knowing the true name of a spirit gave her power over it. There was only one god whose true, magical name she did not know. This was her father, and the father of all the gods, Ra.

The story of how Isis learned Ra's true name was used by the Egyptians as part of a spell to cure snakebites. The reason for this lies in the curious magic Isis used to make Ra tell his secret. Now Ra was an old god, and though it might seem undignified for a god, the unfortunate fact was that he dribbled a great deal. Isis knew that if she collected some of Ra's saliva, she could use it as an ingredient in a spell to gain power over him. In the magic of any culture, anything personal to an individual, especially hair and fingernails, can be used in spells directed against him or her. So Isis secretly gathered some of the old god's saliva which had fallen to earth, and baked it into the clay model of a snake.

She then put a spell on the clay snake to make it come to life at the right time. When

This Utchat talisman is an example of the kind of sumptuous amulet which a rich Egyptian might have worn. It features the 'eye of Horus', a god often associated with healing magic.

Ra walked by the place where she had hidden the snake, it came to life and bit him. Because his own saliva was part of the snake, the bite caused the god terrible agony. Ra called upon Isis to heal him, but she claimed that she could not cure him without knowing his true name. Ra was reluctant to tell the secret since he knew the power it would give Isis, but in the end the pain was too much. Knowing the god's true name, Isis cured him, and was then the most powerful magician among the gods.

THE IMPORTANCE OF HORUS

Horus, son of Isis, also was an important figure in Egyptian magic. When Seth killed Horus's father, Osiris, Horus sought revenge, but was badly wounded while battling with Seth. Thereafter, Horus was regarded as a mythical, magical figure for his dual role as both saviour – for restoring order after Seth killed Osiris – and victim, having been wounded in noble combat. Horus, variously described as 'the good doctor', 'the saviour' and 'the enchanter', was particularly revered by the kings of Egypt, who respected his duality. In many spells, the sick person would be identified with Horus, so that, like the god, he or she would quickly recover.

Seth was clearly not regarded as a wholly malevolent demon until much later in ancient Egyptian history, for he too was featured in early healing spells. He was portrayed merely as hot-tempered and aggressive, but never evil. One legend tells of Seth's punishment for inappropriate lust: his own semen rushed to his head, resulting in a splitting headache. Thereafter, one of the most popular spells to rid someone of a headache was to call upon Isis to cure Seth at the command of Ra.

POKING FUN AT THE GODS

Such was the magical power of the written word that it was considered risky even to record certain mythological events. It was particularly taboo to hint at the vulnerability of the gods – let alone to represent it in words or pictures.

The great pyramids of Egypt's Giza plateau have mystified generations. Even in the twentieth century, writers have speculated that the knowledge required to construct them so accurately must have been gained by supernatural means.

Even to depict a temporary triumph of chaos over the world order imposed and governed by the gods risked chaos becoming a reality.

Yet some particular spells required examples of godly vulnerability to be recorded. One way around this problem was to belittle specific characters by the manner in which they were portrayed: the god Seth, for example, was depicted as a comically tiny figure compared with the normal-size figures of Horus and Isis. In this way, Seth was ridiculed satisfactorily for the purposes of the spell, but without running the risk of cosmic disorder sweeping in and taking hold.

CONDITIONS FOR CASTING SPELLS

The written word was thought to be a powerful source of magic in itself, and hieroglyphs were an essential part of Egyptian priests' elaborate ceremonies.

While powerful writings and a mighty heritage of mythology were central to the crafts of the Egyptian priests, their ceremonies relied on more than just appeals to mythology. Some of the earliest pyramid texts, dating from the twenty-seventh century BC, reveal a visionary and somewhat ecstatic quality in the narratives, suggesting that as part of their magic ceremonies the priests went into a sort of trance during which they journeyed spiritually to the

'other world'. This suggests that elements of early Egyptian religion grew out of shamanistic beliefs. However, as the importance of the written word increased along with literacy, and temples became rich institutions financed by the Egyptian kings, the early shamanistic quality of the magic ceremonies was replaced by more standard and rigid rituals.

PREPARING FOR MAGIC

Before a magic ceremony, during which the temple priest would try to access the powerful forces of the 'First Time', he needed to purify himself ritually. The night before the ceremony he would abstain from sleeping with his wife, and would eat neither fish nor pork. Sometimes the priest would shave not only his head but his entire body, and undertake a complicated bathing ritual. A sacred space had to be created for the ceremony: a special room was spread with clean sand and scented with sacred incense. Only then could the ceremony begin.

POWERFUL NUMBERS AND RITUAL OBJECTS

Many of the spells that survive from ancient Egypt were clearly meant to be read aloud; many even contain detailed instructions on the intonation to use. The spell usually contained various formulae that had to be repeated. Four repetitions was common. The four times represented the four directions – north, south, east and west – from which malevolent forces might try to counteract a protection spell. Seven was an equally common number and appears in the magic traditions of many cultures. That number is most likely related to the seven visible heavenly bodies: the Sun, the Moon, Mercury, Venus, Mars, Jupiter and Saturn.

The magic that was practised by the Egyptian priests was an expensive business, and was restricted to the temples, which only royalty and priests could enter. Richer citizens commissioned their own magic outside the

This wax figure from second-century AD Egypt was used as a sort of 'voodoo' doll meant to influence another person. An important part of the magic was the human hair pushed into the figure's navel.

Look-alikes, punning priests and gruesome ingredients

Much of Egyptian magic's rationale relied on coincidental resemblances and connections between things. A shell, therefore, which could be said to resemble a human eye, would be regarded as having a specific magical connection with the eye and would be used in a healing spell.

Symbolism played a similar role in most magic ceremonies. Colours were always of great significance. Black and green, signifying regeneration and growth, were incorporated in healing spells. The colour could come from something simple, like a green herb, or it could require the bloody sacrifice of an animal. The blood or milk of black animals was particularly prized in spells which required the colour black, and the essence of the colour was thought to be transferred via the blood. So the blood of a black calf was thought to restore grey hair to black, and spells invoking the ginger-haired god Seth used anything coloured red.

Egyptian priests, rarely noted for their sense of humour or comic timing, were known to use puns in their magic spells. In one spell, Seth was called upon in his role as a thief to protect beer, because the words for theft and beer sound similar in the ancient Egyptian language. Dream interpretation worked on the same principle. To dream of a donkey meant that you would be promoted – the words for 'donkey' and 'promotion' being only one letter different. And to dream of a harp (bnt) meant that evil (bint) would befall you.

Some instructions for the casting of spells seem downright bizarre today. For example, one Graeco-Egyptian papyrus bids the magician to use only an olive-wood stool that has never been sat upon. In fact, this relates to the necessity for purity of both the magician and his surroundings when performing a spell.

By the time the Romans began to rule Egypt in the late first century BC, a new type of secular magician had appeared who was not a temple priest, used written magic, and would sell his services to private clients. Surviving magical texts of the period recorded some of the strange ingredients used by this new breed of magician. Some ingredients were expensive and exotic – notably gold leaf, Syrian honey and frankincense – while others were downright bizarre, such as bat's blood, double-tailed lizards, and the hair of a murdered man. The list goes on: crocodile dung, the navel of a male crocodile, and the semen of the god Amun. However, records reveal that some of the more curious ingredients were not really so strange after all: the dung was in fact Ethiopian soil, the male crocodile's navel was just pond weed, and the god's semen was a humble leek.

An abraxas stone, an amulet popular in the Roman era. It features a figure with twisted legs, a common way of representing spirits or gods with particular associations with magic.

temple and lesser priests were paid to officiate at funerals and perform special spells. There also were certain ritual objects that carried magic powers beyond the temple. One such object was a curved ivory wand covered in magical inscriptions. The wands were usually decorated with one or more creatures believed to have magical significance. The hippopotamus was particularly revered. An ivory wand would have been an expensive item, but there were cheaper wands, which may have been used by more ordinary Egyptians. However, when the great state temples opened their doors to ordinary people during the latter half of the second millennium BC, the wands disappeared.

EVERYDAY MAGIC

It was not only priests who practised magic in ancient Egypt. Some people among the general population practised their own versions of the priest's spells. As early as the third millennium BC evidence exists of officially recognized village doctors who practised a combination of practical remedies and magical solutions called sunu. By the second millennium BC another shadowy figure had appeared, called a sau. A sau, who could be male or female, engaged in both practical medicine and minor magic feats. Most of the female saus were probably midwives, who also made protective charms for pregnant women and children. Another group called rekhets – again, including both men and women – had a slightly more sinister repertoire of skills. They employed a type of magic that had always existed in Egypt, but of which little is known because it was not written about by literate priests. The rekhets were supposedly able to contact the dead and identify the evil spirits who were causing illness in their communities.

This luxurious string of amulets, from the Egyptian Middle Kingdom (c.1991–1750 BC), features golden cowrie shells, which were thought to protect pregnant women.

CHARMS TO WARD OFF EVIL

Archaeological records show that one of the most popular ways to ward off evil and misfortune was to wear a charm or amulet. In ancient Egypt everyone wore such items, and they were exported and copied all over the world.

The ibis-headed Egyptian god Thoth, here shown holding symbols of strength and life, was seen as a primary source of magical knowledge in the first millennium BC.

Women and children were always bedecked with amulets because these two groups were thought to be most vulnerable to attack by the supernatural forces which caused childhood diseases and difficult births. Amulets were made from a great variety of materials. Cowrie shells, resembling the human eye or female genitalia, were commonly worn around the waist on a chain to protect a woman's fertility – the shell's resemblance to a particular part of the body was central to its magic power. Amulets might also be made from cat hair or herbs wrapped in linen. Sometimes honey was incorporated in an amulet, the reason being that if honey tasted sweet to humans, then it must, logically, taste bitter to demons and would therefore drive them away.

DEMONS WHO DO GOOD AS WELL AS EVIL

For most of its history, Egyptian religion did not officially recognize the existence of hostile gods or malevolent demons. It is unclear whether demons were added to the religion later on, or whether ordinary people had always believed in them but their beliefs were suppressed by the state religion. Most human cultures feel the need for an explanation for evil and misfortune, and in a culture dominated by the supernatural, demons were the obvious culprits. Each of the gods had a certain number of lesser demons that appear as servants or metaphysical aspects of the god's power.

Anubis, the jackal-headed god on the right of this picture from the Egyptian Book of the Dead, *was an important source of magic in later Egyptian religion.*

One of the most reviled of the evil gods was the goddess Sekhmet. She had seven demons under her control, known as bau, meaning arrow. In summer and during the harvest season, Sekhmet's bau were particularly feared in case they ruined the crops, and were commonly blamed for disease and pestilence. Yet even this goddess could be used for good. Magicians believed that the demons of Sekhmet, like those of other gods, could be controlled by magic. The seven bau of Sekhmet were even called upon by magicians to counter the evil eye. It might seem strange that Egyptian magicians tried to control gods and demons in this way, but they thought about supernatural spirits as if they were forces of nature

Early Christians invented a myth that the Greek Sibyl prophesied the coming of Christ. In this way the ancient religions were shown to have foreseen their replacement by Christianity.

as much as spiritual individuals. Magic was a kind of technology to control the supernatural.

Magic could be used by humans to control the supernatural, but it was the gods themselves who had to give humans the magical knowledge. The two most important sources of magic during the first millennium BC and the period of Roman rule were Thoth, the ibis-headed god, and Anubis, the jackal-headed god. The ancient Greeks identified Thoth with Hermes, their own god of secret knowledge. Anubis was the guardian of magical secrets and, like other gods of the late period, had a host of messenger demons. These messenger demons carried knowledge and other things of help to humanity, but just as the bau of Sekhmet could be used for good purposes, the magician could use the demons of Thoth or Anubis for evil purposes. The magic and the gods of ancient Egypt were not moral beings as we imagine gods should be, they were simply sources of knowledge and power. As everyone knows, knowledge and power can be used for both good and ill doings.

THE GREEKS AND ROMANS EMBRACE EGYPT

Although by the end of the first millennium BC Egypt was no longer an independent power, its antiquity and great monuments were much admired by other cultures, particularly the Greeks and Romans who dominated the Mediterranean. Egypt's magical traditions attracted both admirers and doubters. Even so, the curious Greeks embraced many aspects of Egyptian magic and religion, fusing them with their own traditions of magic and secret knowledge.

After the conquests of Alexander the Great in the late fourth century BC, the Greek culture became predominant among the civilizations of the Eastern Mediterranean. Under Greek influence the notion spread that magic had originated in Egypt. This is even reflected in the writings of the early Christians. According to Acts 7:22, Moses 'was learned in all the wisdom of the Egyptians, and he was might in words and deeds'. This statement illustrates how during the Hellenistic period Moses was esteemed as one of the great magicians of antiquity. This notion ran entirely contrary to the views of the Jewish tradition, wherein Moses' miraculous powers were believed to have come directly from God, and were not due to any personal magical ability on Moses' part.

The Romans, like many other ancient cultures, sacrificed bulls and used their entrails to predict the future or read the will of the gods.

THE JEWISH REJECTION OF MAGIC
The Jewish religion was almost uniquely unbelieving in magic from an early

Tireſias Thebanus.

Iuno abcæcavit ſed mî pro lumine adempto
Iuppiter omnipotens ſcire futura dedit.

The mythical Greek prophet Teiresias, shown in this seventeenth-century illustration, was struck blind by the goddess Athena after he accidentally saw her bathing. In compensation, Zeus gave him the power of prophecy.

date. The books of Leviticus and Deuteronomy, written around the fifth century BC, contain a set of laws plainly forbidding all manner of magical practices and belief. 'There shall not be found among you any one that maketh his son or daughter pass through the fire, or that useth divination, or an observer of times, or an enchanter or a witch. Or a charmer, or a consulter with familiar spirits, or a wizard, or a necromancer' (Deut. 18:10–12).

This comprehensive list banned all practices that involved contact with any spirit other than the Lord. Since almost all divination practices involved the summoning up of ancestral spirits or minor demons, this meant that only the chief priest to the Lord could act as an oracle. There was only one kind of divination that could be defended as lawful. Men known as 'observers of times' compiled calendars of lucky and unlucky days for particular clients or events. The compilers of these calendars could claim that they were using only 'scientific' knowledge, but they could also be suspected of appealing to spirits other than the Lord.

While the ancient Jewish religion did not actually deny the existence of spirits more minor than the Lord, it did insist that it was useless to seek their assistance. However strongly the biblical laws condemned the use of magic, they did not claim that it did not work. The Jewish king Saul was reported to have consulted a witch who, using necromancy, summoned the prophet Samuel. It is certain that these magical practices continued to be used by many people at the village level of Jewish society, despite the severity of the biblical laws.

CULTURES TURN AGAINST MAGIC

Although the Jewish rejection of magic was an exception in the ancient world, eventually it became part of the dominant tradition of European culture. While the Greek culture in general was highly receptive to the concept of magic, many individuals were highly doubtful of and even openly hostile to magical practices. When this Greek suspicion and the Jewish suppression of magic fused in the development of Christianity, magic came to be condemned. But before this condemnation, in fact for most of its history, ancient Greece embraced magic and its use was widespread.

MAGIC BEGINS TO LOSE ITS GRIP

Unlike the Egyptians, the ancient Greeks had no coherent structure in which magic could be elaborated and practised professionally. The Greek priesthood was divided into small, local cults that could not altogether define the nature of the gods and dictate how they should be contacted and worshipped. Religion was largely a civic affair, which increasingly excluded magic. From the fifth century BC Greek philosophers called Sophists (from the Greek for

A popular story theme from ancient times tells of a sorcerer with a bag magically containing great winds. This woodcut shows a sorcerer selling his bag, which is tied with three knots.

'wisdom') developed a form of rationalistic thought which formed the basis for systems of logic and philosophy that are familiar today.

In due course, the philosophers formulated the idea of a rational deity who ordered creation for the eventual benefit of humanity. Within this rational universe, it became difficult for the educated classes of Greek society to embrace magic in all its traditional forms.

Nevertheless, magic continued to be practised in the Greek and Roman worlds, with witches and magicians making numerous appearances in Greek and Latin literature. But magic was always marginalized and isolated from civic religion. The traditional gods continued to be worshipped as a civic necessity, and some forms of divination were practised as part of their cults – such as reading the intestines of sacrificial animals. But many other aspects of magical beliefs were viewed as suspect, tainted with dubious foreign influences. Yet even though magic was scorned by so many, it was nevertheless practised widely in Greek cities and the countryside. Indeed, Sosiphanes, a fourth-century BC poet, remarked that 'every chit of a girl in Thessaly can command the moon down from the heaven by magic incantations – believe that if you will'.

One of the earliest appearances of a diviner in Greek literature is the blind man Teiresias, in Sophocles' play *Oedipus Rex*. Teiresias can predict the future and reveal secret knowledge. 'Lore sacred and profane, all heavenly and earthly knowledge are within your grasp,' says King Oedipus to Teiresias, yet when the blind man's utterings displease the king, Oedipus dismisses him as a 'scheme-hatching magos'. Although the term 'magos' just means magician, it was used here as an insult. The term magos also referred to Persian priests who practised certain types of divination, and to wandering magicians who would foretell the future for a fee, in much the same way that fortune-tellers today demand that customers cross their palm with silver. These practices continued to be denounced by Greek commentators as blasphemous and giving a poor impression of the gods.

Magic in the Greek culture survived largely through various tales and legends, with pieces of hearsay evidence thrown in for good measure. In these magic fables, exotic images were conjured up. There were monstrous and mysterious happenings, more often than not foreign, to add to their allure. Homer's *Odyssey* tells of the adventures of the Greek hero Odysseus (also known as Ulysses) as he attempted to sail home after the Trojan War. Having angered the gods, Odysseus and his crew are led into strange and dangerous

Magic in the Greek culture survived largely through various tales and legends, with pieces of hearsay evidence thrown in for good measure.

lands. Naturally, the story contains a fair amount of magic, and some of the more captivating incidents have been retold in myths and legends throughout the centuries.

BAG OF WIND

In one incident, Odysseus is given a gift – a leather, ox-skin bag – by his host, Aeolus. Aeolus had been given 'charge of the winds' by the god Zeus and had 'imprisoned the boisterous energies of all the winds'. The gift was intended to prevent Odysseus's ship from being blown off course. But unfortunately his greedy crew was convinced that the bag contained gold and silver, so they opened it and their ship was blown completely off course.

This is the earliest appearance of the 'magician with a bag of wind' motif. It returns in stories in the Middle Ages and later still in nineteenth-century German folk tales. But in the medieval European recounting of the tale, the purpose of the bag of wind is to make a ship sail faster, rather than prevent it from sailing in the wrong direction.

An eighteenth-century engraving showing Circe, the great enchantress of Greek myth, performing her spells, equipped with a wand and surrounded by snakes and spirits.

CIRCE THE ENCHANTRESS

Homer's tales also introduce a witch figure – the earliest such appearance in Greek mythology. She is Circe the enchantress, daughter of the Sun. Shortly after their disastrous experience with the bag of wind, Odysseus's crew make landfall on an island and set out to explore. The men come upon a clearing in a glade where there stands a beautiful house built of polished stone. Nearby are wolves and lions that unaccountably begin to fawn over the men – little do they know that the animals are under Circe's spell. Circe emerges

Circe turns Odysseus's men into pigs in this engraving of 1610. Here Circe is imagined as an ugly witch figure, rather than the minor goddess of the Greek legend.

from the house and invites the men to a feast. But the food is laced with a drug that leaves the men in a stupor. After the feast, Circe turns the befuddled men into pigs and drives them into a pigpen, locking them in securely. Brave Odysseus sets out to rescue his companions despite dire warnings from the handful of crew members who had managed to escape from the island.

Fortunately, Odysseus is a favourite of Hermes and the god appears to him in a forest and gives him the antidote to Circe's drug, a powerful herb called moly. Odysseus uses it to force Circe to turn the pigs back into men with the help of a special ointment, and once free they set sail again for home. At the time of Homer's Greece, folk medicine – secret herbal remedies, tinctures, potions and ointments – was used for healing, rather than Egyptian incantations and ceremonies. So it is not surprising that the enchantress Circe should have among her medical supplies herbal drugs to dull the senses, as well as ointments to reverse the effects. These drugs and poisons were regarded by the Greeks as magical creations rather than simply natural substances.

THE FIRST WITCHES

The fact that it was mainly the women of the Greek household who administered medicine gives further credence to tales of Circe and her cornucopia of herb-based pharmaceuticals. But just as the women of the Greek household had a knowledge of healing medicines, it was likely that they would also possess the skills to concoct harmful drugs and poisons. The folktale figure of a witch arose directly from this fear and was compounded by men's fear of women's disruptive powers. Indeed, the god Hermes warns Odysseus not to be lured into Circe's bed unless she makes a sacred vow not to harm him. Otherwise, Hermes tells him gravely, Circe 'will rob you of your courage and your manhood'. The threat that Circe would render Odysseus impotent is a charge that was levelled against witches in almost every society, most commonly during the witch-hunts of the sixteenth and seventeenth centuries.

APPEALING TO THE DEAD

The earliest account of necromancy also appears in the *Odyssey*. After Odysseus has defeated Circe, he wants to resume his homeward journey. But Circe tells him that he must first travel to Hades, the underworld, and consult with the blind prophet Teiresias. Circe gives Odysseus directions and tells him that when he arrives he must dig a trench as long as a man's forearm, and then pour offerings to the dead into the trench, including milk, honey and wine, sprinkled over with barley. Then Odysseus must pray to the dead and, if they assist him, make further offerings, such as animal sacrifices. Until Teiresias finally appears, Odysseus must threaten ghosts with his sword to prevent them from eating the offerings.

AMORALITY AMONG THE GODS

In the early Greek myths, gods wielded their magical powers as they pleased, often with no regard for natural justice. Even in Homer's works there appears some discomfort with the gods' amoral actions.

In the *Iliad*, the story of the Greek war against Troy, a Greek warrior kills a Trojan with the help of the god Poseidon's magic. In the middle of a duel

Having angered the gods, Odysseus and his crew are led into strange and dangerous lands.

between the two warriors, Poseidon 'bewitched the Trojan's shining eyes, made moveless his bright limbs, so that he could not run backward, neither evade him, but stood like a statue or a tree with leaves towering motionless'. The Trojan, unable to fight or run away, is speared by his enemy. Homer commented that while it was admirable that the gods could perform such magic, they ought not to do so. War was meant to be an honourable contest between warriors, and for the gods to use magic to help their favourites was seen as cheating.

TRAGIC MISUSE OF MAGIC

Medea uses her reputation as a sorceress to convince the gullible daughters of King Pelius to cut him up and boil him as a magical way of restoring his youth.

When magic and religion ceased to be compatible, malevolent magic in mythology became identified with powers outside the Greek world. Circe, the enchantress who lived 'at the far edge of the known world', is one example. Another frequent character in Greek mythology is Medea, who also lived far from Greece in a city called Colchis, on the Black Sea. Like Circe, Medea was descended from the Titans, the older generation of gods who had

been overthrown by the younger Greek gods of Olympus. Circe was the daughter of the Titan god, the Sun, and Medea's father was Aietes, the son of the Sun. Medea's story is an example of the tragic consequences of the use and misuse of malignant magical power.

The Greek hero Jason was seeking to avenge his father who had been cheated of his throne of Ioclus, a Greek city, by an enemy called Pelius. Pelius had been warned by the Delphic oracle (a female seer who foretold the future) that he would be deposed by a man wearing just one sandal. When Jason entered Ioclus wearing a single sandal, Pelius, greatly alarmed, rushed him off on a quest that he hoped would get rid of him permanently. The quest was to find the fabled Golden Fleece, and Jason set out with a band of companions on the ship *Argo*. After various adventures, Jason reached the

Jason's adventures live on in the Ray Harryhausen movie Jason and the Argonauts *(1963). Here, with the aid of Medea's magic, he fights skeletal warriors spawned from the dragon's teeth King Aietes forced him to sow.*

TELEPHE GUÉRI PAR LA ROUILLE DU MÊME FER DONT IL A ÉTÉ BLESSÉ.
Telephus cured by the rust of the same spear that had wounded him.

Des Telephus verwundung und Cur.
Telephus genesen door den roest van't geweer waar meede hy gewondt was.

The wounded son of Hercules is healed with rust from the sword that injured him. Sympathetic spells of this kind are the most common form of magic throughout history.

exotic city of Colchis, where the Golden Fleece was held by Aietes, the king of Colchis. Like all the Greek heroes, Jason was the favourite of a particular god. It is never explained how the gods chose mortals as their favourites. Jason was under the protection of the goddess Athena, and when he reached Colchis, Athena made Medea fall madly in love with him. With Medea's help, Jason would be able to succeed in his quest.

Medea then plotted against her own family, and helped Jason accomplish the tasks that her father, King Aietes, had set him in the hope of killing him. First she gave him a magic ointment that would protect him from fire and metal. This enabled him to yoke the fire-breathing, brazen-footed bulls, kill the dragon that guarded the fleece, and kill the armed men that sprang from the dragon's teeth when they were sown in the ground. While helping Jason escape, Medea killed her younger brother and sliced his body into pieces, delaying her father who stopped to gather up his son's corpse. Medea had thus destroyed her own family with the aid of magic – an act for which witches were greatly feared.

Once Jason and Medea had returned to Ioclus, Medea was soon up to her tricks again. She so impressed Pelius, the king of Ioclus, with talk of her magical rejuvenation potion that she persuaded him to try it out. But in the course of the treatment she boiled the king to death. As punishment, Jason and Medea were driven from the city and fled to Corinth. There, Jason rejected Medea and married a Greek woman. Scorned and furious, Medea took her ultimate revenge by murdering her children by Jason. The moral of the story seems to be that however powerful magic may be, to use it for selfish purposes only leads to grief. The heroic Jason was later killed when a rotting timber from the *Argo* fell on his head!

CURSE TABLETS AND SCARY DOLLS

Medea and Circe were extraordinary and exotic mythical women who practised malevolent magic. But during the same time, a number of ordinary men and women almost certainly practised some form of magic that might also be described as malevolent. Archaeological records reveal many 'magical' objects from a very early period. Mainly there are two types of objects, both intended to cause some kind of harm to others by magic – one is curse tablets, the other is voodoo dolls.

The latter, more familiar today as the almost fabled magical objects from modern Haiti, were used widely and frequently in ancient times. In the Greek period, small human-like figures stuck with pins were intended to influence or control another's behaviour, not necessarily to injure them. Sometimes a voodoo doll might have had pins stuck in its mouth, for example, which was most likely intended to prevent someone from speaking out at a particular

time or revealing something confidential. Some dolls had written spells attached to their bodies specifying that the 'victim' was not to give evidence in court. Other dolls may have their feet tied behind their head, or the head or torso might have been twisted back to front. These were all different ways to symbolize the 'binding' of the victim to the particular wishes of the curse.

Curse tablets were usually small thin sheets of lead with spells inscribed upon them. The tablets were also intended to influence someone's actions or affect the welfare of a person or animal. A cache of 22 such tablets was discovered in a fifth-century BC

Medea killed her younger brother and sliced his body into pieces, delaying her father who stopped to gather up his son's corpse. Medea had thus destroyed her own family with the aid of magic – an act for which witches were greatly feared.

Demeter, a Greek nature goddess known to the Romans as Ceres, was one of the chthonic deities in whose shrines people hid curse tablets appealing for aid.

Did curse tablets really work?

Curse tablets were used extensively in the ancient Greek and Roman worlds, and clearly many people believed that they actually worked. If a curse failed to achieve any visible effect, as it surely frequently must have, it is puzzling that people continued to believe in their efficacy. But the failure of one magical action rarely shakes a belief in magic in general. The failure of a curse could easily be explained, for example, by assuming that the intended victim had access to even more powerful counter-magic.

In a society where there was widespread belief in magic, it would be more than likely that any intended victim would have already acquired a protective amulet or counterspell. The most distinctive type of amulet was a roll of inscribed papyrus, or a gold and silver foil sheet, hung around the neck in a copper tube. Amulets could be made for general protection against magic, against a specific disease, or against any secret curse tablets that might be directed at the wearer. A magical 'arms race' developed for tablets that could counter the effects of amulets.

The sort of situation that would drive someone to make a curse on another would usually be a bitter and public conflict, such as between two opponents in a court case. In that situation, both parties might feel that it was important to take magical steps to defend themselves, in case the other party did so. Any apparent failure of the curse spell would be masked by this magical 'arms race'. To curse someone magically was always considered to be a wicked act and was usually illegal. The use of lead as the base material of the curse tablet might seem curiously mundane, but this actually revealed the intensity of the curse-maker's

motivation. The lead was probably taken from the public water pipes found in all ancient cities. This was a dangerous act, which was easily discovered, and considered grossly uncivilized.

Making a curse was also dangerous. The dark powers invoked could easily rebound on the maker. Most early tablets do not name the maker of the curse, so that the spirit called upon to carry out the curse could not return to persecute the maker. Making a curse was a serious business, and could create enough psychological fear in the intended victim for the symptoms of magical harm to be perceived. Equally, any other unfortunate event that occurred could be interpreted as being the result of the curse.

However, if the curse was made in secret, particularly given that it was illegal, then how could psychological pressure be heaped on the victim? In all likelihood, the maker of the curse would discreetly inform the victim that he or she had been cursed. Not all people believed in this form of magic. The great philosopher Plato, in the early fourth century BC, argued that curses only worked on people who believed in them.

A Roman bulla talisman, showing the serpent-haired Gorgon. This was an expensive amulet meant to protect the wearer from malicious magic.

Greek colony in Sicily. So popular were curse tablets that by the second century AD they had spread throughout the Mediterranean. They have even been dug up in Roman remains in Britain.

Surviving curse tablets can be divided into five categories. The first are 'litigation curses', designed to affect the outcome of a trial. This type of tablet was common in ancient Athens, a fiercely competitive and litigious society, where citizens frequently settled their differences in court. Another type of tablet was used by groups of actors. Businessmen, too, had a whole class of 'trade curses' which they had inscribed on their tablets. A late addition to the various categories is the 'love curse', designed to break up a relationship or prevent one from starting, or to attract the victim to the curse maker. The final category was not a curse spell as such, but a prayer for justice.

A CURSE FOR ALL OCCASIONS

The sheer number of curse tablets and their apparently malevolent intent might give the impression that ancient Greek society was nothing but a seething mass of competitive, malevolent citizens. But this was not quite the case, since the conventions of magic traditionally exaggerate the negative quality of magical actions. The convention was that magic could only be used to 'bind' or inhibit another person. Therefore, if a trader wanted to become successful, he could only use magic to restrain the activities of a rival trader. Similarly the early love curses could only be used to attract someone if the curse was directed against the victim's possible attraction to someone else.

Binding magic worked according to several principles. Firstly there was an aspect of 'sympathetic magic', the idea that a similarity between one thing and another could make a magical connection between them. For this reason the material of the binding spell was often twisted or rolled into a tube. Just as the magic object was bound, so too would the victim be bound. The words on curse tablets were often written in a spiral, or with lines written alternately from right to left, and left to right. Twisting was seen as magical in itself. Hephaestus, a god associated with magic, was often portrayed with twisted legs.

The curse tablet also needed to draw power from a source. The souls of the recently dead – especially those who had died young or violently – were thought to have power, and many curse tablets have been found buried in graves. This also provided a source of sympathetic magic. Just as the corpse could not speak, so too the victim of the curse would be unable to speak.

> Sometimes a voodoo doll might have had pins stuck in its mouth, for example, which was most likely intended to prevent someone from speaking out at a particular time or revealing something confidential.

The Trojan Aeneas, fleeing from the Greek sack of Troy, is welcomed to Carthage by Queen Dido. Their love affair ends in tragedy as Dido takes magical revenge upon Aeneas.

Other tablets appealed to chthonic deities, the gods of the underworld, and were buried in their sanctuaries. The most popular chthonic deity for this purpose was Demeter, who also was an agricultural goddess. Tablets that were not buried in graves or chthonic sanctuaries tended to be pleas for justice. Since these were not malevolent in intent, they could be placed in the sanctuaries of ordinary gods.

Early curse tablets were extremely basic, often giving just the victim's name. They were used by ordinary men and women who knew only basic curses and could not write beyond a simple level. Roman writers went into more detail about the types of people who used magic. At the most basic level there were village wise men and wise-women. The writer Ovid described a spell made by an old village woman to stop spiteful gossip. Using three fingers, she placed three bits of incense over a mouse hole. The mouse hole represented the hidden ways gossip could be passed around the village. Next she muttered incantations over some string and tied the string around a piece of lead. Finally she smeared a fish head with pitch, sewed up its mouth and roasted it! Such women were consulted on all sorts of matters, from curing bee stings to sorting out marital problems.

LOVE SPELLS AND HEALING HERBS

There is an abundance of women in Roman literature who use love-curse magic for their own ends. In Virgil's *Aeneid,* the tragic Queen Dido, in revenge upon her faithless lover Aeneas, stages a complex magical rite. With the help of a witch, she builds a pyre and recites the appropriate spells, finally throwing herself upon the fire so that she will haunt Aeneas as a demon.

The poet Horace wrote several tales about a witch called Canidia, whose love spells became increasingly exotic and gruesome. Horace made fun of Canidia in one poem which describes her 'roaming abroad, with her black cloak fastened, her feet bare and her hair undone, uttering shrieks'. To perform her magic she and another witch tore apart a living black lamb with their fingernails, then poured the blood into a hole in the ground as an offering to evil spirits. Unfortunately, in the course of this sickening ritual, Canidia's false teeth fell out of her mouth and her wig fell off! While Roman writers considered magic to be particularly associated with women, they are contradicted by the evidence of the love-curse tablets themselves, most of which seem to have been made by men.

CURIOUS RITUALS

Other forms of magic were performed by 'root cutters' who, as their name implies, were believed to have extensive knowledge of the medicinal and magical uses of various plant roots. (They also knew which herbs and which animal parts should be used in spells.) When gathering herbs and plants, various rituals had to be performed to preserve their magical qualities. For example, the root cutter should stand facing away from the wind and anoint himself with oil. Some plants had to be gathered at specified times, such as at dawn or dusk. A peony could be dangerous to a male gatherer's eyesight if he dug it up during the day – it was more hazardous still if he did this while being observed by a woodpecker.

The magical powers of wise men, wise-women and root cutters were ambiguous. They could be used for good or evil. Some of the plants gathered for beneficial purposes were also known to be potentially poisonous, so root cutters were always regarded with some suspicion.

The souls of the recently dead – especially those who had died young or violently – were thought to have power, and many curse tablets have been found buried in graves.

HEALING ROGUES

Wandering healer-magicians were well known in Greece around the late fifth century BC. Many Greek intellectuals of the time vilified them. The scientist and doctor Hippocrates described certain travelling magical doctors as 'purifiers, begging-priests and humbugs' who, although they claimed to be virtuous and to have special knowledge, were really 'impious rogues'. One such rogue, Empedocles, was the founder of a medical school, of a kind, in Sicily in the fifth century BC.

In a fragment of writing attributed to him, Empedocles claims to be able to teach his students how to 'cure all the sufferings of old age, to stop the force of the winds that destroy the fields, and to bring back the soul of a man from Hades'. He also claimed to be able to teach his students – if they wished – to use their magical powers in reverse and cause rainstorms and droughts. As far as we know, nothing came of Empedocles' magic school, and he disappeared from history, a strange example of the underbelly of magic in Greek civilization.

BENEVOLENT AND WICKED DAEMONS

As the Greek world absorbed influences from surrounding civilizations after the conquests of Alexander the Great, magic increased in complexity and attracted some of the educated and richer members of the Hellenized world. The curse tablets of later centuries made appeals to all sorts of spirits and gods, particularly those from the Egyptian and Jewish traditions. As the spells used in curse texts became increasingly complex, often using garbled foreign words as magical incantations, they required professional curse makers. Such people might have been either astrologers or quack doctors, but they were certainly willing to perform curse magic for a handsome fee.

The power of these magicians was attributed to spirits of various kinds, known as daemons. These were either the spirits of heroes who could intervene in human affairs, or the spirits of the restless dead. The latter kind could be particularly dangerous, causing disease or crop failure. There were other kinds of demons who kept watch on judgments and wicked actions, presumably punishing the guilty. According to one early source, these daemons were the souls of the 'Race of Gold', who preceded humanity in the mythological past.

Magician-doctors such as Empedocles might diagnose an illness as being caused by a daemon punishing an individual for an immoral act, possibly committed by an ancestor. The cure would involve purification ceremonies and other rites in which the magician claimed to be able to control the daemon.

GOOD AND BAD ANGELS

In some accounts, daemons appear as winged messengers between gods and humans. In others they remain light, airy beings but with too many earthly qualities to dwell in the highest heavens with the gods. They also possess some earthly passions, and can therefore be dangerous, although the best of them are benevolent. The philosopher Plato rationalized beliefs in daemons by equating a person's good daemon with his soul. The notion in present-day folklore of a person having a good and a bad angel observing him or her throughout life has its origins in these ancient beliefs about an individual's daemons.

A PHILOSOPHER MEETS HIS DAEMON

In the biography of the third-century AD philosopher Plotinus there is a story about the philosopher meeting his own daemon. An Egyptian priest offered to invoke his daemon so that the philosopher could see it. The ceremony was evidently a complex one, involving the sacrifice of chickens, and in due course the daemon appeared. The priest was astonished because the spirit that appeared was not an ordinary daemon but an important god. The purpose of the story was to illustrate what a great man Plotinus had been.

Plotinus was an important influence on later developments in Christian theology. However, Christian theology rejected the idea that personal daemons

The Greek god of medicine was Asklepios, known to the Romans as Aesculapius. He was frequently called upon for help in healing magic.

Tiberius, Emperor of Rome from AD *14–37, had many people executed for practising magic. This lithograph from 1891 shows the magician Pituanius about to be thrown off the Tarpeian Rock in Rome.*

could exist and have power independent of God. They were considered to be either messengers of God, angels, or evil spirits who would try to prevent Christians from worshipping God. The daemons of antiquity evolved into the demons that plagued Christians throughout the medieval period.

MAGIC IS OUTLAWED

Already distrusted by the fifth century BC, magicians and witches came under increasing disapproval in the Roman period. At the beginning of the first millennium Emperor Augustus passed a law making it an offence to consult practitioners of magic. A report dating from the time of Emperor Tiberius (AD 14–37) records that 45 men and 85 women were executed for practising private divination and magic. These unfortunates would have been relatively rich Roman citizens, probably victims of the high-level political paranoia of the time. The intention of Augustus's law was probably to discredit magic, however, rather than to start a witch-hunt.

MYSTERY CULTS

In the early centuries AD Roman intellectuals were becoming concerned about the increasing gullibility of the urban population of the Roman Empire. The magician Alexander of Abonuteichos, borrowing from his knowledge of cults and ceremonies, and using his own stage illusions, managed to convince the citizens of one small town to build a sanctuary for

(continued on page 52)

Orpheus, the legendary Greek musician, was the inspiration for a Greek mystery cult that sought the secret wisdom they believed Orpheus had known.

49

τhe mystery of egypt's secret texts

The 'hermetic' texts – reputed to be works of secret magical wisdom – were a collection of Greek literature written in Egypt between the first and the fourth centuries AD, created by the Greek-speaking citizens who dominated Egyptian literature. In the texts, the Egyptian god Thoth – whose Greek counterpart is the god Hermes – is shown teaching Asklepios, the Greek god of medicine. In another version of the same story, the teacher of the secret wisdom is Isis, who instructs her son Horus. Most of the texts were allegedly the work of a legendary Egyptian sage, Hermes Trismegistus, who lived at the same time as Moses. While claims were made that the books dated from ancient Egypt, they are in fact a mixture of Greek, Jewish, Persian and Egyptian ideas brought together in the melting pot of northern Egypt, particularly the city of Alexandria.

The hermetic texts fall into two distinct groups. One group was a mixture of magical arts including astrology and alchemy (the attempt to turn base metals into gold). The other group was philosophical and theological, mostly preoccupied with the mystical search for the soul's freedom. Often the texts that discussed alchemy were really describing a mystical quest. Both alchemy and astrology were wrongly said by the hermetic texts to have been of Egyptian origin.

Astrology of one form or another had existed in many ancient societies, but the elaborate system that exists

today did not appear until the first millennium BC. The full twelve signs of the zodiac were in fact developed by Greek astronomers, who fused their knowledge with Egyptian and Mesopotamian star lore. Alchemy was also attributed to Egyptian priests. This was a misconception, partly due to the influence of the Greek writer Zosimus of Panopolis, who described the baking furnaces used by the priests of Memphis as alchemical ovens. These furnaces were actually used to bake magical figurines, rather than transmute lead into gold.

A seventeenth-century illustration of the mythical Hermes Trismegistus, the presiding deity of alchemy.

Although the hermetic texts were not authentic Egyptian magic books, their existence encouraged certain people in the ancient world to believe that there were yet more books waiting to be discovered. Others suspected that the supposedly undiscovered secrets of Egyptian magic were hidden in code in the existing works. Until the seventeenth century the hermetic texts continued to receive considerable attention from many intellectuals in the Western world who still believed them to somehow incorporate ancient Egyptian magical secrets.

When the English scholar Isaac Casaubon accurately dated the hermetic texts to the early centuries AD, the search for 'hermetic wisdom' ceased to be a credible enterprise. Nonetheless, the mystique of ancient Egypt retained its appeal, and secret societies from the eighteenth century onward have often borrowed Egyptian themes for their symbols. Esoteric groups such as the Rosicrucians often wildly misunderstood the nature and meaning of the Egyptian symbols they had borrowed. There exists to this day a great deal of wild speculation and sheer fantasy concerning Egyptian religion and magic, which ultimately stems from the ancient but erroneous belief in the existence of secret hermetic texts.

A fifteenth-century representation of the Hermetic Arcana, by the German alchemist Basil Valentine, showing two groups of seven and three, used in hermetic magic.

The magician Simon Magus is held aloft by demons invisible to the spectators. Simon's diabolical magic is banished by Saint Peter.

a fictional cult dedicated to a sacred snake, Glychon. The late Roman world was fascinated by mystery cults and associated traditions of secret magical wisdom, usually thought to derive from Egypt. In fact mystery cults had a long-standing Greek heritage.

The earliest mystery cult was the Orphics, whose name was derived from the mythical figure Orpheus. Orpheus was a musician so talented that even animals flocked to hear him. In one myth he descended to Hades to bring back his deceased wife, and his music so charmed the gods of the underworld that they released her. He was also said to have been torn to pieces by the Maenads, the female worshippers of Dionysus. The Orphics appeared as early as the sixth century BC and sought mystical immortality through the practice of asceticism (abstention from all forms of pleasure). Very little is known of this secretive cult, but others thought they had secret and possibly magical wisdom.

MYSTIC CULTS AND MIRACLES

The mystic traditions of cults such as Orphism and various philosophical speculations became part of the mix surrounding exotic ideas about secret magical wisdom in the early centuries AD. Christianity became increasingly important in the Roman Empire from the third century AD. At the same time, some of the leading philosophers and priests, and magicians of the various mystery cults, developed the practice of theurgy. Theurgists were reputed to use magical ceremony and paraphernalia to produce 'miracles' (some resemble contemporary stage illusions) demonstrating the reality of the pagan gods. Theurgists wanted to prove that the old gods still operated in the world, and that those who were initiates of secret wisdom were protected and loved by the pagan gods, just as were the mythical heroes such as Odysseus and Jason.

The Christians took a dim view of the theurgists and sometimes produced caricatures about their activities. The best known of these theurgists is Simon Magus, who appears in the Acts of the Apostles (8:9–24), offering Christ's disciples money in return for the ability to do the miracles that they had performed after the Crucifixion. The incident showed that Simon Magus – and others of his kind – had entirely misunderstood the Christians' supernatural abilities. Christian miracles were not magical in origin, but were a gift of grace from God. It was not the Christian saint who performed a miracle, but God himself who worked through the saint.

The Christians did not deny that the pagan priests and magicians could work apparent miracles. The early Christians believed entirely in the existence of the daemons that the magicians claimed to summon. Simon Magus also appeared in the early apocryphal Gnostic Gospel of Saint Peter. Thanks to his spells, Simon Magus had almost convinced Emperor Nero to believe in his unique relationship with the divine, and was asked for a final demonstration of his power. The magician prepared to perform a public ceremony in which he would fly to Heaven – this would be considered by the Christians to be a parody of the Ascension of Christ into Heaven. However, as Simon Magus began ascending high into the air, Saint Peter was kneeling in prayer in the public square. Suddenly, on hearing the saint's prayer, the hosts of Hell that were keeping the magician suspended in the air fled and Simon Magus crashed to his death.

For Christians, all the incantations and spells employed by magicians were merely a mask for illusions willingly performed by evil daemons that sought to corrupt humanity and lead it away from God and salvation. As Christianity began to dominate the late Roman Empire, the complex magic of the theurgists, the old public ceremonies worshipping the pagan gods, and the simple forms of magic practised by ordinary people, were all denounced as being associated with the Devil. No longer were spirits or daemons ambiguous – possibly helpful or possibly dangerous – there were now only evil spirits and the true Christian God.

The late Roman world was fascinated by mystery cults and associated traditions of secret magical wisdom, usually thought to derive from Egypt. In fact mystery cults had a long-standing Greek heritage.

CHRISTIANITY takes ON magic

In AD 312 the Roman Emperor Constantine the Great converted to Christianity, and by the end of the fourth century AD the worship of all the old pagan gods of Rome had been outlawed and their ceremonies and rites forbidden. Christianity was already widespread in the Roman Empire, among the urban populations as well as the educated elite, and eventually it was even embraced by the fearsome Germanic tribes who dominated the empire in the course of the fourth and fifth centuries. Christians took to mocking those who worshipped the old pagan gods, haughtily dismissing them as pagani, literally 'dwellers in the countryside', from which the term 'pagan' derives. Today they might be described as 'country bumpkins' or 'yokels'.

Yet there were many in Roman high society who remained true to the old gods. In AD 410, after Rome was sacked by Alaric and his Visigoth army, rumour was rife that the invasion – an event that deeply shocked the Roman world since the city had been free of foreign invasion for nearly a thousand years – and the fall of Rome had occurred specifically because the old gods had been outlawed. So gravely did the Christians regard these rumours that they urged Bishop Augustine of Hippo (later Saint Augustine) to take up his pen and thoroughly denounce them. The early parts of his great work of theology, *The City of God*, railed against the notion that human prosperity depended on the whims and appeasement of the old pagan gods. His intention was to draw the more educated pagani into the Christian understanding of the world.

Christianity brought a new spiritual order to Europe. Heaven was ruled by a single God consisting of three persons: God the Father, the Son and the Holy Spirit. Christians often depicted the human mother of Christ, the Virgin Mary, enthroned in Heaven as a lesser power to which Christians could appeal for help and mercy.

Saint Augustine of Hippo wrote one of the earliest true autobiographies, which movingly described his youthful temptations to dabble in magic and heretical religions.

A SAINT'S TEMPTATION

The Confessions, another of Saint Augustine's great works, presents a vivid picture of religious beliefs at the turn of the fourth and fifth centuries. Although Augustine's mother was a Christian, he himself was attracted to the quasi-Christian heresy of Manichaeism, which decreed that the material world had been created by the Devil, whose power was equal to that of God. But heresy was not the only temptation.

The young Augustine taught rhetoric (the art of public speaking) for a living and entered a theatrical competition in the hope of winning a valuable prize. He was approached by a 'wizard' who offered to ensure that he would win the competition in exchange for a particular 'payment'. Augustine was sorely tempted, but upon discovering that certain 'foul mysteries' would be involved in the payment, including making a sacrifice to demons, the highly scrupulous young man declined the wizard's offer, saying, '…though the garland be made of imperishable gold, I would not suffer a fly to be killed to gain me it'.

LICENCE TO SIN

Augustine was less scrupulous, however, in consulting 'mathematicians' – who were in fact astrologers – because they seemed neither to make sacrifices nor pray to any spirits for their divinations. According to Augustine, astrology implied that a sin was caused not by the person who committed it, but by planetary influences. After due consideration, Augustine rejected astrology, deciding that it was in fact an abuse of God's mercy towards humanity and, moreover, a licence to sin.

Through Augustine's writings, and that of other church fathers, Christians defined their rejection of magical beliefs and practices of the past. But it was not just through theology that Christians sought to discredit pagan beliefs. Christian holy men were held up as examples of the power of the Christian faith against pagan magicians.

SAINTS, MIRACLES AND MAGIC

Curiously, it was in Egypt, the country that Christians described as the 'mother of magicians', that the first Christian holy men appeared in the third century AD. Their very holiness was based on asceticism, the denial of the body through fasting, and poverty. Christian belief spread rapidly in third- and fourth-century Egypt, and stories of Christian miracles flourished.

During the persecutions of Christians, carried out by the pagan Roman Emperors until the end of the third century, some holy men fled from the towns into the deserts. There, in the wilderness and wastelands, arose the practice of solitary ascetics making their homes in the ruined tombs and temples of

the old Egyptian gods. Saint Anthony, the most famous of these early Christian hermits, was credited with bravely resisting the attacks of hosts of demons who were driven from the towns by Christianity and hid out in these ruins that rightfully belonged to the old religion.

A BROKEN BIRD

Contemporary dramatic accounts of holy men resisting the assaults of demons effectively discredited magic, the stories clearly indicating that magic-making spirits had no real power except to tempt and torment mentally. Another way in which Christian saints attacked pagan magic was by physically destroying its symbols and temples.

The story of Saint Anthony, the hermit saint of Egypt, powerfully moved medieval Christians. Here he is shown tormented by devils in the stony desert foreground.

In the fourth century AD, Abba (Father) Macedonius, a bishop of Egypt, set out to destroy a temple of the goddess Isis, situated on the Nile on the island of Philae. One of the rites of Isis involved worshipping the image of a falcon, and during ceremonies at the temple, a lifelike model of the creature flapped and fluttered about in a seemingly magical fashion. The bishop knew very well that the bird was just a mechanical device, and on one occasion, claiming to wish to make a sacrifice to Isis, he crept around to the back of the altar and quietly smashed the bird-contraption to pieces. When the temple priests found the broken wings and feathers, they were so sure that Isis's worshippers would kill them when they discovered the damage to the shrine that they fled in terror to the desert. Soon afterwards Bishop Macedonius managed to track down the frightened priests and converted them to Christianity.

It was not only in Egypt that Christian leaders deliberately violated and destroyed pagan shrines and temples. In Gaul, modern-day France, the bishop Saint Martin of Tours (c. 316–97), an ascetic holy man, was renowned for his 'miraculous' destruction of pagan centres of worship. In many cases the destruction amounted to nothing more than cutting down a few sacred trees. Even so, legends surrounding Saint Martin grew rapidly after his death. His biographer went so far as to credit him with having the ability to summon down lightning from Heaven to destroy pagan shrines.

MANLINESS IS A VIRTUE

Christians at this time wholeheartedly believed in the reality of miracles. They expected holy men to be able to perform miracles, and believed that the power of prayer also might make them occur.

We might think it strange, but Christians thought miracles were the opposite of magic. Magic was merely an illusion created by demons, while miracles were acts of the true God. Holy men, who performed God's miracles, possessed virtus or virtue, which in Latin originally implied something between manliness and power. Magic was acquired through an unholy knowledge of spells and through favours granted by the pagan gods, while miraculous 'virtue' was gained through grace and a heroic faith in Christ. While the distinction between magic and the Christian faith was clear to the more sophisticated, educated Christians of the time, it was most likely far less obvious to the common man or woman.

In many respects the legends that grew up around the power of the saints

While the distinction between magic and the Christian faith was clear to the more sophisticated, educated Christians of the time, it was most likely far less obvious to the common man or woman.

were remarkably similar to legends about magical feats. Magic healers and witches, for example, often relied on ointments and tinctures in their treatments. A Christian Egyptian hermit called John of Lycopolis gave out healing oils to all those who came to him seeking cures for their ailments. Although his remedy was doubtless just ordinary cooking oil – albeit blessed by the holy man – people flocked to him from near and far, clearly believing devoutly in his healing abilities.

VISITED BY ANGELS

Christian legends were keen to emphasize the difference between magic and miracles: A magician would be surrounded by his 'familiars', or demons, while the early Christian hermits were visited by angels. In one legend, a group of desert-dwelling hermits was reputed to receive the Eucharist from an angel of God every Sunday. The Egyptian bishop Paphnutius found four ascetics who also claimed to be the recipients of a miraculous daily consignment of bread 'warm and fresh as though straight from the oven'. Whatever wonders pagan magicians might claim to accomplish in legend, Christian authors were determined that their wonders, appropriate to Christianity, would be even greater and more profound.

A horror story from the thirteenth century. A monk is drowned in the River Tiber in Rome. However, Christians believed that devils could only influence people's actions – they couldn't do physical harm themselves.

The remains of Saint Augustine's Abbey in Canterbury, England. The monastery was founded in the early seventh century by Saint Augustine, sent to convert the English to Christianity.

DEMONS, DEMONS EVERYWHERE . . .

Stories of the Egyptian saints focus on the immense ascetic and spiritual sufferings necessary to achieve a life free from demons and blessed by angels. This form of 'miraculous literature' found its way into Western Christianity, particularly through the writings of Pope Gregory the Great (590–604) about the miracles performed by the Italian saints. But the powers of the Italian saints had to be adapted for a Western audience. Where the Egyptian saints cowed crocodiles, the Italian saints tamed savage bears and wolves.

Command over the animal kingdom, demonstrating the power of the Christian saints, was one of the major themes in the literature of this period. Before his fall from grace, Adam had held sovereign power over all the animals in the Garden of Eden: consequently saints were believed to embody some of this power. It automatically followed that saints also had power over the demons that tormented people in their everyday lives. The collective view of the miracle stories written in the medieval West was that possession by demons was the principal explanation for ills of both body and mind.

MAKING CONTACT WITH GOD

For people living in medieval times, demons were as real and as omnipresent as germs are for people today. Since almost anything bad could be explained away as 'possession by demons', it was necessary for ordinary people to have some means of eradicating or warding off demons. The general clergy relied upon exorcism and the sacraments to give people contact with divine power. Throughout the Middle Ages, many people believed that simply attending Mass could be a powerful protection against the devils that crowded around them, waiting for any opportunity to pounce and do harm. Indeed, the paraphernalia of the Christian Church itself had connotations of quasi-magical power for the people of Northern and Western Europe during the period of conversion from the sixth to the eleventh centuries.

Even as late as the sixth and seventh centuries, Anglo-Saxons evidently continued to believe in magic and magicians.

A WISE KING RELENTS

Even as late as the sixth and seventh centuries, Anglo-Saxons evidently continued to believe in magic and magicians. The first English historian, Bede, writing in the early eighth century, recorded the reaction of Aethelbert, the king of Kent, in AD 596 when Christian missionaries visited his small kingdom. To convert Aethelbert to Christianity would have been something of a coup, since as overlord of the southern English kingdoms he was one of the most powerful men in the British Isles at that time.

The court of King Aethelbert should already have been familiar with the outward forms of Christian worship, since Aethelbert's French wife Bertha was a Christian and had even brought her own bishop to England with her. Yet when the missionaries arrived, led by the future Saint Augustine of Canterbury, the king ordered them to remain on the Isle of Thanet, on the north coast of Kent. Aethelbert sent supplies to the island and eventually went to visit them, but he took care to remain in the open air. Apparently he was scared that if he met the missionaries inside a building and they turned out to be practitioners of 'magical arts', they would cast a magic spell that would give them power over him.

In the end, however, the king was so impressed by the missionaries that he allowed them to preach in the old abandoned Roman churches of Canterbury. According to Bede, the monks led such holy and pure lives that people were greatly impressed and eventually the king's entire court converted to Christianity.

DEMONS CHASED FROM THE CHURCHES

Pope Gregory the Great subsequently advised missionaries on leading the English gradually towards Christianity. Pagan temples, usually located on a

Bede was the first historian of the English, in the eighth century. He recorded not only the deeds of kings, but the miracles of the early English saints.

hill or in a clearing in a wood, were not to be destroyed, he said, but rather converted to Christian use. First, however, any loitering devils or pagan gods had to be eliminated by consecrating the site with holy water and by enclosing holy relics in the Christian altar. These were generally the bones of saints and martyrs, or occasionally more exotic items purporting to be fragments of the Cross, for example. Once again Christianity had found a parallel with the magic of the ancient world. Where once people would have worn amulets appealing to certain gods for protection, now Christians were encouraged to believe that the bones of holy men had the power to protect.

Compared with other northern pagan countries, the progress of Christianity was particularly rapid in England. But confusingly, although the worship of pagan gods had completely disappeared by the end of the eighth century, people still believed in sorcery and magic. Archbishop Theodore of Canterbury (668–90) found it necessary to condemn those who invoked fiends to bring about a change in the weather, for better or worse. But this was not the end of the matter. More than 50 years later in 747, a major council of the English church instructed priests to preach against the belief in sorcery, incantations and other practices. Christianity may have been relatively widespread at this time, but it did not prevent Christians from believing just as firmly in the existence of magic and witchcraft.

THE SURVIVAL OF MAGIC

Bede tells the story of a young man captured in a battle between two English kings in AD 679. Imma was a young noble in the service of the brother of King Egfrid of Northumbria, and during a battle with King Aethelred of Mercia, Imma was knocked unconscious. When he woke he was captured by the Mercians, and to avoid being killed he claimed to be merely a peasant who was there only to bring provisions to the Northumbrian army. The Mercian nobleman who had captured Imma had his wounds treated and placed him in irons so that he could not escape. Evidently they planned to sell Imma into slavery.

However, Imma had a brother who was a priest, and assuming he was dead, the brother had Masses sung for him so that his soul would be released from purgatorial punishments. Since Imma was still alive, the Masses caused his chains to fall off each time they were secured to him. The Mercian nobleman wondered at this and asked Imma whether he 'possessed any written charms like those mentioned in the fables'. Imma denied having access to such magic, but admitted that he was really a nobleman and that his brother was a priest. Eventually Imma was able to buy his freedom and return home. The story shows us that many Anglo-Saxon noblemen believed in magic, and carried magical charms to protect themselves. But for Bede, Imma was an example of noble Christian faith; he did not rely on magic, but only on his faith in Christ. For Bede, the story demonstrated the superiority of Christian worship over pagan magic. While the magic to which the Mercian nobleman referred was an old superstition, the story of Imma, according to Bede, was genuine.

Maleficium was the Latin term used by the clergy to denote harmful magic.

A DEADLY FRENCH QUEEN

Over the next few hundred years, despite criticism from generations of churchmen such as Bede, most ordinary people continued to believe in the efficacy of magical charms and in the possibility of harmful magic being directed against them by their neighbours.

One of the earliest instances of belief in witchcraft – of a kind – appears early in the post-Roman history of Europe. In the fifth century much of Roman Gaul had been conquered by a Germanic tribe called the Franks, whose name was eventually given to the country as France. The early Frankish kings were called the Merovingians, after the founder of their dynasty, Merov. They ruled until the middle of the eighth century, but suffered from lethal competition for power within the ruling family itself. In one incident accusations of witchcraft became a political tool.

In AD 580 Queen Fredegund's two young sons died during an epidemic. She blamed her stepson, Chlodoric, accusing him of asking his mistress's mother to make maleficia to kill the two boys. (Maleficium was the Latin term used by the clergy to denote harmful magic; it is usually translated as 'witchcraft', though it literally means 'evildoing'.) The woman was arrested, confessed to the crime under torture and was subsequently burned as a witch. When another son died of dysentery, the queen blamed his death on her political enemies, and they too were accused of witchcraft and tortured to death.

In fact these events had as much to do with politics as they did with witchcraft. The queen probably believed that these individuals were using witchcraft against her, but it is more than likely that she wanted to get rid of them because they were her political opponents.

For Bede, Imma was an example of noble Christian faith; he did not rely on magic, but only on his faith in Christ.

HALF-HEARTED BELIEF IN WITCHCRAFT

The Merovingian rulers of France were not alone in their belief in witchcraft in the early Middle Ages. The Lombards, a Germanic tribe who ruled part of Italy in the same period as the Merovingians, and the German Saxons, who were conquered by Charlemagne in the eighth century, were both known to have pursued and killed suspected witches in private vendettas.

In AD 814 Emperor Charlemagne passed a law denouncing those witches who caused storms, destroyed crops, dried up milk and cheese, and caused disease through the summoning of demons. The punishment for these acts of maleficium was death. Yet no one was ever brought to court to face these charges. The clerical elite, who were crucial in governing Charlemagne's empire and educating its nobility, simply refused to believe in the possibility of witchcraft. Under the influence of the Christian clergy, belief in witches and the possibility of harmful magic faded in intensity, and became a superstition of the peasantry that was not shared by the rulers of Europe.

SYMPATHETIC MAGIC WIDESPREAD

If witchcraft was a relatively minor phenomenon in the early Middle Ages, the use of magic for beneficial purposes was much more widespread. Evidence of the prevalence of magical charms comes from a surprising source – the clerical elite itself. This is surprising, because the clergy, above all people, should have adhered strictly to the theological position that all magic was ultimately sinful, dependent on demons and therefore potentially damning to the soul. However, monasteries, the centres of learning, were more than religious institutions. Medical knowledge, which was mostly dependent upon a few texts inherited from the Romans, was kept alive by monks. Apparently some monks who practised medicine felt that magic could provide solutions to disease that were otherwise lacking.

CHARMS FOR EVERY OCCASION

The range of surviving charms is extensive. There are Latin charms for various problems in pregnancy, including miscarriage. Others are to prevent arthritis, shivering fits, dysentery and fevers in general. Toothaches, chilblains or frostbite, ear- and eye-aches are all covered, too. There are charms to staunch bleeding and even a charm to heal a horse with a sprained leg. Other charms offered protection against theft, venom, infectious diseases, against the tricks of witches and elves, and 'against the atrocities of all fiends'.

Many of the charms recorded in medical manuscripts invoked 'natural' magic. Since they were comprised mainly of plant material, it is understandable that a monk could use them with a clear conscience. For a swelling, one charm instructs, 'take a root of lily and sprouts of elder tree and a leaf of garlic, and cut them into very small parts and pound them well, and put them in a thick cloth and bind on'. Certainly this is folk medicine, but it depends on the principle of

Charlemagne (AD 742–814) united most of Italy, France and Germany under his rule. The Pope crowned him the 'Holy Roman Emperor' as if the Roman Empire had returned.

sympathetic magic for its effect. The three ingredients used are 'swellings' themselves. The act of cutting them up and pounding them is, in a sense, a ritual action to destroy the actual swellings. Once they are bound onto the injury, the parallel between the destruction of these natural swellings and the injury itself was hoped to have a magical healing effect. The principle at work is the same one that is used with a voodoo doll.

Other charms show various ingenious uses of the sympathetic magic principle. A remedy for baldness uses the bark of willow and ash trees as ingredients: The two trees were renowned for their astonishing regenerative growth. Hair, it was promised, would sprout up from a bald head upon the application of a willow leaf, just as the willow shoots up from a bald trunk.

Cheap charms and costly cures

These relatively simple charms were undoubtedly used by village wise-women, who probably passed them on to the monastic doctors. The doctors then recorded them for posterity. Other medicinal spells were a great deal more complex, and called for resources that only a wealthy household could have possessed.

Broken bones required extremely complex and costly spells. As with healing spells in most cultures, the important aspect was not the nature of the injury itself, but the nature of the cause. Thus the spells for broken bones specified whether they were to be used for a wound caused by iron (an axe, for example) or for the man who had been 'hit with a tree or a stone'.

One general recipe for a bone salve begins with an extensive, and expensive, list of ingredients that include rue, radish, dock, iris, feverfew, vervain, carline, thistle, celadine, beetroot and betony – plus an additional 25 herbs. There should be equal quantities of all these, and they must be pounded in a mortar together with a sprinkling of ivy berries. But the spell does not stop there. It also requires the bark of an ash tree, twigs of willow and more parts from five other types of tree. All these must be gathered on the east side of the trees, close to the ground. The pieces should be cut and boiled together in holy water, then mixed with the ground herbs. Next the fat from a hart or stag, a he-goat, a bull, a boar, and a ram should be melted together in mulberry wine. Then old butter should be boiled together with the herbs and the bark. The whole mixture should be placed over a fire to form a tarry substance. To this should be added wine, nine cloves of hallowed garlic and more herbs and incense. Lastly, the marrow from an old ox and an

The clerical elite, who were crucial in governing Charlemagne's empire and educating its nobility, simply refused to believe in the possibility of witchcraft.

eagle should be mixed in. (The eagle and the ox were animals noted for their strength, so this adds an aspect of sympathetic magic to the ointment.) The entire preparation should be performed to an accompaniment of Christian Latin hymns. The final tar should be poured out in the form of a circle, and around this circle should be poured the grease from bones pounded with an axe. (This aspect of the spell again relies on the sympathetic magic of the bones and the axe, to reverse the injury caused by an axe to the recipient of the ointment.)

Magical charms were used to protect against disease, but for the devout Christian such remedies were unthinkable. In this medieval image, monks suffering from plague are blessed by a priest.

It is highly unlikely that a spell requiring so many and such exotic ingredients could possibly have been assembled by an ordinary villager. This spell was certainly exclusive to a monastic apothecary. Nonetheless, some of the practices mentioned in the spell would also have been carried out by everyday people.

Gathering herbs in special ways is a characteristic of magic that goes back to ancient Greece at least, but some of the particular instructions found in English charm spells suggest a folkloric origin. Herbs often had to be gathered on a particular date. One charm to prevent liver complaints instructed that vervain for a remedy had to be gathered on Midsummer's Day, around June 21.

Many aspects of the charms were derived from the monasteries' classical records. One charm relied on the Greek legend of the Seven Sleepers of Ephesus, and was clearly copied from a Greek original. Others were derived from Christian prayers or the power of the sacraments. Some of the Latin tags that are part of the spells turned out to be quotations from ancient Roman texts.

One charm to prevent miscarriage involved walking three times over the grave of a dead man, while repeating a short Latin verse three times. Once the woman had become pregnant, she was to recite another verse to her husband, then go to her local church altar and swear by Christ that the baby had manifested.

The saints provided a valuable source of sympathetic magic that could be accessed by ordinary people. Saint Lawrence was martyred by the Romans, and according to tradition was broiled to death on a gridiron. Thus it was natural that Christians called upon Saint Lawrence to heal burns. Saint Nicasius was supposed to have suffered from smallpox and to have prayed to God that whoever carried his name with him would not carry that disease.

METHODS TO PREVENT TRICKERY

Other charms had even stranger components. In a charm to prevent trickery by witches and elves, a special 'formula' had to be written in Greek letters (in reality the letters read as gibberish) on a piece of parchment. Next blackberry,

Greek letters were often used in spells, since they were thought to contain magical power. Here the Greek vowels are inscribed on a pendant as a magical amulet.

lupine and pennyroyal had to be pounded together on the parchment to make a powder. The powder was then placed in a bag under the altar of a church and left there for the duration of nine Masses. After this, the powder was added to milk, and holy water was sprinkled over it. The final potion was to be taken three times a day and also could be given to animals.

MAGIC TO PUT FOOD ON THE TABLE

Understandably in early medieval times when deaths from starvation were commonplace, most people's greatest concern was ensuring that their harvest provided enough food to keep them alive. It is no surprise, then, that Christianity was expected to provide some sort of magical protection for the fields where crops were grown. Priests are known to have carried out annual blessings on the fields, and in later centuries these ceremonies evolved into elaborate communal events. However, no detailed descriptions exist of how such village ceremonies were actually performed in the early Middle Ages. But in the medicinal books there is an agricultural charm that may describe something similar to the ceremonies performed in most villages, even though it was written by monks for their own use.

The field charm specifies that it can be performed to improve the fields or to undo any damage caused by sorcery or witchcraft. Four sods of earth were to be dug from each side of the land. Then oil, honey, yeast, milk from all the cattle on the land, and a part of every well-known herb (except for burdock, for some unexplained reason) were to be gathered together. Holy water was poured on top, then the mixture had to be dripped three times on to the bottom of the sods of earth – the number three was particularly significant, for it was hoped that it would invoke the power of the Holy Trinity. After this the sods were to be blessed with a Latin tag bidding them to grow, multiply and fill the earth, 'in the name of the Father, the Son and the Holy Ghost'. The Lord's Prayer was then to be recited.

Afterwards the sods were taken to a church and their green sides were turned towards the altar. The priest then said four Masses, one for each corner of the land. Before the setting of the sun the four sods had to be returned to their original sites, and the four evangelists were to be invoked – again, for each corner of the land. Next, seed was given out to beggars, and then incense, fennel, hallowed soap and salt were placed in the holes along with the sods of earth. The lengthy ceremony was completed with a prayer to the earth that the 'omnipotent, eternal Lord grant you fields growing and

One charm to prevent miscarriage involved walking three times over the grave of a dead man, while repeating a short Latin verse three times.

69

eaRLy enGLisH charms — not pagan ReLics, But simpLe RHymes

Scores of written charms have survived from the Anglo-Saxon period, mainly in medical manuscripts. While some might argue that this is clear evidence that pagan folk beliefs survived into Christian times – and certainly there are elements of simple village magic in some of the surviving charms – there is in fact a remarkable absence of evidence concerning the survival of pagan religion. Simple charm magic is a different class of belief from the worship of pagan deities, and could have emerged without any influence from a pagan past.

Snakes have been associated with evil magic since ancient times. This sixteenth-century engraving from a Protestant pamphlet portrays the Catholic church leaders as venomous snakes.

Charm magic could nevertheless invoke pagan gods, implying some cultural memory of pagan mythology. Only one among the many surviving written charms actually mentions a named pagan god. This spell is for healing snakebites:

'A worm came crawling,
it killed nothing
For Woden took nine glory twigs
He smote then the adder flew into
nine parts.'

This verse recalls a mythical event about the god Woden, the Anglo-Saxon equivalent of the Norse god Odin. By relating the snakebite to this event, it was hoped that the power of the god would be invoked against the venom.

Woden was remembered relatively well in early English culture. Most of the lineages of the Anglo-Saxon kings were believed to have originated with Woden. The god's name also survives in many English place names, as well as in the middle day of the week, Wednesday. In Norse culture, Odin was regarded as the source of all charms and spells.

This single surviving English charm invoking Woden may actually represent the influence of ninth- and eleventh-century Danish settlers, rather than the survival of any specifically English pagan mythology.

If some of the monastic writers of medical manuscripts were willing to record charms that lay clearly outside the boundaries of orthodox Christian belief, it is all the more remarkable that so few charms revealed any pagan influence. If pagan belief had survived to any degree in Anglo-Saxon England, more such examples would have been recorded. Christianity dominated the people's world view. Belief in magic survived but it had lost any connection with the pagan past, and was limited by the Christian understanding of the world.

thriving'. Lastly, a few words of ceremonial church Latin were uttered over the fields.

KEEPING THE BEES AT HOME

Other, less complex charms also could be used to protect food supplies. Honey was particularly important to the Anglo-Saxon economy, as it was the only sweetener available at that time, and it was also used in many medicinal remedies. Thus there developed a charm to ensure that a swarm of bees would stay in its own hive, rather than fly off to a neighbour's. Earth was to be taken in the right hand and placed under the right foot, while the spell maker declaimed: 'I catch it under my foot, I have found it. Lo, earth had power against all creatures, and against malice and against ungratefulness, and against the mighty tongue of man.' When the swarm of bees flew off, the spell maker was to throw sand after them, while presumably trying to avoid actually hitting and annoying the bees. A verse accompanied this action: 'Settle victorious women [the bees], sink down to earth. You must never fly wild to the wood. Be as mindful of my welfare as every man is of food and home.'

THE SAGAS

The twelfth century witnessed an explosion of literature across Western Europe, from the sagas of Scandinavia to the Arthurian legends of France and Britain. In all this literature, the magical and the supernatural play a substantial part. The sagas of Iceland were recorded from the twelfth century onwards. Although by then people had embraced Christianity, they continued to chronicle stirring myths and legends about the exploits of their Viking ancestors during the pagan era. Although magical acts permeate the sagas, the spells and curses are only imaginary. The authors were simply recounting hearsay tales about their pagan ancestors and the sagas cannot be treated as reliable histories. The stories do reveal, however, people's attitudes towards magic and the supernatural in the time of their ancestors.

The sagas tell of many Viking leaders who were genuine historical figures and whose lives became the subject of legend. One such tale, known

(continued on page 74)

Honey was a crucial part of the medieval economy, and magic was sometimes used to control the bees. This could be a difficult task, as is shown in this illumination from 1300.

eLves and dwarfs — friends or foes?

Elves are largely depicted in the charm texts as sources of evil. Unlike the fairies and 'little folk' imagined in later times, elves were usually thought of in the early Middle Ages as tall and beautiful, more like the elves of Tolkien's stories in The Lord of the Rings. *Dwarfs, too, were seen as evil, supernatural creatures with their own secret kingdoms. Diseases were attributed to both much-maligned groups, so naturally charms were developed to protect against them. One particularly nasty illness was known as 'water-elf disease', and special salves were considered necessary to protect against 'elf shot' – an ailment that caused heart attacks and that could afflict cattle and horses as well as humans.*

B ut paradoxically, although Christianity generally regarded elves as evil fiends, they occasionally performed acts of kindness as well. There are elf elements in a number of Anglo–Saxon names which hint at their potentially helpful nature. Alfred (Aelfred) means 'the counsel of elves', and the Anglo–Saxon word 'aelfsciene' means 'bright as an elf'. So it seems that elves at this time had a somewhat ambiguous reputation, similar to that of demons in ancient Greek culture.

Stories about elves that emerged in the twelfth century still contained hints about their ambiguity, as well as great variety in the descriptions of their natures, with some being described as tall and evil, and others being tiny and friendly. Gerald of Wales told a story concerning a priest

of his acquaintance. When he was a small boy learning to read, the priest had run away from the harsh treatment of his teacher, who frequently beat him. He had remained hidden for several days when a pair of tiny men appeared and promised to take him to a land where 'all is pleasure and playtime'. The boy went with them, through an underground tunnel and into a beautiful country of rivers and meadows, woodlands and plains. The country was dark, however, as the sun did not shine there, and at night there was no moon or stars. The country had no religion, but its inhabitants were dedicated to telling the truth at

Dwarfs and midgets were thought to have supernatural origins or powers by many societies. This nineteenth-century illustration shows a dwarf in the Roman imperial court.

all times, and also had abundant amounts of gold.

Unfortunately, the boy became entranced by the fairy gold, and tried to steal some of it for his mother. For this crime he was exiled from the fairy kingdom, and had to endure the brutal discipline of his teacher in the mundane world. Eventually he grew up to be a priest, and told this story to all who would listen. The writer, Gerald of Wales, clearly did not believe in this imaginative fable, but thought it had a useful moral.

The story contrasts the deceits, complexities and struggles of the real world with an imaginary place of childhood perfection. In this fable at least, the little people were clearly not being portrayed as fiends.

Elves are presented in a far more sinister light in a story from Sunderland, in northern England. A young labourer called Richard, on an errand for his master, encountered three tall young men on the road: 'Their clothes were all green and so were their horses, and they themselves were beautiful of stature and countenance.' They took him, against his will, 'and they came to a valley which opened to them of its own accord. So Richard was led into the desert by a spirit of fantasy, that he might tempt him thrice, if so be, and that he might be held prisoner by a company of devils'. The youths brought him to the court of their king, where he was 'fed among the fairy youths and maidens'. Richard was given 'in a green horn liquor in the likeness of new ale'. He refused to drink the liquor, being suspicious of its contents, nor would he take part in other 'unlawful pleasures' that were offered to him. Although

angry with him, the green people finally allowed Richard to leave, but struck him dumb.

Once restored to his family, Richard was cured of his dumbness by an appeal to Saint Cuthbert, the great seventh-century hermit and bishop of Northumbria. The excitement of the story, for a medieval audience, was the picture of an ordinary young peasant caught between the titanic spiritual forces of good and evil.

The monstrous and the supernatural were embodied in two fairly broad categories. Elves and dwarfs comprised one category, and even reflected civilized society, since they had their own kings and customs. The other was the Wild Men, who appear in art and literature throughout the Middle Ages. The Wild Man took many forms, but he was often imagined to be a solitary, hairy creature who dwelled deep in the woods, far from any society.

There were several variants on the Wild Man; giants, trolls and ogres all made regular appearances in literature and folklore. One of the earliest examples is the monster Grendel in the Anglo-Saxon epic poem *Beowulf*: 'some strange, vicious creature that hunts only at night and that no one has seen'. Beowulf was a warrior hero, and his killing of Grendel and Grendel's even more monstrous mother is undertaken with a sword 'hammered by giants'.

In medieval times, prehistoric flint arrows were thought to be of elfin origin, and therefore full of magical power which could be used to make protective amulets.

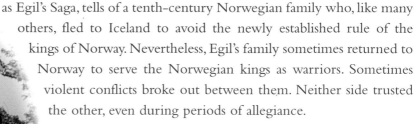

A rune stone from Lake Storsjön in Sweden. In local legend the now-incomprehensible runes bind a monster to the bottom of the lake until someone deciphers the inscription.

as Egil's Saga, tells of a tenth-century Norwegian family who, like many others, fled to Iceland to avoid the newly established rule of the kings of Norway. Nevertheless, Egil's family sometimes returned to Norway to serve the Norwegian kings as warriors. Sometimes violent conflicts broke out between them. Neither side trusted the other, even during periods of allegiance.

In one incident, Egil was present at a feast attended by King Eirik and Queen Grunnhild. Egil was carousing with a band of warriors led by his friend Olvir. The men were becoming enthusiastically drunk on flagons of ale supplied by the queen and her servant, Bard. Egil offended Bard by singing a verse accusing him of withholding the ale with the excuse that it had to be put aside for sacrifices to the gods. While Egil continued to pour beer down his throat, Bard told the queen about Egil's offensive behaviour and the two of them concocted a poisonous horn of beer. When Egil was handed the horn he must have become suspicious, for he stabbed his knife into the palm of his hand, then carved runes upon the horn, rubbing in his blood. He then spoke this verse:

> *I hatch runes on the horn*
> *Help seal each spell with blood*
> *Now, hear the nostrum I've*
> *Notched on this wild-ox horn*
> *Let's booze as we think best*
> *Beer those cheerful girls poured.*
> *Bard's marked it. What's that mean?*
> *Mischief? Well, let's find out.*

This was evidently a spell, for it caused the poisonous horn to break and 'the drink poured down into the straw'. At this point Egil's friend Olvir became dizzy with drink, and Egil took him outside for some fresh air. Bard followed them. While Olvir was vomiting and passing out, Egil killed Bard and fled the scene, returning to safety in Iceland, out of the king's and queen's power. The queen remained furious with Egil for his behaviour, and her attempts to have Egil killed make up much of the rest of the saga.

If this incident seems somewhat absurd for a heroic epic, then it was probably meant to be, in part. Christian Icelanders did not look back at the antics of their pagan ancestors without criticism, for they believed that sins were committed in an atmosphere that fostered them. One sin led to another, was the contemporary opinion, and drunkenness, violence and the practice of magic all inevitably occurred during the feasts of pagan gods. Nevertheless, Egil was presented as an admirable and even heroic figure. He drank the most alcohol at the feast and, unlike his friend Olvir, managed to remain on his feet in a manly fashion. His facility for spontaneous verse was considered as admirable as his capacity for brawling, and all these accomplishments resulted in his having certain magical powers. Egil's magic is usually used for good or neutral purposes – his spell here, for instance, was used only in self-defence.

These two rune stones from c. 900–1100 now lie in a Danish church. The runes of the larger stone contain a curse to prevent their destruction.

HERO WITH A KIND HEART

Later in the saga Egil reveals that he also has a command of healing spells incorporating runes. Runes were only used in special circumstances, often of a memorial or religious nature. This gave them a natural role in magical ceremonies as conduits of power. Runes were used for a variety of problems, all familiar from the magical practices of other societies. They were used to ensure victory in war, to ensure fertility, to attract the opposite sex and to improve the weather.

A group of people were attempting to cure a sick woman by carving runes into a whalebone. However, the correct runes had to be used and all attempts to cure the sick woman failed until Egil appeared. Our hero carved the right runes into the whalebone and the invalid was instantly cured. This sort of practice is even corroborated by

archaeology. A fish bone fashioned as an amulet was found in Lindholm, Sweden, with runes specific to a particular pagan god carved upon it.

The saga provides a contrast between the benign magic practised by Egil and the darker magic practised by the king's wife, Grunnhild. She was 'of all women the loveliest and wisest, and she had considerable knowledge of magic'. The queen is credited with having learned the practice of magic from the Sami of Lapland, the indigenous people of northern Scandinavia. In later centuries the Sami developed shamanistic traditions, in which their holy men were said to be able to leave their physical bodies while in a trance. It is likely that the Sami had similar beliefs in the early Middle Ages. In Egil's Saga, Grunnhild practised a form of magic that involved going into a trance. While in the trance she could perform any magic act or see into the future.

The queen used her power to persuade Egil to leave his safe home in Iceland so that she might be able to find some way to kill him. In the end, Egil fell into the clutches of King Eirik and the queen. At this dramatic stage of the story, when Egil seems doomed, the conflict is temporarily resolved without violence. It is Egil's talent as a poet which softens the heart of the king. Egil, on the spot, composes and declaims a long poem in praise of the king, and

A Scandinavian hero conjures up favourable winds for his journey in this sixteenth-century illustration for Olaus Magnus's history of the northern peoples.

persuades the king to show mercy. For the Icelandic audience, this incident showed the superiority of song and poetry, the arts of peace, over war and magic, the arts of violence. As so often in the sagas, however, the story did not end there, and the cycle of violence began again.

EGIL SHOWS HIS TEMPER

Although essentially something of a hero, Egil later used magic with ill intent, as his conflict with King Eirik grew even fiercer. In a fit of fury with the king and queen, he took a pole and thrust it into the cleft of a rock that faced an island which the king and queen had wrongfully claimed. On the pole, which Egil called a 'mocking pole', he fixed a horse's head, saying, 'I turn this mockery against the spirits who guard this land so that they may all wander astray, none reaching nor finding his home until they drive King Eirik and Queen Grunnhild from the land.' Then Egil carved a specific set of runes into the pole, and recited the full curse, which is not recorded by the saga (it being unwise, perhaps, to do so).

As Christians would have defined it, Egil's curse was an act of maleficium or witchcraft. The use of spirits to bring about curses demonstrates that Norse magic was similar to that of other societies. It is possible that other spells, even those using runes, may have been thought to depend on spirits as well as the innate power of the written word. Other curses in the sagas are more specific about the kinds of spirits invoked.

A Lapp shaman lies on the ground with his magic drum on his back, preparing to go into a trance to receive divine messages.

ROLE MODELS DISCOURAGED

The sagas, at first glance, seem to regard the use of magic as an almost acceptable part of the conflicts that were rife in Norse Viking society in ancient times. The leading characters frequently have some knowledge of magic, of both a benign and a malicious nature. But the authors of the sagas were careful to incorporate a note of disapproval into their tales. While stories about the heroes of old were certainly meant to be enjoyed and relished, and the characters to be admired in many respects, the saga authors did not wholly approve of them and took care not to present them as role models to be imitated. The magic acts recounted in the sagas were most likely meant to be rather shocking, and the contemporary readers − while admiring the noble sensibilities of the heroes and enjoying their boisterous adventures − were probably secretly rather relieved that society had become more civilized and magic was no longer a threat.

Grunnhild practised a form of magic that involved going into a trance. While in the trance she would be able to perform any magic act or see into the future.

In the early Christian period, fear of witchcraft remained widespread. In eleventh-century Denmark the newly Christian Danes believed their priests practised magic, and feared them accordingly. Women and priests were obvious targets to accuse of causing storms and pestilence, and the accused women − but not the priests − were often put to death as punishment. In 1080 Pope Gregory VII wrote to King Harold of Denmark condemning the killings of the women and forbidding any belief in witchcraft. This was the standard reaction of the church authorities at this time. They refused to accept that witchcraft was remotely possible because God would simply not allow it, and they even considered a belief in the possibility of magic to be sinful.

KING ARTHUR − MYTHICAL MAN, OR JUST A MYTH?

Despite the efforts of rational churchmen, belief in magic just would not go away, and Norse societies were not the only ones to record their fascination with magic in their literature. In Britain and France in the twelfth century, the genre of literature known as Arthurian first appeared. Like the sagas, Arthurian literature looked to the past, even if this one was wholly fictional. Nonetheless, in this ideal of Arthur's court, magic could flourish comfortably. Ironically, the authors of most Arthurian literature were the highly educated clergy who were supposed to toe the party line and take a dim view of belief in magic.

The origins of the myth of King Arthur are obscure, but it can safely be said that there is no genuine historical figure that remotely resembles the

King Arthur's Round Table in the Trehorenteuc church in the French Forest of Brocéliande, where many of the medieval adventures of Arthur's knights were set.

legendary Arthur. One sixth-century British chronicle survives, written by the cleric Gildas. Gildas was highly critical of Britain's rulers and made no mention of any illustrious noble that could be compared to Arthur, let alone one called by that name. The earliest sign of a burgeoning Arthurian myth appears in the dubious ninth-century chronicle of the Welsh writer Nennius; his Arthur was leader of all the kings of Britain, and won 12 battles against the invading Anglo-Saxons.

Arthur, as he appears in the earliest legends, is far from being the familiar, civilized Christian king of a sophisticated court. Rather, he was a warrior king. In the first substantial surviving account of the Arthurian legend, completed in 1136, the Breton cleric Geoffrey of Monmouth emphasized Arthur's status as a titanic warrior.

In one story, the king slew a Spanish giant who had kidnapped the daughter of a duke, sunk many ships by hurling huge rocks at them, and had eaten alive any warriors sent to fight him. Arthur's great strength enabled him to withstand the giant's massive club smashing against his shield. And because of his agility and speed, Arthur managed to inflict dozens of wounds on the giant before finally thrusting his sword into the giant's massive head.

THE CLASSICAL ARTHUR

Geoffrey of Monmouth's stories of Arthur, and his other legendary tales of ancient Britain, derived from Breton and Welsh legends, as well as his own vivid imagination. And although Geoffrey wrote a heroic narrative for Arthur, he omitted many of the supernatural elements usually associated with the most familiar version of the legend. Either the themes were developed later, or Geoffrey suppressed them, being more eager to present Arthur as a pseudo-historical figure than a pseudo-mystical one. He did, however, include Arthur's sword, Caliburn – in the later stories called Excalibur – but failed to mention that it was the gift of the spectral Lady of the Lake.

In Geoffrey's version of events Arthur is mortally wounded in his last battle against his nephew Mordred and is taken to Avalon so that his wounds might be attended to. Perhaps the later stories of the king who returned from his otherworldly resting place already existed in Geoffrey's time, but he suppressed this millennial fantasy. Geoffrey wrote in the hope of gaining the approval of the Norman kings of England, who might have been slightly piqued at the prospect of a legendary king who was expected one day to return and possibly seize their thrones.

In fragments of surviving Welsh legends about Arthur, he certainly appears as a more supernatural figure than in Geoffrey of Monmouth's version. An eleventh-century Welsh poem has Arthur wandering with a group of companions. Two of them are familiar from later stories. They are his knights Kei (Kay) and Beduir (Bedivere). Kay, Arthur's steward in Geoffrey's version, was often drawn as a comic and somewhat pompous figure in the later romances. But here he is

Merlin as a prophet, a kind of a holy man, was always imagined to be celibate in medieval legend, but romantic artists have depicted the aged man tempted by young women.

MERLIN AND VIVIEN

described as a 'destroyer of lions and witches' and vanquisher of the demon cat, Cath Paluc. Also among Arthur's companions are three figures who can be identified as Celtic gods: Mabon, Manaurdan son of Llyr, a Welsh equivalent of the Irish sea god, and Lluch Llauynnauc, derived from Lugh, the Irish god of storms and the sun.

The cycle of Arthurian literature that is most familiar today derives more from the tradition of literature known as romance, so called because it was written in a romance language, primarily French. It was in this tradition, founded upon the story traditions of the Bretons, that the magician Merlin became identified with Arthur and mysterious magical quests were developed for the knights of King Arthur.

The Holy Grail appears to King Arthur and his knights in this stained-glass window in a church in Brocéliande, France. The legend of the Grail first appeared in the twelfth century.

Most famous among these quests, and most mysterious in meaning, is the quest for the Holy Grail. The mythical origins of this object were lost with the original Breton stories, and it seems that even in the twelfth century storytellers were not sure exactly what the Holy Grail was. It appears sometimes as a 'platter of plenty', which magically provided feasts, and in other stories it appears in the form of a stone or a goblet. The Grail was always connected with a wounded or sick king, and the hero of the story is a knight of King Arthur's court, who is able to cure or relieve the king of his burden through some symbolic and mystical act. This part of the Grail legend is obscure in all the early versions. Later versions connect the hero's successful quest to relieve the Grail king with the rejuvenation of a wasteland, the Grail king's country. It wasn't until the thirteenth century that the Grail itself came to be identified with the goblet of Christ's Last Supper.

MAGIC OBSESSION INSPIRED BY THE SAINTS

In romance literature, magic resided mainly in objects, unlike the Icelandic sagas where magic was identified primarily with words and writing.

the myths of merlin

The magical figure most commonly associated with Arthur is the magician Merlin. Merlin appears in early Welsh legend as the prophetic poet Myrddin. Myrddin's prophetic abilities were supposed to have developed during a period of madness when he lived alone in a forest except for one companion – a little pig. The character Myrddin is related to the legendary Suibne (Sweeny) in Ireland and Lailoken in Scotland. These were prophetic Wild Men, whose fate was to die three times, or rather by three mortal injuries delivered at once. They also had the ability to predict the death of others.

In Geoffrey of Monmouth's version of the Arthurian cycle, Merlin is identified with yet another figure from an earlier Welsh legend, a clairvoyant boy who was nearly killed as a sacrifice by the tyrannical King Vortigern. Vortigern was trying to build a great tower as a base for his power over Britain, but every attempt ended in the building's collapse. The king's court magicians advised Vortigern that the tower would only stand if a sacrifice was made on its foundations. The sacrifice should be a boy who did not have a human father. Merlin's mother was a cloistered nun, but his father was an incubus demon (this was a kind of devil that medieval people thought visited women in their sleep to have sexual intercourse with them). Once King Vortigern's men found Merlin, they brought him to the tower to be sacrificed.

Because Merlin's father was a demon, the boy had prophetic powers and was able to show the king the real reason why his tower would not stand. Merlin convinced Vortigern to excavate the foundations of the tower where they found a red and a white dragon fighting. With this discovery,

Vortigern abandoned his attempts to build the tower, but kept Merlin as his court magician.

Merlin outlived Vortigern, and advised the next king of Britain, Uther Pendragon, and then his son, King Arthur. Geoffrey also invented the bizarre story that on Merlin's orders Stonehenge was transported from Ireland to Britain. He did this, apparently, because the stones 'are connected with certain secret religious rites ... Many years ago the Giants transported them from the remotest confines of Africa'.

The dragons beneath the tower disappear from the story as soon as they are discovered, but Geoffrey used them as symbolic figures in the prophecies he attributed to Merlin. The prophecies used the red and white dragons as symbols of the wars between the Saxons and the British. Geoffrey meant the prophecies to depict the eventual triumph of the Norman conquerors of Britain. This was intended to please Geoffrey's patrons, the Norman kings, by fabricating evidence that their rule had been predicted centuries before, and that they were the true heirs of Arthur.

There were two Merlins in legend, the Wild Man alone in the forest, and the boy prophet. The nineteenth-century artist Aubrey Beardsley imagined this image of the magician as a feral Wild Man.

Arthur's weapons and armour quickly took on a magical aura. Layamon, the first to write Arthurian tales in English, has Arthur wearing an apparently magical helmet named 'Goose-White' and a corslet, a body-armour, wrought by an elvish smith. Layamon was also the first author to arrange Arthur's knights around a circular table, which itself soon acquired magical properties. Many of the magical items in Arthurian literature were made by the elves in Faerie, the supernatural land where elves dwelled separately from the mundane world. Others have strictly Christian associations, such as a sword with the name of Jesus carved on it, or with relics placed upon the handle.

It was in fact the influence of the cult of the Christian saints that inspired Arthurian literature's distinctive obsession with magical objects. From the early centuries of Christian dominance in Western Europe, relics of the saints – bits of bone, tooth or hair, or scraps of their clothing, for example – were believed to have extensive healing and protective powers. The church also spent much of its wealth on magnificent decoration for its churches, and vast amounts of gold and silver were used to decorate the reliquaries or shrines containing the sacred relics. It was this background of venerating anything connected with the Christian saints that influenced the magical objects of romance literature.

'THE HANDSOMEST KNIGHT IN THE WORLD'

Another profound influence on the Arthurian legends was the Christian emphasis on the power of virtue itself. Many of the magical objects and places in the tales of Arthur could only be used or reached by knights who were very virtuous indeed. In the earlier stories, one of the most virtuous was Sir Lancelot. Later his virtue would be tarnished as the tale of his adultery with Queen Guinevere increased in popularity. However, in the thirteenth-century *Book of Lancelot,* his knightly virtue was in itself powerful enough to undo a magical enchantment.

Lancelot came upon a band of knights and damsels in a wood who were dancing around a chair upon which had been placed a golden crown. Lancelot cheerfully joined the dance but immediately lost his memory and was trapped in a continuous round of dancing. Finally, he sat upon the chair and the dancers placed the crown on his head. As soon as this was done the enchantment was broken and all the dancers recovered their memories. They explained to Lancelot that the enchantment had been laid on them years

In the fully developed Arthurian cycle, the aged and wounded king is taken to the mystic Isle of Avalon by three fairy queens, including his old enemy and half-sister, Morgan le Fay, centre.

before, and could only be broken if the 'best and handsomest knight in the world' sat on the chair and wore the crown. Lancelot's virtue made him magical in and of himself. He did not need to know how to break the spell, nor had he even intended to do so.

REMARKABLY POTENT OINTMENTS

In many of the adventures about Arthur's knights, attractive damsels are usually on hand to administer magically healing unguents or ointments when the plot requires the knights to go on living. Some authors ridiculed this sort of magic in farcical scenes. The great fifteenth-century writer Malory includes an episode in which Sir Gareth and his betrothed, Dame Lionnesse, are trying to sleep together before their wedding. Dame Lionnesse's sister, Dame Linet, is horrified and sends a knight to attack Gareth as soon as Lionnesse creeps into his bed.

Gareth swiftly beheads the knight, but Dame Linet saves the day by smearing a magical ointment upon the dead knight's head and neck. She then sets the limbs together, and they 'stuck as fast as ever they did'. The knight thus survives to launch an attack at Gareth the very next time he and his intended arrange a prenuptial tryst. Again the knight is beheaded, and this time Gareth chops his head into a hundred pieces, which he throws out of the window into a ditch. Undaunted, Dame Linet gathers up all the 'gobbets' of the head and glues the knight back together again with her special ointment. Gareth complains bitterly at Dame Linet's behaviour – the tale is silent on the reaction of the twice-beheaded knight – but Linet explains herself by claiming that she acted as she did only to protect the betrothed couple's honour.

From the early centuries of Christian dominance in Western Europe, relics of the saints – bits of bone, tooth or hair, or scraps of their clothing, for example – were believed to have extensive healing and protective powers.

MAGICAL WOMEN ARE FEARED

The leading exponent of magic in later Arthurian tales is Morgan le Fay, Arthur's half-sister. In the earlier stories she was only one of a number of characters with connections to the magical world of the fairies. Sir Lancelot himself, in some versions, was kidnapped by a fairy while an infant and plunged into a lake that became the fairy castle where he was raised. Morgan was frequently presented as a helpful figure in the early cycles – for example, Morgan's healing the hero Yvain of madness by means of an ointment. According to Malory, however, Morgan was schooled in a nunnery as a child and there 'she learned so much that she was a great clerk of necromancy'.(Malory used the term necromancy to describe magic in general.) In Malory's version of Morgan le Fay, unlike earlier versions, it becomes clear that by the fifteenth century, women who worked magic were regarded in a much harsher light than in earlier centuries. Malory's Morgan is depicted as almost exclusively evil in her use of magic. Malory sees her essentially as a witch, and after one of her evil plots has nearly caused the death of Arthur himself, 'then all had marvel of the falsehood of Morgan le Fay; many knights wished her burned'.

Sir Lancelot fights another knight before King Arthur, Guinevere and his court, in an early fourteenth-century manuscript illustration of Arthurian legends.

ARTHUR ANNOYS THE CHURCH AUTHORITIES

In the twelfth century, when the Arthurian tradition began, magic and witchcraft were of no great interest to the church. But the wealth of marvellous and magical elements in the Arthurian tales provoked disapproval from some of the more serious-minded clerics. One abbot complained that his monks had a habit of sleeping through his sermons, but if he blurted out the name 'Arthur' in a loud voice, the monks would wake up in a state of excitement. Many churchmen viewed the Arthurian stories as a frivolous waste of time.

It was principally the aristocracy who recounted these tales of courtly love and heroic quests to each other, and it did not greatly matter to the church whether or not these idle nobles diverted themselves with stories about magic and elves. It was a different matter, however, when ordinary peasants believed in magic.

THE RISE OF MEDIEVAL MAGIC

Beginning in the sixth century, the Christian clergy engaged many hundreds of monks in producing detailed manuscript books called 'penitentials', prescribing penances for various sins people might confess to their priests. These manuscripts consistently referred to the belief and practice of magic as sins throughout the Middle Ages, providing clear evidence that belief in magic remained widespread in Europe at this time despite people's embrace of Christianity. Some clergy even criticized the penitentials for reminding people about various unsavoury practices they might otherwise have forgotten.

Morgan le Fay, King Arthur's half-sister, shown here practising her evil magic in Frederick Sandys' painting of 1862–63. Morgan was only seen as wholly evil late in medieval tradition.

The practice of magic was considered a particularly serious sin if a priest committed it, and such a priest would be dismissed from the clergy. In sixth-century Ireland the penalty for making a love potion 'for the sake of wanton love' was a year on a diet of bread and water.

Later penitentials were less drastic in their punishments for witchcraft. In eighth-century Germany, the penitential of Theodore stated that a woman who performed 'diabolical incantations or divinations' should do as little as 40 days' penance, depending on the nature of the offence.

Lancelot confronting a knight and rescuing a damsel in a painting of 1886. The shields hung on the tree represent the other knights defeated by Lancelot's opponent.

SPELLS AND BAD WISHES

Diabolical incantations varied in form. Swineherds and cowherds were known to pronounce spells to protect their animals from disease or pests and shift the problems onto a neighbour's animals. The spells might be cast over a loaf of bread, herbs or knotted cords, and left in a significant place, such as a tree at a boundary or crossroads.

Women, it was claimed in the penitentials, used charms to draw all the potential milk and honey in the neighbourhood to their own cows and bees. Other spell makers, mostly women, were even more malevolent in their desire to be better than their neighbours, and boasted that they could kill chickens and piglets with a single word or glance.

In eleventh-century Germany and England, it was common for the penitentials to mention tempestarii. These were people – charlatans, no doubt – who went about the countryside extorting money from simple peasants by threatening to cause storms that would destroy their crops. But these charlatans played a dangerous game. Those suspected of witchcraft were sometimes lynched by villagers or townspeople. In the ninth century a German bishop, Agobard, rescued three men and a woman who were about to be stoned to death by peasants accusing them of being tempestarii. Others were not so lucky. In Bavaria in 1090, in the absence of a resident bishop, three women were accused of being poisoners and 'destroyers of people and crops'. They were flogged and immersed in water, but would not confess to the crime. Eventually they were burned to death. But stories such as these are extremely rare during most of the Middle Ages: only occasionally did such an event occur, and even then just a few people would have been involved. The great age of the witch-hunts came after the medieval period.

Accusing one's neighbours of witchcraft carried a considerable risk. In most countries secular law prevented malicious prosecutions by punishing the accuser if he failed to prove his accusation. Accusing another of witchcraft could lead to one's own punishment by death, particularly since maleficium was extremely difficult to prove. But occasionally such cases did occur. As late as 1451 a man in Strasbourg was judicially drowned for failing to prove an accusation of witchcraft.

MAGIC BEGINS TO DECLINE

The protective or malicious magic undertaken at the village level was a constant practice in Europe, but it was not in any sense connected with the old pagan religions or organized into any recognizable system of magic. Such magical practices were merely collections of techniques that were thought to help peasants in their constant struggle to sustain their lives. In a society such as ancient Egypt, the common magical solutions of the village might have been bound into a coherent system of magic and religion developed by the temple priests. Without that system, village practice in the Christian medieval period would always have been a purely practical assembly of folk knowledge and belief, with a few trappings from general Christian beliefs in the power of saints and their relics.

The idea of magic as an intellectual system disappeared from Western Europe with the collapse of the Roman Empire and the subsequent domination of the Christian Church from the fourth century onwards. The surviving

(continued on page 92)

Alchemy became as much natural philosophy as the pursuit of magic itself. Here the Sun and the moon are symbolic matches to the alchemical couple harvesting 'alchemical dew'.

89

Were there really medieval Witch-hunts?

It is a common assumption that the great witch-hunts began in the medieval period. The words 'medieval' and 'witch-hunt' are often spoken together when comparisons are made with certain modern instances of persecution. Until recently, general histories of witchcraft stated that witch-hunts began in 1275 in the south of France, in Toulouse, with the burning of one witch. In 1335 the first mass trial was said to have occurred, with the burning of almost 100 men and women. By 1350, 400 people were said to have been executed at Toulouse, with some 200 people burned for witchcraft in Carcassonne. In Italy, too, there was supposed to have been mass hysteria over witchcraft, with hundreds more being killed in the diocese of Novara between 1341 and 1352.

An illustration of a mass burning of 400 witches in Toulouse. This event happened in 1577, over 200 years after the fictional witch-trials mentioned by Lamothe-Langon.

None of these events actually occurred. The much-reviled medieval Inquisition, which was said to have been behind the events at Toulouse, was set up by the Papacy in the thirteenth century to seek out and suppress heretical beliefs. However, it was rarely involved in witchcraft trials, and was usually more concerned with halting such trials than pursuing them. All that happened in Toulouse in the fourteenth century was the imprisonment for life of one monk who had been discovered trying to make a love potion. But it is not the fault of the general public that witch-hunts are generally regarded as medieval. For a century and a half, from the early nineteenth century, historians believed that mass trials of witches took place in the fourteenth century.

The main villain in this embarrassment for professional history was a popular nineteenth-century French writer called Baron Lamothe-Langon. The baron was a minor aristocrat who, by his late teens, had already written a voluminous amount

of poetry and fiction. He soon turned to writing historical romances, and was among the earliest mass-market authors. His output of cheap adventure stories was huge, running into hundreds of volumes in the course of his life.

Relatively early in his career, Lamothe-Langon wrote a history of the Inquisition in France, and it was here that the mass trials of Toulouse first appeared in modern history. The baron did not actually create these events entirely in his own imagination. He relied partly on the late medieval chronicler William Bardin. Bardin was a careless chronicler and prone to inventing much of his material. In the fifteenth century it was not unusual for historians to make up events that happened a hundred or more years before.

However, Bardin did not create the mass trials that appeared in Lamothe-Langon's history. The baron himself seized upon Bardin's story and added many of his own details. He increased the number of people executed to make the story more exciting, and even fabricated the involvement of the Inquisition.

Lamothe-Langon's history of the Inquisition was accepted as genuine for a long time before scholars checked his sources and began to uncover the deceit. Historians accepted the truth of these singular events in Toulouse only because, like most people in the nineteenth and twentieth centuries, they felt that the witchcraft trials were an irrational horror that was appropriate to the supposedly barbaric medieval past. The causes of witchcraft hysteria in the sixteenth and seventeenth centuries must have had their origins in a 'backward' medieval past, because the modern, rational culture that was growing between 1500 and 1700 should not have been capable of such barbarity. After the horrors of World War II and the Holocaust, we now feel less optimistic about the rational and civilized nature of modern societies. We can now see clearly that the general European witch hysteria emerged only with the beginning of modern European history, in the Renaissance of the fifteenth century.

Witch persecution was relatively rare in the Middle Ages, but there were many legends of witches, including this twelfth-century English story of the witch of Berkeley, who was carried off by the Devil.

Eastern Roman Empire, known as the Byzantine Empire, provided no more of a refuge for the written magical tradition of antiquity. The rise of Islam in the seventh and eighth centuries brought forth another monotheistic religion as hostile to magic as Christianity. Islamic civilization soon stretched from India to Spain, and appropriated the old centres of religion associated with magic – Persia, Babylon and Egypt. Intellectual life in general flourished across the Islamic world and many of the philosophical and scientific works of antiquity were preserved by its scholars. Magic may not have been an acceptable part of official religious life, but in the general atmosphere of comparative intellectual freedom, astrology and other magical traditions survived.

ISLAM BRINGS CULTURE TO EUROPE

Western Europe was essentially a backwater of civilization until the twelfth century. As trade expanded and cities grew, a secular intellectual elite began to rise along with the foundation of the earliest universities. It was in this climate that the philosophical learning of the Islamic world began to stream into Western Europe, along with many otherwise lost manuscripts of the ancient world. Only in this context could magic begin to reappear in the form of a complex and intellectual art. Certainly much of the growth of astrology in the later Middle Ages was derived from Arabic learning. Twelfth-century culture was marked by its admiration for the writers of classical Rome and Greece, and images from those ancient writers filled the imaginations of Western Christians. As a result, magicians appeared in the pages of literature long before any individual appeared in society

The pagan figure of Saturn was seen in the fifteenth century as the ruler of two signs of the zodiac, Aquarius and Capricorn, and the many earthly activities pictured below.

Roger Bacon was a thirteenth-century Englishman renowned as a natural philosopher. However, his experiments in alchemy also brought him under suspicion of being a sorcerer.

claiming to be an authentic practitioner of magic. This makes Geoffrey of Monmouth's fictional Merlin one of the first European magicians.

'REAL' MAGICIANS APPEAR

The first sign that there were real men in Europe, not mythical figures like Merlin, who believed themselves to be magicians came from the complaints of some of the clergy in the thirteenth century. In 1267, the English philosopher and scientist Roger Bacon complained that charlatan magicians were producing writings – using pompous and overblown language, specifying demons that could be invoked and sacrifices that should be made to them – that purported to contain the magical wisdom of Solomon. Bacon himself was occasionally suspected of sorcery, due to his practical experiments in physics and chemistry, which involved alchemy. The line between magic and science was not yet clear.

Among the works of classical civilization that were new to the medieval West was the *Testament of Solomon*, written in Palestine in the first century AD. This was a tome of obscure medicinal magic, in its own time claiming to be the wisdom of the still more ancient biblical King Solomon. This book inspired self-styled magicians to write more books of magical instruction. This kind of magical writing consisted largely of lurid and fanciful descriptions of devils and demons that could be summoned by magic. The names of the demons were derived from the Bible, but these charlatan magicians invariably claimed to have gleaned their knowledge from secret books from the East. Since a wealth of ancient books of learning and legend in Greek and Arabic had only recently started to become known in the West, this seemed to some at the time to be a plausible claim.

WHY MEN SUMMONED DEMONS

Would-be magicians who summoned demons undoubtedly did so with the motivation of personal gain. Those interested in this kind of magic were inevitably highly educated men, at least able to read Latin, if not Greek and Hebrew as well. They believed that the demons could bring them knowledge of science and the arts, preferably esoteric knowledge that would benefit them in some way. The magicians, often clerics with expectations that demons could bring them success in their careers in the church or in government, usually had a patron, a powerful figure who would want to manipulate the magicians' skills to harm his enemies. Books of magic contained maleficia, spells to cause disease, 'provoke men to theft and murder', demolish wells and even sink warships.

ALCHEMY TAKES HOLD IN EUROPE

One of the main centres in which the study of magic developed in the West was the court of Emperor Frederick II. Before he became king of Germany in 1212, and subsequently the Holy Roman Emperor, Frederick was the king of Sicily.

Books of magic contained maleficia, spells to cause disease, 'provoke men to theft and murder', demolish wells and even sink warships.

Sicily was perhaps the most important meeting place for Christian and Islamic culture. The island had been Moslem for centuries before it was conquered by Norman adventurers in the late eleventh century. Moslems remained highly respected in government under Christian kings, and the island became a place where Jewish, Islamic and Christian scholars could meet to discuss their ideas and pool their knowledge. Magic was part of the cross-fertilization of culture, and alchemy was one of the magical practices that were introduced to Western Europe partly through Islamic influence.

Frederick II, a keen patron of science and philosophy, was interested in all forms of learning. Inevitably magic was included in his interests, and he instructed his court astrologer to compile an encyclopaedic work on astrology and related subjects. From this and other surviving commentaries on magic, the belief had emerged that demons could be summoned and controlled by carrying out certain rituals. Demons had to be summoned by name and then imprisoned in a bottle or a ring, so the magician could control them. As demons were more creatures of spirit rather than mortal flesh, magic could confine them in objects. But the magic required that a sacrifice had to be made to the demon to entice it into the trap. Since demons were said to have a taste for human flesh (despite their 'spiritual' nature, they did have material appetites), it was advised that the magician use flesh from a corpse, or even slice off some of his own for the sacrifice.

Emperor Frederick II (1194–1250) of the Holy Roman Empire was possibly the most powerful man of his time. His court was a centre for all kinds of learning, including magic.

SUMMONING DEMONS

In the fourteenth century an Italian astrologer, Cecco d'Ascoli, described similar practices, as had Frederick II's tutor at an earlier time. D'Ascoli claimed that his knowledge of magic derived from the tradition of Zoroaster, an ancient Persian religious figure who was wrongly thought by Europeans to have been a magician.

In d'Ascoli's conception demons were grouped in hierarchies, headed by four spirits 'of great virtue', which represented the four corners of the earth: east, west, north and south. They were named Oriens, Amaynon, Paymon and Egim, and each of them controlled 25 legions of lesser spirits. These spirits could only be controlled by being given human blood to drink, or at the very least fed with cat's flesh. This new 'tradition' of the summoning of demons was probably not something that derived from Arabic learning, however much magicians boasted of having secret Eastern knowledge. The Western European rituals of demon-summoning were probably the inventions of the magicians themselves.

D'Ascoli admitted that the rituals involved in the summoning of these spirits were contrary to the practice of Christianity. Nonetheless, the rituals were influenced by Christian beliefs. The magician had to become something of a holy man in order to control the demons successfully. While the clergy worried about magic because they believed that the summoning of spirits involved their worship, the late medieval magicians claimed to be controlling the demons by the power of the Christian God. Thus a magician would remain chaste, and he would fast and pray devoutly in preparation for a ritual. His instruments – staff, sword and sickle – had to be consecrated with the recital of the psalms. And once the demon had been summoned he was to be controlled, rather than worshipped.

The church made only occasional attempts to suppress this kind of magical activity. Churchmen warned that demons could not be controlled, and would only appear to be under the magician's control in order to lead him farther into sin and damnation.

Those philosophers and early scientists who tried to develop theories of magic and its relationships to God and the natural world were often very careful not to specifically mention demons in their writings. Anyone who openly believed in the usefulness or naturalness of demonic magic was in grave danger of being arrested and brutally punished as a heretic by the church authorities.

> Since the scientific revolution of the seventeenth century, Western Europeans have tended to think of the universe as mechanistic – that is, that it works according to strict laws whereby objects react to each other in a direct and predictable way.

THE LINK BETWEEN DEMONS AND STARS

Intellectual magic, based on written esoteric traditions rather than village folk practices, was not just a shady practice of ambitious and amoral clergy. Early scientists hoped to use astrology and alchemy to understand the nature of matter. Since the seventeenth century, Western Europeans have tended to think of the universe as mechanistic – that is, that it works according to strict laws whereby objects react to each other in a direct and predictable way. This is the universe that was described by such seventeenth-century thinkers as Sir Isaac Newton, whose laws of physics were at the foundation of modern science. But Newton was also interested in magic. Even as he developed his revolutionary new laws, he dabbled in alchemy and astrology.

Before the seventeenth century, philosophers believed the world operated in a way quite different from our 'mechanistic' universe. All materials were thought to be imbued with some kind of 'spirit' or virtue which could affect other materials from a distance in a magical fashion. Astrology is based upon this idea.

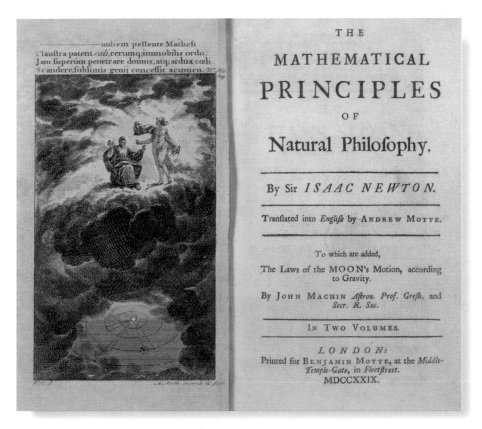

Sir Isaac Newton, the seventeenth-century mathematician renowned as the founder of modern physics, was also interested in alchemy, the practise of which had not yet been entirely discredited.

aLchemy — the greatest quest of aLL

Alchemy first emerged in the early centuries AD in Alexandria in Egypt. It was then practised in the Byzantine Empire and Arabic civilizations, before passing into Western Europe during the twelfth century. The basis of alchemy was the belief that all materials were formed from combinations of four elements: air, earth, fire and water. It was thought that all metals were formed by sulphur, representing fire, and mercury, representing water. Alchemists attempted to use their knowledge of the elements to turn base metals, such as lead, into gold.

An alchemist is pictured between furnaces and chemical paraphernalia used in his experiments to transform base metals into gold.

Alchemists generally did not see themselves as merely pursuing a base desire for wealth. Alchemy was seen as a spiritual quest to discover the nature of the elements and therefore God's Creation. Alchemical research could therefore only be successfully performed by those living a pure life, and alchemists had a reputation for ascetic living. Many alchemists were monks, despite the church's condemnation of alchemy as a dangerous form of magic.

Alchemy remained a common intellectual pursuit into the seventeenth century, and alchemical experiments fostered the development of science, particularly chemistry. In the alchemists' search for the basic building blocks of the universe, and the answer to the question 'how was the world created?', alchemy can be compared to today's theoretical physics.

As true scientific knowledge grew in the seventeenth century, the basic theories of alchemy were shown to be incorrect, and the practice was finally discredited.

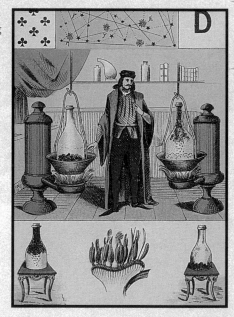

Just like in modern-day astrology, the planets had certain 'virtues' that affected all things within their sphere of influence. Often the 'virtues' of celestial bodies were personified as demons, so astrologers were believed to have dealings with these demons: The astrologers themselves viewed the demons as part of the workings of the natural world and as such they could not be inherently evil. In their view demons were really a kind of angel. These angelic demons served God as 'natural' forces in the world, rather than remaining in Heaven with traditional angels. It remained dangerous for Renaissance philosophers to state this theory openly, and most chose to

hide the extent to which they used demons in their astrology.

Some of the other magic practices that existed at this time did not involve demons but were based on the notion of objects and materials having 'spirit'. The theologian Saint Thomas Aquinas admitted the existence of a form of 'natural magic' that a Christian could use with impunity. Certain herbs and minerals were thought to have natural magical qualities. These qualities were seen as 'sympathies', in which one object had a mystical connection with another object or person. Properly used, the sympathy of one object with another could produce a physical effect, such as healing.

Alchemy had four stages, which revolved around the four elements — earth, water, air and fire. This engraving also shows the four degrees of fire balanced on the personified elements.

MUSIC AS A SPIRITUAL FORCE

Many Renaissance philosophers developed elaborate schemes of 'natural philosophy' that attempted to use and explain magical ideas in describing the

This strange beast is the Mercurial demon of alchemy. The demon was related to the Greek God Hermes, or Mercury to the Romans, a god of secret knowledge with an uncertain temper.

universe. One of these was the late fifteenth-century Italian writer Ficino. Much of his magical system was based upon music, because he thought that music was a spiritual force that could connect with and control all the other spiritual forces in the universe. Certainly he considered music a powerful medicine, acting on the human spirit through the air, just as food related to the physical body.

Ficino's music also was astrological in nature. By the performance of music as part of a magical ceremony, the music could balance the astrological forces that acted upon the body. In this way, Ficino claimed to be able to control nature through his music, while firmly denying that when performing his musical rituals he was invoking demons in any way. When performing a hymn to the Sun, for example, Ficino was hoping only to make his own spirit more receptive to the 'natural' astrological influences of the Sun. His critics objected, citing the possibility that a demon might hear the hymn and produce some magical effect or illusion.

It seems that Ficino was not entirely honest about his true beliefs in his public writings. The ancient authors who influenced his thinking certainly thought musical rituals like this were direct communication with demons, and one of Ficino's own disciples wrote clearly of demonic magic. All the thinkers who discussed magic ran the risk of censure by the church, but many of them saw no contradiction between their Christianity and their practice of magic.

A late dabbler in magic, the Elizabethan English courtier Sir Walter Raleigh was able to declare more openly that 'the art of magic is the art of worshipping God'. His contemporary, John Dee, a famous magician in England, claimed that he took great care only to summon 'good' demons.

MAGIC'S SECRET CODE

It is often difficult for scholars to understand Renaissance writings on magic, and many of the authors deliberately made their works obscure because they felt that the knowledge within their access would be dangerous to most people. Renaissance magicians considered themselves to be elite, specially graced to rediscover the knowledge of the ancient world. Magic works tended to circulate around Europe only in manuscript form, even though printing presses had become available. In keeping their work secret the magicians were protecting themselves from the church authorities, but they were also concerned about containing their secrets within their own charmed circle.

An alchemist working at his furnace, from the compendium of science The Philosophical Pearl, *first published in 1503. Behind him is an apparatus for the distillation of gases.*

The esoteric writer and ex-monk Giordano Bruno, who openly called for

Nostradamus — hero or villain?

Not all of the esoteric figures of the Renaissance were men of serious intellectual qualities – some were charlatans or failures. One of the most famous of this group was the French 'prophet' Michel de Nostradamus. He was born in 1503 in St. Remi, Provence, into a Jewish family that had recently converted to Christianity. His childhood was not rich, but his family managed to educate him in Latin and mathematics and send him to Montpellier to study medicine. After some early wandering years, following the deaths of his first wife and children, Nostradamus married a wealthy woman and had an enviable practice as a doctor. He was rumoured to have used secret – possibly magical – remedies to cure infectious diseases in Aix and Lyon. After his success and the welcome notoriety that came with it, Nostradamus began to believe in his own ability to make prophecies. In 1555 he published a book of prophecies.

Nostradamus pictured in the 1690 edition of his prophecies. Nostradamus claimed to have divine inspiration for his nonsense verses, but few people took them seriously.

This publication brought him even more notoriety, and the queen of France, Catherine de' Medici, summoned him to her court in Paris to cast horoscopes for the young royal princes. In 1559 King Henri II died of a wound inflicted during a jousting tournament, and people convinced themselves that Nostradamus had predicted the event. Yet none of Nostradamus's colleagues took him seriously, and by the time he died in 1566, most people thought him an impostor.

After Nostradamus's death, others began to use his 'prophecies' to comment on contemporary politics, and in the seventeenth century he was a useful foil to attack powerful government ministers. These uses of Nostradamus's writings were purely satirical in intent, and no one really believed that they were genuinely prophetical. The sheer obscurity and generality of his writings have nonetheless allowed people to claim the veracity of his predictions for almost any subsequent event.

a new religion based on an enlightened 'hermetic' priesthood of an ancient Egyptian kind, was burned to death as a heretic for his speculations.

One of the ways in which way magicians kept their secrets was to write in complex codes. A German Benedictine monk, Johannes Trithemius (1462–1516), wrote a book on the summoning of angels and spirits. It has been claimed that the incantations in his book, which were long and nonsensical, are in fact codes, and that the book itself was really a cipher manual. Certainly Renaissance magicians contributed to science through their interest in cryptography and mathematics, which developed significantly in this period. In addition, the complex ciphers that they developed were of great interest to monarchs and governments who wanted to spy on their rivals.

MESSING WITH MAGIC LEADS TO A GRIM END

Many saw magic as a highly dangerous activity, while others who were doubtful of the claims of magic held magicians in some contempt. At the height of the fashion for intellectual experiments with magic in the sixteenth century, the famous legend of the magician George Faust began to appear in Germany. In this legend, a scholar, after many years of failure, finally learns

> In keeping their work secret, the magicians were protecting themselves from the church authorities. But they were also concerned about containing their secrets within their own charmed circle.

The legend of the magician Faust, who summoned the Devil to satisfy his thirst for knowledge, then power and pleasure, has been told in many versions since the sixteenth century.

103

The arteries of the human body, originally described by scientist-magicians, depicted in an 1805 edition of Culpeper's Herbal, *a compendium of practical and sometimes magical medicine.*

the true secrets of magic and succeeds in summoning a demon. Unfortunately the demon that Faust summons is the Devil. Faust has various adventures in the different versions of his story, but in all cases he comes to a grim end. Like the first-century magician Simon Magus, Faust is dashed to the earth while using his demonic powers to fly. There were many magicians at the time who may have provided a real-life model for the Faust story, including a George Faust who was rumoured to practice necromancy in Germany. Whatever the origins of the story, it was hugely popular in Germany and England in the sixteenth century and was turned into a masterpiece by the English playwright Christopher Marlowe.

In the course of the seventeenth century, philosophers such as René Descartes provided intellectual arguments which undermined belief in magic, and the new science destroyed the assumptions that served as its foundation. Educated opinion ceased to believe that magic had any reality, and rather than coming to an abrupt end like Faust's ability to fly, widespread belief in magic slowly ebbed away over many decades.

MAGIC – A DEAD END, BUT FRUITFUL

The efforts of Renaissance magicians seem wasted from a modern-day point of view. But even though magic became discredited, many of the achievements of the scientific revolution originated in the attempts of Renaissance scientists to make magic a useful system that would explain the universe. Indeed, many Renaissance figures combined studies and disciplines now regarded as separate, but at that time they were thought of as being intimately linked. The great German doctor Paracelsus (1493–1541) practised alchemy, cosmology and

The pre-scientific universe was seen as a series of circles, with earth at the centre, the moon as the first circle, followed by the planets, enclosed by the spheres of Heaven.

magic, all as part of his medical science.

The mystical conviction that numbers contained the keys to all mysteries fostered the revival of mathematics. Astrological inquiry led to new precision in the observation of planetary movements. Esoteric writers helped to spread Copernicus's revolution in cosmology – even biological discoveries, such as the circulation of blood, were originally encouraged by magical thinking. Magic turned out to be a dead end, but it was not wholly without fruitful consequences.

CUNNING FOLK AND WISE-WOMEN

hile Renaissance magicians continued with their esoteric research in the sixteenth century, ordinary men and women did their best to get by in a harsh world. To help them in their daily struggle, people relied upon a whole range of magic and rituals. Some of these day-to-day superstitions and magical practices were sanctioned by the church, some were tolerated and others were condemned.

A great many people, from the poorest to the richest, consulted a 'wise-woman' or 'cunning man' at some point of trouble in their lives. Indeed, Robert Burton complained in the *Anatomy of Melancholy*, published in 1621, that sorcerers were all too common: 'Cunning men, wizards, and white witches as they call them, in every village, which, if they be sought unto, will help almost all infirmities of body and mind.' Other descriptions for these people included conjurers, wise-women, wizards, charmers and blessers, but often they were collectively described as 'cunning folk'. The cunning folk were called this because they were thought to have special knowledge and skills. 'Cunning' simply meant intelligence and knowledge. But already in the seventeenth century the word was beginning to acquire its modern meaning, which implies deceitful scheming. People depended upon the cunning folk, but did not always entirely trust them.

The cunning folk existed within a vast web of practices and beliefs that were magical to some extent, or depended upon beliefs in the commonness of spirits and other supernatural creatures. In Europe, magic became ever more visible from the sixteenth century onward.

Self-styled wizards tried to convince people of their magical abilities and knowledge by dressing in exotic robes and cluttering their rooms with strange objects and impressively ancient tomes. The wizard's clientele was likely to be illiterate, as he himself might be, so it mattered little what the books actually contained.

Robin Good-fellow was a comical make-believe fairy figure to some, but to many he could be a much more dangerous spirit, possibly helpful but sometimes malevolent.

At this time there was a growing gap between the culture and beliefs of the rich and those of the poor working people. Some of the educated rich began to take an interest in the beliefs and customs of the poor who lived around them, and started to record them. These folklorists were the forerunners of the historians and anthropologists of modern times, and their notations add helpful information. The amount of information from folklorists increased dramatically in the eighteenth century, but the largest amount of information about the sixteenth and seventeenth centuries comes from court records. Across Europe, the governing and clerical elites tried to suppress the superstitions and magical practices of the common people.

While petty magic of various kinds was made illegal, the courts were not able to stop people from resorting to magic, since it was simply too widespread and too much a part of everyday life. Many of the superstitious practices emerge as incidental details in witchcraft and sorcery trials. The cunning folk sometimes found themselves charged with witchcraft and explained their practices in detail, trying to show that they were not involved in evil magic. We might expect the cunning folk to be particularly vulnerable to charges of witchcraft, but in reality they were no more likely to be caught up in witchcraft trials than other people.

ACCIDENTS WAITING TO HAPPEN

Until modern agriculture and medicine developed, life was insecure, and the sixteenth and seventeenth centuries were times of frequent plague and famine. For their crops to flourish, people were dependent upon not just the weather, but their tools and animals as well. Consequently the sickness of a single animal, the accidental loss of a tool, or the theft of a few small items could endanger the livelihood of any poor family. The possibility of an accident occurring was a constant fear, and many people turned to magic to explain mishaps and misfortunes and to guard against them.

RITES AND RITUALS FOR EVERY ACTIVITY

Everyday work was surrounded by rituals. It was common in England in the sixteenth century to leave out a little food or drink for spirits who might cause small mishaps in the household, so a bowl of milk would be set out for Robin Good-fellow, a sort of fairy spirit. All working objects, too, would be blessed at the end of the day. Right up until the twentieth century in the Outer Hebrides in Scotland a spinning wheel would be blessed before being put away for the night, cows were blessed before being milked, and tools were blessed when returned to the workshop. The decorations made on spinning wheels or on containers for crops were not whimsical additions. Crosses and other mystical or sacred insignia were incorporated in their decorations as protective devices for food or machinery.

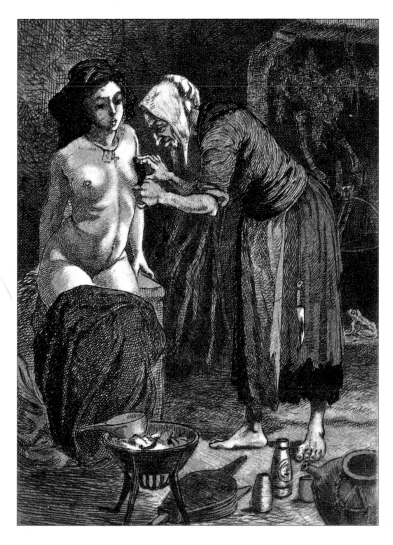

A French wise-woman treats her patient with secret herbs in Jules Michelet's 1862 history of witchcraft, which he saw as a form of peasant protest against an oppressive social order.

COMMUNITY MAGIC

At the beginning of the sixteenth century, communities across Europe held many ceremonies and festivals to mark important times of the year. These were not merely festivals for pleasure, they were meant to protect communities by honouring the saints that they called upon in times of need or to banish harmful spirits. Parish priests were often central to the most important agricultural rituals, which included blessing trees and reading the Gospel over streams to ensure the purity of the water. To

A king being baptized by a bishop in a sixteenth-century illumination. The holy water used in baptism was thought to be a powerful, even magical, remedy for many ills.

guarantee the fertility of their crops, after Mass had been said by their parish priest, the community would make processions around the parish boundaries and across the fields.

KING WITH THE MAGIC TOUCH

The magical or miraculous atmosphere that permeated the culture at this time extended to the highest ranks of society. Kings in particular had a magical aura. In England, the king's touch was supposed to be able to cure scrofula, a disease of the lungs which caused blisters, sores and tumours on the neck, head and eyes. Special services were performed and lengthy queues of the afflicted would assemble before the king. While a clergyman read out appropriate verses from the Gospels, the sufferers would kneel one by one in front of the king to be touched lightly on the face.

Once the whole assembly had been treated in this way, everyone came forward again to receive a gold coin strung on a white silk ribbon from the king. While in this sense the ceremony was an act of ritual charity that dated as far back as the eleventh century, people were generally muddled as to its religious significance. Some regarded the king's power as a gift from God, others thought the power was inherent in the king himself, and still others believed that the power lay in the words spoken during the ceremony.

Theologians might claim that these rituals were not magical in any sense, since they merely called upon God's blessing in good Christian faith. God might respond or not, depending on His mysterious will, or perhaps whether the people who called on him were deserving enough. Magic, in contrast, was supposed to work every time, as long as the spell or ritual was carried out properly. No one needed to 'deserve' the magic to work, it would do so anyway. Most people would not have recognized the distinction between magic and religious ritual based on faith, for all the various Christian prayers, rituals and church ceremonies frequently made up part of the magical practices of village belief. Many other customs at this time also blurred the boundaries between religion and magic.

PESTS OUSTED BY CHURCH OR BY LAW

One such custom was the following of the saints, in which people appealed to the past holy men and women of Christianity for help in all aspects of their lives. The reverence paid to the saints was condemned by the Protestants, who believed it to be riddled with superstitious magic. In 1580 the French essayist Michel de Montaigne wrote that the people of Augsburg claimed to be free 'not of mice, but of the large black rats with which the rest of Germany is infected'. They attributed this absence of vermin to one of their bishops, who was buried in the town, and regularly took a little soil from his grave and sprinkled it in places where rats would normally be found.

Most ordinary people at this time believed that saints had the power to keep away vermin and insects. In the fifteenth century, in a village near Toledo in Spain, the inhabitants made a vow to Saint Barnabas and built a chapel to him. In return, the saint filled the trenches they had dug with dead locusts. The villagers claimed that since that day they had never suffered from that particular pest. In 1736, in the Palatinate in Germany, Jesuits observed the peasants using 'Ignatius-water', holy water blessed with the relics of Saint Ignatius, to rid themselves of a plague of caterpillars.

Most village communities had to rely on their parish priest for all matters spiritual and superstitious. One commonly held superstition among village folk was that evil spirits manipulated insects to cause trouble. This meant that the spirits had to be exorcized. In Italy, in 1588, the following magic formula was recited by a priest to rid his village of unwanted wildlife:

'I exorcize you pestilent worms, mice, birds, locusts and other creatures, cursing you; wherever you are, may you be accursed, shrinking and shrivelling into yourselves from day to day, until none of you remains.'

If the priest's warning went unheeded, the villagers occasionally took matters to a higher authority, such as the ecclesiastical courts, which sometimes obliged by excommunicating the troublemaking pests or animals. This course of action was particularly common in regions around Switzerland. In 1500 the inhabitants of a prime vine-growing region of Burgundy applied for legal action to be taken against the flies that were attacking their vines.

Some theologians disapproved of people drinking holy water to cure disease, regarding it as a superstition rather than a Catholic practice.

DOMESTIC RITES AND RITUALS

Other customs were less strange. Particular foods had to be eaten at particular times of the year as symbolic acts. For example, on Christmas Eve in the south of France frugal food had to be served to offset the fruitfulness that they hoped would come in the spring. Christmas itself was the spark that caused the spring to come again. In Sicily, no one would bake on a festival day in case it offended the saints. Many other simple but significant rituals surrounded the eating of food. In Languedoc the head of the household would make the sign of the cross with a knife over a loaf of bread before cutting it, saying as he began cutting, 'We do not know whether we will finish it.' The gesture was to keep misfortune at bay.

BLESSING THE HOUSE AND ITS ANIMALS

Across Europe rituals were carried out at Christmas, Epiphany and New Year to bless the internal parts of a house: a priest would trace crosses on the windows, for example. In Romania the walls and foundations of a new house were blessed by a priest. Priests could also help to provide protection for animals. In many parts of France from the fifteenth to the nineteenth century, medallions depicting Saint Anthony were hung around the horns or necks of animals. In southern Spain small bracelet-shaped rolls were baked on Saint Mark's Day, one for each person or animal, and blessed by the priest.

Holy water was a common ingredient in healing spells and other magic rites. Some theologians disapproved of people drinking holy water to cure

disease, regarding it as a superstition rather than a Catholic practice. But most churchmen took a tolerant view, arguing that if it was carried out in good Christian faith, then it was permissible. They held the same moderate view about many other charms and protections relating to Christianity.

A witch feeding her demonic familiars, two monstrously large toads and a cat, as imagined by an illustrator in 1579. The witch's brew was probably meant to be blood.

HOLY CHARMS

As a protective talisman, many people wore a piece of paper, tucked or pinned inside their clothes, or a medal with Gospel verses written upon it. The most common Christian amulet was a small wax cake inscribed with a lamb and flag. This was to protect against a host of evils, such the Devil, thunderstorms, drowning or death in childbirth. According to the official doctrine of Christianity, these charms were not considered to be magical because they were only a kind of prayer to God.

However, most ordinary people believed that these 'Christian' charms were magical. The charm was believed to work in an almost mechanical way (which is much the same as believing it worked in a magical way), while the effectiveness of a prayer depended on the virtue of the person saying it.

A forged magic book of recent origin, called The Book of Shadows, *and purporting to be an old collection of spells used by witches. The sort of magic used by village wise-women was never formally organized into instructions in this manner.*

Whereas the Christian saint was believed to have miraculous power through his extraordinary holiness, the cunning folk believed the power of their charms and spells was mechanical, or automatic. The cunning folk were also thought to have some sort of inherent power. This power was supposedly 'secret', but some practitioners of magic were persuaded to explain themselves when required to do so in court. In 1638 Thomas Hope claimed that he had acquired his powers while in Rome as a boy, where he was washed in particularly powerful holy water.

GRUESOME SACRIFICES

While some superstitious practices were tolerated and even encouraged by the church, many others were expressly condemned. Even so, these condemned practices were widespread. It was common at this time for sacrifices to be placed under the foundations of a newly built house, especially under the threshold, to provide protection against external dangers. These sacrifices could be as harmless as statues, bottles, pots, coins, paper charms or old shoes, but some were more grisly.

In Ireland, it was not uncommon to find horses' skulls buried under foundations. Cats were buried under British foundations from the late Middle Ages, and this practice continued into relatively modern times. Animal bones were placed in the foundations of the first Blackfriar's Bridge in London, built in the 1760s. And in 1897 a horse's head was buried in the foundations of a Methodist chapel in Cambridgeshire, with beer added for good measure.

Live animals were also sacrificed to halt the course of certain diseases thought to be caused by witchcraft. A Scottish woman called Margaret Bow was brought to court in 1650 for sorcery because she had buried a lamb under the threshold of her stable. She admitted the crime, claiming that she had done it in 'simplicity' – that is, without knowing that it was illegal – on the advice of an old woman whose own animals had died. The old lady had assured her that the sacrifice would prevent her animals from dying of the same disease. In 1604 in Huntingdonshire it was recorded that a local farmer who had lost many of his animals to a sudden disease had been advised to burn a sick horse alive. This he did, and it was reported that the rest of his herd recovered.

In 1629 in Dunbar, Scotland, a local woman, Isobel Young, was accused of burying a live ox and a cat with some salt as a sacrifice to the Devil so that the rest of her animals would remain free of sickness. As in all such cases where uneducated peasants were involved, the woman would not have had any notion of making a sacrifice to the Devil or indeed to any other spirit. The practically minded peasants merely believed that they were carrying out a simple, traditional magical rite as a means to ensure a particular end. It was the educated men of the courts, with their far more extensive knowledge of theology, who considered any act not specifically directed towards God to be directed at some diabolical spirit or demon.

A sensational publication from 1619 recounting the trial of a group of witches. Pamphlets such as these were common at the time and helped to fuel further witch hysteria.

MAGICAL CAUSES OF DISEASE

Diseases could be attributed to a wide number of causes in the sixteenth and seventeenth centuries, including astrology. Astrology was a complicated practice that in the fifteenth century was only well-

THE
WONDERFVL
DISCOVERIE OF THE
Witchcrafts of *Margaret* and *Phillip*
Flower, daughters of *Joan Flower* neere *Beuer*
Castle: executed at Lincolne, *March* II. 1618.

Who were specially arraigned & condemned before
Sir *Henry Hobart*, and Sir *Edward Bromley*, Judges
of Assize, for confessing themselues actors in the destruction of *Henry*, Lord *Rosse*, with their damnable prac-
tises against others the Children of the Right
Honourable FRANCIS Earle of *Rutland*.

Together with the seuerall Examinations and Confessions of *Anne
Baker*, *Ioan Willimot*, and *Ellen Greene*, Witches in *Leicestershire*.

Printed at London by *G. Eld* for *I. Barnes*, dwelling in the long Walke
neere Christ-Church. 1619.

Irish shefroes, a type of fairy, dance around a toadstool in an 1862 collection of Irish folklore.

known among educated men interested in esoteric learning. During the sixteenth century, knowledge of astrology spread more widely among ordinary people, who simplified the complex practices of the educated astrologers for their own practical use. The basis of astrology is the belief that the movements of the planets were highly significant. Certain diseases were blamed on the influence of astrological movements. Well into the eighteenth century, at least in London, unexplained deaths were frequently attributed to 'planet', or the influence of the heavenly bodies. A number of innocuous phrases in use today date back to astrological explanations for disease, such as 'moonstruck' and 'starstruck'. Some wise-women offered 'planet water' to treat these illnesses. In 1619 a wise-woman named Anne Baker was accused of witchcraft and during her trial she gave an elaborate account of astrological illnesses. According to her theory, each planet had a colour – for example, black always portended death – and she claimed to be able to see the different colours of the planets that attacked her patients.

Spirits and witchcraft also were worrisome sources of disease. Cooking meat could be a high-risk activity in magical terms. When making black pudding from pig's blood, men were excluded from the kitchen and the doors and windows were closed to avoid envious local women who might give the inhabitants the 'evil eye'. Cooking also attracted fairies and other spirits including the ghosts of dead children, who had to be appeased with gifts of food.

Fairies caused diseases, but they could cause other problems too. For example, they might disapprove of the prospective site of a new house. In Ireland, much care was taken not to offend the fairies by avoiding building across one of their 'pads', the places where the fairies were supposed to live or hunt. In County Tyrone a man would stick a spade into the earth and leave it overnight. If it was still there in the morning, the fairies were not displeased

A woman from Edmonton, near London, confessed to witchcraft without torture in 1621 and was executed. Cases such as hers were very rare, but confirmed people's fear of witchcraft.

and building could commence. Another ritual was to place a line of stones on the site and leave them overnight. Again, if the stones were undisturbed then the fairies were content.

THE CUNNING FOLK'S CREDENTIALS

There were a great many folk healers across Europe, and almost every village would have easy access to at least one such character. 'Wise-women' remained popular in some places well into the twentieth century. In the 1790s in the Gironde area of France, an official reported that there were 50 irregular 'medical' practitioners. He also noted that the local priests often worked as healers, too, using many of the same methods.

Most cunning folk did not have any special 'magical' start to their careers,

A fifteenth-century blacksmith at his forge. Blacksmiths were often associated with magic since forging metals appeared to enable them to transform one substance into another.

though some superstitions gave credence to their supernatural abilities. In many places in Europe, the seventh son or daughter was thought to have special powers. This belief was later transported to America. In some places in the United States, until relatively recently, the seventh son of a seventh son was thought to be a physician by nature. A more common reason for having magical power was to have been breech born. Also in a few places in Europe, around the Alps in particular, a child born with the placenta over its head was thought to have some mystical powers.

Certain professions had magical associations. Blacksmiths were believed to be able to heal wounds; this belief was particulary strong in Italy. In early nineteenth-century France many folk healers were believed to have gained their powers by rescuing or restoring statues of the saints during the French Revolution. Above all, however, it was the women throughout Europe who acted as midwives, a difficult and mysterious occupation, who were the most likely to expand their expertise to other forms of healing and other magical practices.

THE POWER OF PRAYER

The techniques used by the cunning folk to cure diseases often contained elements of Christian worship. One village healer questioned by the authorities in 1528 in London said that to heal someone she would first kneel and pray to the Holy Trinity to rid the patient of his enemies. She would then advise him to recite various prayers each night and would prescribe herbs according to each illness – some diseases required holy water, too. In 1557, one cunning man reputed to be more than 100 years old asserted that he always prescribed prayers alone for any disease. Folk medicine relied heavily on invoking the saints, particularly in countries which remained Catholic. In Portugal, the wise-women were considered to be the means by which the saints would produce cures.

WRITTEN CHARMS

Among the ancient Greeks and Egyptians, specific myths were an essential part of the magical charm. The same was true in early modern Europe, but the mythology was Christian. A cure for toothache was to write three times on a piece of paper, 'Jesus Christ for mercy sake, take away this toothache.' The paper was to be read aloud three times and then burned. Christian Europeans were not alone in these kinds of practices. Among Moslems in

> Blacksmiths, particularly in Italy, were believed to be able to heal wounds.

Nigeria, a similar practice exists: verses from the Koran are written on pieces of paper as protection against disease.

TALKING GIBBERISH

Some of the more esoteric magic of the Renaissance magicians filtered down to a popular level. The clearest evidence of this was the use of Hebrew words in some popular charms, such as Saboath, Adonay and Yhvh (Yahweh spelled in its four-letter form, known as the Tetragrammaton, was thought to be particularly powerful). Village wizards also used a mixture of names that were neither one language nor another, but a confused muddle of elements of names from a variety of languages including Hebrew, French and Italian, for example Ravaronne, Hur, Asmobias, Mebarke or Geballa. A foreign-sounding name impressed the uneducated folk who made up the vast majority of a wizard's clientele. Indeed, many of these wizards were not well educated themselves, having perhaps the ability to read a little Latin and maybe recognize a few Greek letters. The wizard was just as likely to be impressed by gibberish as by any genuine snatches of ancient or Eastern languages.

The Tetragrammaton, the Hebrew spelling of Yahweh (shown here in a 1385 illustrated service book), combined in its letters the elemental power of creation, and was often used in written magic.

BELT-MEASURING AS A CURE

Other techniques were more folkloric and show few signs of educated influence. In the 1570s in England, Janet Pereson was brought before the Durham church courts on a charge of witchcraft for using 'measuring belts' and advising mothers to wash a sick child in a south-running stream. The practice of belt-measuring was a strange means of diagnosing illness. It was thought that a person's belt would vary in length according to their health and could be altered, particularly if the wearer was 'haunted with a fairy'.

This might seem a rather curious belief, but it is another example of the traditional 'magic of sympathy'. Those objects most closely identified with a person are naturally imbued with that person's nature. Undoubtedly the belt was not expected to show any visible changes of shape except to the person with the expert, magical eye. The principle here is an ancient one, with the oldest of spells depending upon the use of bits of hair or nail from the person being treated. Belt-measuring as a practice in England dates back at least to 1438, when a Somerset woman, Agnes Hancock, confessed to treating children suffering from the 'feyry' (fairy) by inspecting their girdles. As an extension to the practice of belt-measuring, Agnes also measured the children's shoes.

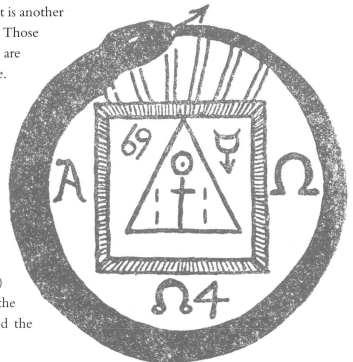

A CHARMING WAY WITH WORDS

The written charms that appeared in the sixteenth and seventeenth centuries continued, in one form or another, to spread throughout Europe. Some English charms are almost identical to charms found in Germany and France, and they also can be related to charms dating back to the Anglo-Saxon period. Some surviving charms even contain elements of classical spells.

This design for a charm amulet against diseases carries the instruction that it will be particularly effective if it is worn for some time by a maiden under her left breast.

Charms to counter disease generally contained a command to the illness to go away. In the Limousin region of France, one healer used the following verse to recite over a patient suffering from arthritis:

Ache from cold
Ache of Anthony
Go away to the sea
Where you will find
Plenty of stones and rocks
To rub against

The Anthony mentioned is Saint Anthony, who was associated with a number of diseases relating to pains in joints and bones. The English courtier

(continued on page 124)

Were witches and cunning folk always women?

The witches of folklore were invariably female, and many of the practitioners of magic throughout history have been women. In most traditional societies it has been the primary concern of women to care for children and the sick. This was still largely the case in early modern Europe, particularly in the countryside, where the only medical expertise available to most people might be the herb lore and magical preparations of an impoverished elderly widow.

However, even though many women practised magic, the 'professional' practitioners of magic at the village level were divided between men and women in the sixteenth and seventeenth centuries. A small majority of these full-time cunning folk, white witches and village wizards were women, but there were significant numbers of men involved as well. Many women practised magic as a 'part-time business'. Acts of magic were a way of earning a little additional income for those who were desperate, and women were significantly more likely to become economically needy than men. But it was risky to practice magic because of official disapproval. Therefore, much of our knowledge about village magic comes from the records of the women and men who were brought before the courts accused of practising sorcery or some other magical misdemeanour. The village magic practised by the cunning folk was not normally regarded as related to witchcraft, and the punishments for practising their charms and cures were relatively mild.

In normal circumstances, the cunning folk were not regarded as witches at all, but when a witchcraft trial began, normal circumstances often disappeared. During the great witch-hunts of the sixteenth and seventeenth centuries, any connection with magic could bring with it the suspicion of witchcraft. Some people today regard the witch-hunts as specifically directed at women, 'wise-women' in particular. This was not in fact the case. Male wizards and wise-women were equally likely to become involved in a witchcraft trial.

It was not usually the cunning folk themselves who were the first to be accused of witchcraft. In some cases one of their clients, involved in some village quarrel, was accused of using witchcraft to harm a neighbour. The cunning man or woman was then summoned to court to give their evidence, and could end up being charged with witchcraft themselves. Sometimes the cunning folk avoided these accusations even when caught up in a witchcraft trial. In 1581 a German woman, Ursula Fladin, who was accused of witchcraft, claimed that the spells she had used were harmless ones she had learned from a wizard in a nearby village. He was duly called to court to explain himself, but luckily he was only charged with deceit, rather than with witchcraft.

Overall, it is difficult to discover how often the cunning folk became caught up in witchcraft trials. It seems obvious that any practitioner of magic would be vulnerable to witchcraft accusations, but the historical records show far fewer witchcraft trials involving the cunning folk than one would expect. Since the cunning folk always had to be careful in their dealings with authority, they were perhaps better equipped than most people to avoid witchcraft accusations. It can be said with certainty that female 'white witches' were no more likely to be prosecuted for witchcraft than were their male colleagues.

Surviving statistics from the witchcraft trials show the true scale of the persecution of both men and women. In the Pays de Vaud region of France between 1581 and 1620, 970 people were condemned for witchcraft, 325 men and 624 women (the gender of the 21 others is unknown). In other areas the statistics show an even greater bias against women. In southwest Germany between 1561 and 1684, 1,050 women were condemned as opposed to 238 men, that is, 82 percent of the accused were women. In some mass trials in Germany women made up 90 percent of the accused. There was a strong vein of misogyny in the witch trials, which may have had its roots in the hysterical anti-witch texts of the fifteenth century, notably *The Hammer of Witches*. This text, particularly well-known in Germany in the sixteenth century, took the view that women's customs and natures led them naturally to witchcraft.

Villagers accuse a poor old woman of witchcraft, while three doubtful magistrates on the right look on. Magistrates were often reluctant to pursue witchcraft accusations.

123

In the woodcut: "Lord, haue mercy on London." "I follow." "We fly." "Wee dye." "Keepe out."

Death rules over London during a plague epidemic, in a woodcut of 1625. People turned desperately to charms and amulets to protect themselves from the merciless disease.

Robert Cecil suffered from worms, and in 1604 he consulted the healer Goodwife Veazy. She tried to expel the worms with the command 'Thou canker worm, begone hence in the name of the Father, the Son and the Holy Ghost'.

More elaborately, commands could be repeated over a number of days, increasing the magical pressure on the disease to leave. For example, a cure for worms might be repeated every day for 10 days or so, with each recitation of the charm claiming that the worms' numbers were decreasing day by day.

During the Great Plague in London in 1665, the writer Daniel Defoe noted a practice of a similar nature. Some Londoners wore an amulet around their necks to protect themselves against the plague. The amulet was a written formula, repeating the famous magic incantation 'abracadabra' in a triangle form, with each successive line missing off a letter from the end. The shrinking of the magic word was supposed to act upon the plague, also shrinking it to nothing.

HERB LORE AND IMAGINATIVE ANTIDOTES

Aside from written charms, the most common elements in magical cures were herbs and roots that had been used over centuries by many different cultures. There were several explanations for their effectiveness. According to medicine at the time, for good health a human body needed a balance of the four 'humours': dryness, wetness, heat and cold. Disease could occur when these humours were out of balance. Strictly speaking this is not a magical explanation for disease, since the theory of the humours, originally developed in ancient Greece, was thought to describe the real biological nature of the body. The idea of humours which governed the body's health was fairly well-known among ordinary people, and their understandings of the idea mixed this early form of 'scientific' medicine with their own magical remedies. Many plants were thought to be effective in balancing the humours of the body. Since lettuce is cold and moist it could be used to soothe overheated skin. The poppy-like herb celandine, being 'hot and dry', could draw out rotten blood, phlegm and melancholy.

The old practice of drawing blood from the veins of someone who had a fever was another practice based on the ancient principle of balancing the body's humours. A fever was considered to be hot and wet, like blood, so if a patient was suffering from a fever he needed to lose some blood to bring balance to his humours. This unhelpful and even dangerous 'cure' remained part of respectable doctors' normal practice until the

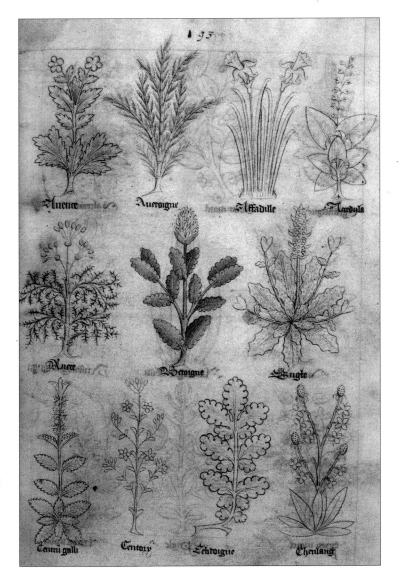

Eleven herbs from an English herbal. Herbals were compilations of the medicinal healing properties of plants, which also often included magical recipes and folklore.

125

nineteenth century, when modern medicine finally rejected the idea of humours entirely.

THE SIGNATURE THEORY

Most herb lore worked according to more strictly magical principles. Many plants bore signs that indicated to which organs they were related. This is known as 'signature theory'. Lungwort was regarded as a cure for consumption because its leaves, which were flecked with white, were thought to resemble tubercular lungs. Figwort was prescribed for scrofula (a swelling of the lymph nodes) and piles because of its knotty roots. Gromwell was used to dissolve bladder stones because the hard seeds were thought to resemble these stones. Liverwort was naturally used for liver ailments because the shape of its leaves slightly resembled the liver. The seeds of viper's bugloss resembled a snake's head, consequently this herb was used for snakebites.

SHADES OF MEANING

It was not just their shape that gave herbs and roots their natural magical properties. Someone suffering from jaundice would have a yellow tint to his skin, so a yellow object, plant or flower could be used to counteract the illness. Similarly a red washcloth could be laid against a sore throat, since red was associated with blood and a sore throat was thought to be a disease of the blood.

Although the reasoning behind these herbal remedies is flawed, some of the concoctions of herbs probably did have some beneficial effects. Various plants, roots and herbs have been used in almost all traditional societies throughout history as the only available source of medicine.

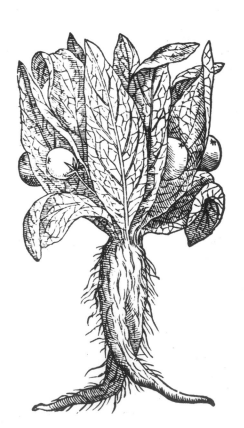

Male and female mandrake plants (left and right, respectively) were both thought to be especially powerful in magic, and became associated with witchcraft in the late Middle Ages.

A 'HAIR OF THE DOG'

A less effective solution was a rather literal approach to snakebites which involved killing the snake and placing its skin on the wound. This is based on the principle known as 'the hair of the dog that bit you', which is more familiar today as an unwise cure for a hangover. The Spanish writer Cervantes told of a young man who was bitten by dogs while visiting a gypsy camp: 'The old gypsy who undertook his cure took some hairs from the dogs, and, after washing the bites with wine, applied the hairs, which she had fried in oil, and covered them with a little chewed rosemary. She then bound up the wounds with clean cloths, and made the sign of the cross over them.'

CALLOUS CURES

Peasant societies wasted no sentiment on animals, and considerable pain was deliberately inflicted on them for the purpose of some magical cures. In Portugal, a lizard could be used to cure a tumour, but it had to be killed by blows using the index finger. A seventeenth-century English cure for consumption required a cock to be killed, flayed and beaten into pieces so that it could be made into a medicine. It seems that the more the animal suffered, the greater would be its efficacy in a cure. Among the many magical cures for plague was a particularly gruesome remedy recommended in 1615 where a pigeon should be cut in two and applied to the sufferer's skin. There are echoes of these customs in certain cures used in the nineteenth century in the United States. For example, the blood of freshly killed pigs and cows was smeared directly onto the skin of an eczema sufferer.

Toads were frequently thought to be witches' demonic familiars, and a source of witches' powers, allowing them to fly.

127

toads, moles, hare's livers and crab's eyes

Toads were famously associated with witches who performed wicked spells and were themselves associated with evil. Indeed, a number of accused witches in England were forced to admit to having a toad as a 'familiar' evil spirit, or that they could turn into a toad at will. Somewhat inconsistently, it was common for toads to be used in protective spells; dried toads were commonly worn around the neck in times of plague in the hope that they would ward off infection. Since toads were poisonous, it was believed that they had the power to counteract poison. This worked through the principle of similarity – things that are similar to one another have a 'sympathy' between them and can exert influence over each other.

A specific connection, such as between a cure for poison and a poisonous animal, was not strictly necessary. Moles were used in some cures because of the belief that anything which burrowed in the ground had a sort of demonic power of its own. A mole's power could be transferred to a person simply by killing it, and the hand that had killed the mole was thought to have great healing power. The unfortunate animal's body parts could also be used in healing spells. A French medical book from 1758 recommends placing the paws and head of a mole around the neck of a sickly baby.

Animal parts were commonly used in a number of cures, usually according to the principle of similarity. The dried liver of a hare was used for liver complaints, a fox's lung was used for lung complaints, while the eyes of a crab were placed upon the neck to ease swollen eyes.

In a sense, many of these cures were not thought to be magical. Beyond the observable world, it was believed that there was an unseen web of influences binding the spirits of all things together, and village healers and people in general believed they were simply exploiting the natural properties of any given thing.

In an absurd and nightmarish flight of fancy, a demonic toad flies to the witches' Sabbat on the skeleton of a small animal in Collin de Plancy's Dictionnaire Infernal *(1863).*

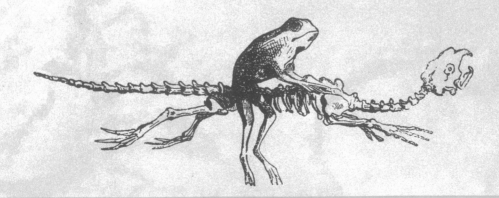

128

FOUL MAGIC

In addition to animals' parts, magical ingredients included a range of other unsavoury offerings, including several cures involving the use of urine or animal excrement. Burned male excrement or goat's dung mixed with honey served as a salve for breast cancer, while excrement, again treated in various ways, was often used for burns. Some of these cures worked by sympathetic magic.

According to a sixteenth-century French cure for dropsy (also known as edema), the invalid should 'piss for nine mornings in a row on a hoarhound plant before the sun has touched it, and as the plant dies, so will the belly subside'. Another sixteenth-century French cure from Marseilles involved urinating before a fever fully took hold, kneading a loaf of bread with the urine, and then feeding it to a dog. The unlucky animal would receive the disease and the patient would be cured.

Medieval medical practices from about 1200. On the right hand, physicians cauterize wounds. On the top left, the physician reads from a scroll as his assistant prepares a recipe.

Sometimes when witchcraft was suspected to be the cause of a disease, the patient's urine could be used to make the witch lift her curse. In the German town of Esslingen, a cloth and some wax would be placed in a glass filled with the patient's urine. This was supposed to bring the witch to the house within 12 hours, and she could then be forced to help her victim. To prevent her from leaving the house once she arrived, bread, salt and a broom were placed over the door. This 'spell' was to prevent the witch from using her own magical power to escape. No doubt in reality the angry members of the patient's family were all that was needed to trap the witch. At this point, the witch was forced to offer a magical cure in return for her freedom. People did not think of witches' magic as irredeemably evil.

Although a witch was likely to cause harm by her magic, she could also use it to cure people, if she wished.

CURED BY REVERSING AND STEALING

Magical power could also accrue from reversing normal events and customs. In Suffolk, England, it was customary never to use the words 'please' or 'thank you' in dealing with a folk healer. In the Limousin, in France, a cure for a toothache involved attending Mass, but doing everything backwards. When the congregation rose up, the patient should kneel down, when the others knelt, the patient should stand. There was a limit to how much anyone could do backwards without annoying the priest, as well as the rest of the congregation, but the symbolic power of a few actions would have been seen as effective. Sometimes it was even necessary to break the law, since occasionally ingredients for cures had to be ritually stolen.

Rue was frequently used in folk medicine, and in exorcisms. It was thought to have powerful healing properties because it was associated with Christ's suffering.

Beliefs dating back to medieval or even classical times persisted that herbs had to be gathered at certain times of the year and in specific ways. A French book from 1597, *La Maison Rustique*, describing the customs and daily life of the peasants to a curious aristocratic audience, noted that fern spores should only be gathered on the eve of Saint John's Day, the 23rd of June. Most Christian festivals were assigned to one herb or another. Vervain, according to a woman questioned by the Spanish Inquisition in 1615, should be gathered on Midsummer's Eve (around the 21st of June) and placed under the altar cloth so that, unbeknownst to the priest, it would be blessed the next morning at Mass. The herb could then be used to ask the Virgin Mary for wealth. Many plants acquired similar Christian associations: rue was often used in remedies because it was associated with Christ's suffering – the precise link is unknown. Once gathered in the appropriate magical fashion, it was not always enough for the herbs to be consumed like a medical drug. Herbs were usually just one of the ingredients in a magical cure.

VERVAIN THE WONDER HERB

Perhaps the best-known chronicle of herbal cures and herbal magic, Nicholas Culpeper's seventeenth-century *Herbal* represented general practice in its own time and borrowed greatly from folklore's classical sources. According to Culpeper, vervain was remarkably potent and was prescribed to strengthen the womb and ease jaundice, dropsy and gout. Furthermore it could expel tapeworms from the belly and cure

mouth ulcers. Vervain also protected against witchcraft and could be used in love potions. According to another source, it had to be crossed and blessed when gathered, and a special verse should be recited at the time of gathering:

Mistletoe has been used throughout history in magic and medicine. Its power was not confined to curing diseases; it was also used to extinguish fire and open locks.

> *Hallowed be thou Vervain, as thou growest on the ground*
> *For in the mount of Calvery there thou was first found.*
> *Thou healedst our Saviour, Jesus Christ, and staunchedest his bleeding wound,*
> *In the name of the Father, the Son, and the Holy Ghost,*
> *I take thee from the ground.*

There is no biblical evidence that vervain was used to heal Christ's wounds, but its association with Christ's resurrection provided a neat mythological

context for its magical efficacy.

Mistletoe was reputed to be even more powerful than vervain, for as well as curing diseases, it could be used to extinguish fires and open locks. Mandrake, also, was noted for its magical properties, and is even mentioned in the Bible.

A mandrake root shaped like a mother and child. A root with this resemblance would have been used in remedies to protect pregnant or nursing women and their babies.

In Genesis 30, Jacob's wife Rachel eats mandrake in order to conceive a child. In some cultures mandrake was known as 'man root' because of its resemblance to the figure of a man. Sometimes mandrake was said to scream when it was uprooted, which was taken as a sign of its particular magical power. Classical authors also mention the medicinal powers of mandrake. According to Pliny it could be used as an anaesthetic during operations. In was only in the late Middle Ages that it acquired associations with witchcraft.

A DUCK'S BAD LUCK

Healing magic often demanded some kind of bodily contact between the sufferer and the healer. Ointments and salves had to be rubbed on, and massage was often used. Sometimes healers were reported to touch or stroke their clients in order to draw the illness out and transfer it to some inanimate object, such as a stone. In parts of France this sort of healer was called a toucheur, one who touches.

In seventeenth-century England, a woman from Northumberland was reported to have put her lips to a sick child's mouth and 'made such chirping and sucking that the mother of the said child thought she had sucked the heart out of it, and was sore affrighted'. In the same area in 1604, two women were brought to the church courts accused of being charmers 'of sick folk . . . and they used to bring white ducks or drakes and to set the bill thereof to the mouths of the sick person and mumble up their charms'. This odd practice was clearly intended to transfer the disease from the patient to the duck.

SHAMANISTIC RITES

'Transference' is a common form of magic and it is found in cultures throughout the world. Shamans from isolated groups in Amazonia are known to attempt to draw out the evil spirit causing a disease. With energetic stroking of the patient, they pull the spirit out and take it into themselves, whereupon their own powers will be able to dispel it. Likewise, many healers in early modern Europe temporarily took a disease upon themselves. Although they would have used a different sort of ceremony, the magical principle behind the action would have been much the same. Sometimes a healer would advise someone else to take on the disease. One Somerset woman in 1555 was told by a wise-woman to take her sick daughter into her bed at midnight, so that the disease would be transferred to her.

The sixteenth-century French writer Michel de Montaigne recorded a meeting in his youth with an old man troubled by lung disease. The old man proposed that since Montaigne was a young man, the old man could concentrate hard upon Montaigne's youthful and healthy face and cure

Shamanistic religion is widespread throughout the world. Pictured are shamans from Tunguska, Siberia, at the end of the nineteenth century.

A fairy-tale witch brandishes her magic wand, while preparing some evil magic in her cauldron. Her grotesque servant gazes at the ingredients.

himself of his disease. Montaigne later ruefully observed that the old man omitted to mention that through this 'cure' the lung disease would be transferred to the youthful Montaigne. Fortunately in this instance the magic did not work.

MAGIC A SHADE DARKER

Much of the magic that was practised at this time had at least a possibility of becoming 'black magic'. In seventeenth-century Italy it was believed that one could get rid of a cold by wiping one's nose on a cloth or paper in which a coin was wrapped. The cloth should then be thrown away. But whoever picked up the 'gift' of the coin would gain something much less pleasant, the original cold. Transference of disease is a persistent belief. Some Americans during World War I believed that syphilis could be cured through sexual intercourse with a virgin. This dangerous belief is now found in parts of Africa, where the same course is taken to cure AIDS.

BLAME THE HEALER

The possibility of disease transference made folk healers in early modern Europe vulnerable to accusations of witchcraft. In 1629 Isobel Young of Dunbar, Scotland, who had already been tried for burying an ox and a cat, was accused of taking a sickness from her husband and transferring it to her nephew. The method of transference was indirect. Isobel was accused of placing the disease in a grain of barley in a barn. Usually healers tried to transfer an illness to an animal, perhaps a cat or dog. But if a valuable animal such as a calf died, the healer ran the risk of being blamed for transferring the disease. A healer and child minder called Marguerite Touret near Quingy, France, was executed as a witch for this exact crime in 1657.

WHEN THINGS GO WRONG

Sometimes the healer lost control of the transference magic. In Dumfries, Scotland, in 1590, Agnes Sampson was tried for witchcraft. She had been engaged in curing a man named Robert Kerr by taking his disease into herself. She struggled with the disease 'with great grieving and torment till the morning' and tried to pass it into an animal by means of a cloth switched from her to the animal. Unfortunately it appears she accidentally passed the illness into another man, who subsequently died.

In this story it is possible to see how magic could seem tangible to people who believed in its reality. Since everyone knew it was possible to draw disease from one person and pass it to another, they attributed the spread of an infectious disease to a human agency. Folk healers could therefore find themselves in a dangerous position when dealing with an infectious disease. People would be more likely to assume that the healer had malevolently passed the disease around than believe that the healer's magic had failed in the first place. Magic is very hard to disprove. Any apparent failure of magic can be attributed to another spell working against the original remedy. The result of any magical remedy, however different from the original intent, can be blamed on some secret agenda of the magic worker.

TREES TAKE ON HUMAN DISEASES

Perhaps it was the inherent dangers of transferring diseases to animals that encouraged the belief that diseases could be transferred to trees. In seventeenth-century France the custom arose to tie oneself to a tree, often at first light while fasting. One should then bite the bark of the tree, untie the rope and leave it by the tree to rot. A less strenuous version of this cure involved leaving a gift of bread in the branches of a hawthorn tree and scattering salt around its trunk, saying, 'Good day, hawthorn, I bring you bread and salt, and fever tomorrow.' A different route had to be taken to return home and a different door used to enter the house. If the house had only one door, a window had to be used for entry, in order to keep the disease inside the tree.

In the United States, a number of methods were used to transfer diseases

Some Americans during World War I believed that syphilis could be cured through sexual intercourse with a virgin.

milk magic

Milk was an important food in the rural economy, and magic was used to protect a household's supply. Theft of milk by supernatural means was feared across Europe, and in Germany there was thought to be a type of witch, a Milchhexe, who specialized in stealing milk. A Scottish woman in 1698 was accused of sticking a pin in the roof of her house that would supposedly draw her neighbours' milk to her own home.

Witches were thought to perform many of their malevolent deeds while in the shape of household animals, such as cats and mice.

In Germany in 1581 Ursula Fladin was accused of milk sorcery. Her crime was to place a reed, dripping with cream, inside a skull hidden in the parish church. She claimed that this was a spell told to her by a village 'sorcerer' to find out who had been stealing her milk. In Scotland amulets were made, usually on May Day (the first of the month), and used to protect cows from having their milk stolen by magic means. A sprig of rowan tree could be curled into a circle and hung in the dairy. Or ivy, bramble or red thread could be tied around cows' tails while a few incantations were uttered.

to trees: nails were driven into the bark, or a hole was made and some of the patient's hair or nail clippings placed inside. Another method was simply to hang clothes belonging to the patient on the branches of the tree.

In addition to trees, healers and sufferers tried to transfer diseases into the earth, a stream or even the air. Throwing a symbol of one's disease over the shoulder was a way of trying to release the illness into the air. It was the custom at a spring in France to kneel and say, 'Spring, I bring you my misfortune; give me your good fortune.' To complete the transfer, patients had to throw a coin, cheese or eggs into the spring over their left shoulder.

Today we often say to a sick person, 'You'll pull through'. The origins of this phrase are forgotten, but it probably refers back to another widespread method of curing disease.

Across Europe there were various rituals for pulling patients through a hole of some kind in order to rid them of their illness. An English antiquarian from the late eighteenth century recorded that in Hertfordshire it was the custom to cut a large cleft in the trunk of a young and flexible pollard ash tree. The cleft would be held open by wedges and a chronically ill child would be pushed through the cleft. After this ritual, the hole in the tree would be plastered with clay. The notion was that if the tree healed, then so would the child.

MAGICAL HEALING AS A RITUAL EVENT

There are relatively few detailed records about the precise ways in which cunning men or wise-women actually performed their cures. This is partly because secrecy itself was an important part of their trade, and it was crucial for every healer to have a 'secret'. Possessing a 'secret' secured a healer's reputation. Indeed, for healers to have any effectiveness at all, it would have been essential for local people to believe sincerely in their power. The 'placebo effect', whereby a patient's condition improves merely if he thinks he is being given an effective and powerful medicine, certainly played its part in the effectiveness of village healers.

The most detailed descriptions of magic cures often come from later European folklorists. In Sicily in 1875, a wise-woman called Ticchi-Ticchi was summoned by a family to a sickbed. She declared that the patient's illness had been caused by 'strong witchcraft'. First she assembled some of the ingredients that she would be using in the course of the healing performance. These consisted of a few dried herbs, incense, some little crosses made of palm leaves that had been blessed in church on Palm Sunday, and a length of virgin flax. Next she dissolved some salt in water and sprinkled it on the floor, muttering under her breath and tracing crosses in the air with her hands. She snipped the flax and made crosses with the threads, all the while gesticulating in a mystical fashion. Placing her hands on the patient's head she recited the Creed. She then moved to his feet and, standing with her arms outstretched, let seven of the thread crosses fall on him while reciting a spell:

> *I greet you, bread and tassu* [a plant believed to combat malaria]*;*
> *Heat and cold I hereby free:*
> *Better the head and worse the feet;*
> *Health come back again!*

In Germany there was thought to be a type of witch, a Milchhexe, who specialized in stealing milk.

Shamans used their magic not just to heal, but to resolve disputes. Here, an equatorial African shaman tests the truthfulness of one man who has accused another man of a crime.

Then she recited the first half of the Hail Mary, which was finished by the other women in the room. Returning to the middle of the room, she burned some of the herbs and scattered incense over them. When the smoke from the incense had spread, she prostrated herself. The other women imitated her. Finally, touching the floor with her bare breasts, she declaimed another verse.

I touch and I do not touch! I see and I do not see you!
Furcu [pitchfork or gallows], Befurcu [snake's tongue]
Lurcu [vampire], Cataturcu [devil]
I put you to bed, I wrench you, I hang you on the gallows.
With water and salt and incense, which all have power!
By the wounds of Jesus which none can resist,
With incense, salt and water at every moment!
Into the ditch with the horrible worms; let them be strangled,
Let their bones be chewed away!

This Italian wise-woman of the nineteenth century probably had a great deal in common with the cunning folk of the sixteenth and seventeenth centuries. By using herbs and the rituals of the Catholic Church, and by combining Christian prayers with verses of a more folkloric origin, the healer was creating a grand spectacle to convince her patient that a great and magical process was taking place.

In general, the healers seemed deeply sincere and would no doubt have wholly believed in the reality and power of their magic. However, some people in early modern Europe dismissed the cunning folk as frauds and liars as part of their overall attack on beliefs in magic and witchcraft. The cunning men and wise-women accused of witchcraft invariably defended themselves by claiming that while they could indeed work powerful magic, they only did so for good, and their sincere protestations in court bear witness to their noble inner conviction.

A SHAMANIC HERITAGE

The performance given by the Sicilian healer to her patients in the nineteenth century probably benefited them psychologically, for they would have been convinced that their disease was under attack from powerful magic. In some ways, however, the people of early modern Europe were relatively deprived of the complete experience of the shamanistic healer. There had been no tradition of shamanism in most parts of Europe for a thousand years or more by the sixteenth century, but the cunning folk retained some similarities with the shamans, though their art was not as highly developed or prestigious.

IMITATING THE CHURCH

Often poor, and with few resources, the cunning folk competed with the priesthood to earn a meagre living, especially in Catholic countries. To simple, uneducated villagers or townspeople, the church, with its elaborate ceremonies and impressive ritual objects, possessed an aura of organized, legitimate magic. It is not surprising then that the cunning folk borrowed its trappings so extensively, from identifying cures with the saints, to holy water, to scraps of Latin liturgy. In an attempt to make their magic seem even more powerful, the cunning folk went farther and imitated the practices that were related by repute to Christian holiness, such as asceticism. William Barckseale, a petty wizard from Southampton in

William Barckseale, a petty wizard from Southampton in England, would fast for three days before performing a magic rite to locate stolen goods.

the Shaman

Shamanic healing in traditional societies, whether in Africa, the Americas or Pacific islands, works on two principles: first, through the shaman's special knowledge of 'medicines' based at least partly on medicinally useful plants; and second, on the shaman's inherent magical power over the spirits or magical spells causing the illness. The European folk healers' contest with illness worked in a remarkably similar way. It also was the healers' secret magic, especially in a malady caused by witchcraft, that was thought to be put to the test in the conflict with the malicious magic.

Shamans have been and remain highly respected leaders of their communities in many societies, particularly for their expertise in traditional medicine and healing magic.

It is in traditional societies where the shaman healer also is the leading religious figure of the community that shamanic healing could reach its most impressive heights. An example is the medicine that was practised well into the twentieth century by the Navaho people of America. Like most shamans, they know a great variety of medicinal plants that can relieve the symptoms of illness, but they also work to diagnose an illness through spiritual inspiration. As part of the curing process the shamans, also known as 'singers', ritually chant lengthy songs and make complex drawings in the sand. Some distinguished singers may know songs enough to fill a hundred hours, which they can recite perfectly. This sort of cultural legacy was simply not available to the cunning folk of early modern Europe.

Navaho healing magic is at its most effective in treating psychological illnesses. If a person is consumed by grief at the death of a loved one, the singers can create a healing singing that offers some clear psychological benefit. The ceremony might begin by singing to remove the presence of the dead from around the living, and then concentrate on turning the patient's mind towards the living. The patient becomes the focus of a prolonged and intense ritual which can draw out suppressed social conflicts surrounding the patient's grief.

southern England, would fast for three days before performing a magic rite to locate stolen goods. Sometimes even lowly village clergymen were caught practising magic themselves. In 1554 a parish priest, William Hasylwood, was discovered to have used a spell to find a lost purse which held 14 silver coins.

In early modern Europe, magic was thought of as a practical aid. All the important stages of life were surrounded by magical customs, but perhaps none more so than the most dangerous time in a woman's life.

MAGIC AND CHILDBIRTH

Around 1600, it is estimated that a married woman would have had a baby roughly every two or three years of her reproductive life. Death in childbirth was a great and very real fear, with about one in every eight first-time mothers dying. Midwives up to the eighteenth century had little practical aid, and were typically equipped with no more than scissors, thread, vinegar to stop bleeding, some sort of lubricant and massage oil. Magic and ceremony were therefore crucial supports.

Childbirth was very dangerous for women before modern medicine, with one in eight first-time mothers dying in labour, so magic charms were routinely used to protect women.

Difficulties while giving birth were attributed to fairies, witchcraft and the Devil. One Scottish woman in 1576 claimed that during childbirth, the 'Queen of Elfdom' visited her and told her that her child would die, and indeed it did. In 1533 the church in Brandenburg told its clergy to instruct women that they were not under the power of the Devil during childbirth, which they apparently believed. In Estonia in the 1650s, a woman fell into a coma for several days after delivering. Blame was attributed to a cat that had climbed on the roof just over the spot where she had been lying. The cat was believed to have been a local witch in temporary animal form.

In Eastern Europe childbirth was often as secret and solitary as possible, so that the mother would not attract the 'evil eye' from any ill-wishing neighbours. In Western Europe the opposite strategy was adopted; a labouring woman was attended by a large gathering of other women. The group could offer some practical support, but it was often said that their main function was to ward off any evil spells that might attack the mother.

A CAPABLE WOMAN

Most villages had their own midwife, known as a matrone, sage femme, comadre, levatrice, goodwife, povitukha or hebamme. Usually in late middle age, she was often a widow with children of her own. Sometimes the office

Men and women had different roles assisting a labouring woman. In this 1587 illustration midwives assist in practical ways, while the men are distracted by astrological enquiries.

of village midwife was handed down from mother to daughter. A midwife's status was a little similar to a cleric, and was the only role remotely close to the clergy that a woman could occupy. She would be involved in a number of important ritual events, such as the baptism of a new baby and other church rituals a woman had to undergo following childbirth. The midwife – often referred to as the 'wise-woman' (the term could be used for a variety of women who practised some form of magic or folk medicine) - would also often lay out the dead and perform other funeral rites. She would carry an emergency vial of holy water to baptize any newborn baby that seemed in danger of immediate death.

The nicotine plant arrived among Europeans soon after they reached the Americas. A variety of beneficial properties were soon claimed for the plant, though it was always used for smoking.

The role of midwife was so important that from the late medieval period the church authorities took care to authorize the appointment of particular women to this office. She had to be instructed in the proper, solemn ritual of baptism, and in some places a church ceremony was held 'consecrating' her as midwife.

In eighteenth-century Angers, France, the ceremony took place at Mass on a Sunday, and the prospective midwife would take an oath while holding a candle by the church font. In England, midwives were licensed by a bishop, and also had to take an oath not to 'use any kind of sorcery or incantation in the time of travail of any woman'. Yet, an English play from 1638 featured a wise-woman midwife who undertook general healing, fortune-telling and the magical finding of lost objects.

In practice, many midwives remained unlicensed, and there were some complaints from the clergy that women preferred the unlicensed sort of midwife. Licensed midwives would have been constrained in their use of magic since they needed the continuing approval of the church. Unlicensed midwives had greater freedom. Also, since childbirth was exclusively the domain of women, a pregnant woman would have felt that an unlicensed midwife, with no connections to male authority, was more appropriate, and maybe even more effective. Various natural herbal aids were used during childbirth, which may have given some relief from pain, such as ergot fungus, balm, bay, mugwort, lilies and tobacco. Most substances were used in a clearly magical fashion, such as when the woman in labour was required to swallow three pepper grains. Three was a symbolic number in traditional magic, representing the Holy Trinity: God the Father, the Son and the Holy Spirit.

BIRTHING CHARMS AND AMULETS

Midwives were known to use various charms and prayers. Charms were written down, sometimes in Latin, and attached to the woman or her bed to speed the birth or alleviate pain. One charm, known in various forms in England and Scandinavia until the twentieth century, read, 'I conjure you infant, whether you be male or female, by the Father, Son and the Holy Ghost, that you come forth, and draw not back and that you do no harm to your mother.' The charm then referred to the miracle of Christ's raising of Lazarus and his coming forth from the tomb. Other charms used nonsense words, or simply wrote 'Jesus'.

Various kinds of amulets were used across Europe. In Germany, special stones – sometimes an eaglestone – were tied around a mother's right knee during childbirth. Pumice stone, coral, special seashells, axeheads, horseshoes and magnets were all used in different regions. If these could not be obtained by the poor, parts of animals were used, such as a donkey's or horse's hoof hung 'near the privities [genitals]', according to one contemporary observer. How these were supposed to work in magical terms is not always clear, but in one case the sympathetic magic aspect is fairly obvious.

The skin discarded by a snake has an obvious connection with birth and was used as an amulet, even though the clergy considered it to be associated with the Devil. Sometimes the peasants were fearful, too. In one area of France, a snakeskin was worn as a belt during childbirth, but it was quickly removed after the birth so that the child would not belong to Satan.

Other types of belts were used, generally with supernatural connotations. In 1576 one Scottish midwife accused of witchcraft claimed that the lace that she tied around women to ease the pain of childbirth had been given to her by a ghost. More conventionally, some women wore belts made of lengths of rope which had been used to ring church bells. Since the ringing of church bells was thought to drive away demons, the rope itself was believed to have

One Scottish midwife accused of witchcraft in 1576 claimed that the lace that she tied around women to ease the pain of childbirth had been given to her by a ghost.

Charms used to protect childbirth included the rope from a church bell, used to drive away demons, and a snakeskin (the snake's own rebirth) could be used to aid human birth.

some similar protective power. Girdles associated with female saints were often used, though male saints could be appealed to as well. Jewish women used belts made of the leather strap that bound together the Torah scroll.

Unmarried women did not usually play any part in the rituals and magic of childbirth. However, in some cases they could have some magical significance. A 'medicine' recipe from seventeenth-century New England gives a complicated spell for easing difficult childbirth:

(continued on page 148)

145

a witch cult that never was

The fanciful notion that witches were a secret cult dating from pre-Christian times until the seventeenth century is a myth that began in the nineteenth century and persists to this day. Even up until the 1970s a few professional historians still lent some credence to this idea. This is remarkable, because after the end of the witch craze in the seventeenth century people did not believe that any witch cult had ever existed and regarded the women who had been put to death for witchcraft as unfortunate innocent victims. This consensus only began to change in the 1830s, when some conservative Catholic historians, obsessed with secret societies in their own time, began to argue that the witch cult had been real after all.

This imagined witch cult would probably have faded from view once again but for a book written by the folklorist Margaret Murray in 1921, *The Witch Cult in Western Europe*. Murray reconstructed the confessions of 'witches', invariably given under torture, as representation of a pagan nature religion. In her view, the remarkable uniformity of the confessions, involving nighttime gatherings of witches where the Devil was worshipped, confirmed the existence of a real, coherent witch cult. For Murray the witches were not evil worshippers of the Devil, but priestesses of a gentle nature-loving religion that embraced both a god and a goddess. She dismissed lurid accusations of sexual orgies and feasting upon babies as the propaganda of the Christian authorities. Of course, these horrific stories were church 'propaganda', since such things never happened. The men who imagined the existence of a witch cult, and spent their lives hunting down and prosecuting the people they thought were witches, believed witches committed horrific crimes during their meetings. However, neither the witch-hunters' idea of a witch cult, nor Murray's peaceful and virtuous witch religion, ever existed.

The startling similarity of the confessions of the so-called witches in the sixteenth and seventeenth centuries suggests that they did not come from their own experience or even their own imaginations. The supposed 'Sabbat' meeting of the Devil and his witches was an idea concocted by churchmen in the fifteenth century. Many educated clergymen and other members of the ruling classes were only too easily convinced that there was an international conspiracy of Devil-worshipping men and women who sought to corrupt and destroy Christian society. This paranoia led some to write obsessively about the supposed crimes committed by witches, and to

The discredited idea of the witches' Sabbat began to make a comeback from the 1830s onwards. The idea grew that the Sabbat had been a real, although not supernatural, event.

lead murderous judicial persecutions in an attempt to root out and destroy the imaginary witch cult. It was the international community of clerical witch-hunters who created and spread the propaganda about witchcraft, telling bizarre stories of witches flying about on broomsticks or animals, having orgies, and practising various sordid rituals including cannibalism.

Murray thought that the obsessive activities of the witch-hunters must have been directed at some real opponent, rather than the fantasy that it really was. She also wanted to believe that women were not completely dominated by the male church hierarchy, with its single male God, so she felt that women should have had their own female religion in opposition to the Christian Church. In arguing for this belief, Murray showed less than complete scholarly honesty in her accounts of the witches' confessions. To present a convincing case that the Sabbats were a genuine underground religious ceremony, she suppressed the more implausible aspects of the confessions. If impossible things happened at the witches' Sabbat, like flying on broomsticks, then it is clear that the entire meeting was imaginary. Murray needed the Sabbat to sound plausibly like a gathering of ordinary peasant women practising a genuine religion, and fantastic stories didn't fit in with her argument. In some of the confessions upon which Murray relied most heavily, many of the stories involved witches turning themselves into various beasts, making horses out of beanstalks, flying long distances, sinking ships while in flight, flying

through tiny holes 'like bees', and other fantastic adventures. Only once these incidents were conveniently omitted could Murray present the confessions as credible evidence of real secret meetings.

In reality there were no secret meetings of witches or nature-worshipping women. The confessions of 'witches' were made under torture, and the men and women accused of witchcraft by the authorities told their persecutors the stories the witch-hunters wanted to hear. Under torture the 'witches' developed ever more fantastic stories to satisfy the expectations of their tormentors.

There is no evidence for Murray's witch cult apart from the now-discredited confessions of the accused women. All the existing evidence concerning the use of magic – for good or evil – shows that it was highly unlikely that any kind of pagan witch cult existed in Western Europe in the sixteenth and seventeenth centuries. The cunning men and wise-women mostly used charms and magical verses with a strong Christian theme and appealed to Christian saints for help. These simple people were not secretly pagan, nor did they worship the Devil, however much the church might claim that magic honoured the devil rather than God.

Margaret Murray's ideas have been remarkably successful for the last 80 years. For many years the *Encyclopaedia Britannica* even published an article by Murray under the entry for witchcraft. The popularity of her theory seems to have more to do with modern wishful thinking than it does with the past.

'Take a lock of virgin's hair of half the age of the woman in travail. Cut it very small to fine powder; then take 12 ants' eggs dried in an oven after the bread is drawn or otherwise make them dry and make them to a powder with the hair. Give this with a quarter of a pint of red cow's milk or for want of it strong ale.'

WHEN MIDWIFERY GOES WRONG . . .

In the misogynistic climate of early modern Europe, it is not surprising that a woman with such public importance as a midwife should attract male suspicion and hostility. A fifteenth-century book describes midwives as essentially witches who 'in various ways kill that which had been conceived in the mother's womb, or when they do not do this, offer the children to devils. . . Midwives surpass all other witches in their crimes. And the number of them is so great that there is scarcely any tiny hamlet in which at least one is not to be found'.

When childbirth went wrong, midwives had to employ different sorts of magic. In a case where a child was stillborn, Walpurga Hausmännin, a licensed midwife of the German city of Dillingenm, buried the corpse of the baby under the doorway of the house so that the woman would have no additional miscarriages or stillbirths. But Walpurga was executed in 1587 for witchcraft, found guilty of having caused the deaths of a woman and child by rubbing a salve on them. No doubt the salve was meant to have had protective properties, but since the childbirth ended in death, the midwife was held responsible.

'Churching' was a ceremony practised up to the eighteenth century to purify a woman after giving birth so that she could fully participate once again in village religious life.

PROTESTANTS, CATHOLICS AND SUPERSTITION

In the course of the sixteenth and seventeenth centuries a growing number of people refused to have anything to do with magic. These people were often Protestant, although suspicion of the practice was appearing at the same time among the educated classes across Catholic Europe. However, the Protestants' focus in their attack on magic was usually on Catholic customs, which the Protestants felt were tainted with magic, and which were seen as

The devil sits enthroned amid the pandemonium of the Sabbat in this engraving from 1730. Male and female witches cavort in a parody of a celebratory feast.

encouraging the superstitions of the village folk. One English Protestant complained that 'About these Catholics' necks and hands are always hanging charms/That serve against all miseries and all unhappy harms'.

One of the former Catholic rituals that roused Protestant suspicion was the tradition of 'churching' women who had just given birth. After childbirth a woman was considered vulnerable to evil influences and had undergo a purification ceremony in church before resuming normal life in her new role as a mother. There was usually a short gap between birth and the churching ceremony. In Wales at the end of the seventeenth century, one English clergyman commented that 'the ordinary women are hardly brought to look upon churching otherwise than as a charm to prevent witchcraft, and think that grass will hardly ever grow where they tread before they are churched'.

The church tried to discourage superstitions attached to churching, but they existed nevertheless in many local traditions. The orthodox Christian view was that the ceremony was simply an act of thanksgiving for a safe birth, but many people regarded women as impure and unholy after childbirth and thought they should be barred from entering a church until the churching ceremony had been completed. At the root of the practice was the idea that a woman was impure for a certain period after having had sexual relations. Childbirth being the ultimate fruit of sex, it too conferred a state of impurity. On these grounds one Anglican clergyman in the early

seventeenth century refused to give communion to menstruating women or anyone who had had sexual relations the day before.

It was in this context that some Protestants in England objected to churching, which survived far into the eighteenth century in the Anglican church. One seventeenth-century radical Protestant objected that the whole practice of churching 'breedeth and nourisheth many superstitions in the simple people's hearts; as that the woman that hath born a child is unclean and unholy'.

It was not just the practice of churching that was felt by Protestants to encourage belief in magic and witchcraft. In his *Discoverie of Witchcraft*, published in 1584, Reginald Scot denounced the witch trials, describing them as attacks on deluded or harmless old women. Scot regarded the Catholic practice of exorcism – 'merely a magical incantation' – as no better than the superstitious activities of 'conjurers'. Exorcism, he declared, was a gift of God to the Apostles alone, and in later times no such miracle could be expected to happen.

Protestants were not alone in turning away from magic in the seventeenth century. The Catholic Counter-Reformation movement also sought to banish the superstitious and folkloric practices that had grown up around church ceremony and traditions. By ridding Catholic customs of some of the magical elements that had grown up around them, they hoped that belief in the central sacraments of Catholic Christianity, such as the belief that during Mass the bread and wine become the real body and blood of Christ, would be made stronger. In spite of their outward disapproval of village magic, many Protestants and reformed Catholics continued to believe in and practise it, even when forbidden to do so by their pastors.

The decline of magic was a complicated process, but it was clearly underway in most Western European countries and America during the seventeenth century. Belief in witchcraft is often rationalized as the only option available to ordinary people in the absence of adequate medical knowledge. Yet effective and widespread medicine did not appear until long after magic had been largely discredited and had become culturally isolated and marginalized. In fact, the decline of magic made medical and scientific advances possible, rather than the other way around. However, just as a rationalistic view of the world was spreading and developing, the fear of witchcraft and harmful magic reached its spectacular height in the great witch trials of the sixteenth and seventeenth centuries.

A lonely peasant woman pictured in the Tales of Hans Andersen. *Many women like her were accused of witchcraft, and like them, she has companions, a cat and a rooster.*

In spite of their outward disapproval of village magic, many Protestants and reforming Catholics continued to believe in and practise it, even when forbidden to do so by their pastors.

tHe HammeR of Witches

Over the course of nearly three hundred years, Europe was gripped by a hysteria that arose gradually and spiralled out of control, resulting in the slaughter of thousands of innocents. At the heart of this hysteria was the belief that certain men and women in a society – whether a village, town or city – belonged to a diabolical sect of witches who worshipped the devil at large gatherings called the Sabbat.

It is hard to believe today that people from all levels of society truly believed that their neighbours were witches. These witches were supposed to fly to the Sabbat by magical means, on animals or on household implements such as shovels or broomsticks. Once at their secret destination, the worshippers kissed the devil's posterior and made a mockery of the Christian Eucharist with a Black Mass, in which elements of the ceremony were performed backwards, and a piece of charcoal took the place of the communion bread. The witches would then consume the devil's feast, which included human babies, and copulate with the devil himself. After the Sabbat, the witches would fly home and use their powers for all types of evil, from causing disease in people and animals, and making men impotent, to ruining crops, spoiling milk and causing a variety of minor mishaps. The witches were not merely considered evil, they were believed to be servants of the devil.

The great witch-hunt craze began in about 1450 and did not die out until after 1750. During that period, approximately 100,000 trials were held across Europe, and between 40,000 and 50,000 people were executed. In many areas, such as Ireland, Wales, Brittany and large parts of Germany, the

Persistent heretics, those who held beliefs at odds with official church doctrine, were frequently executed, most famously by burning. Witches were seen as the ultimate heretics, not merely holding the wrong beliefs, but worshipping the devil himself.

incidents of witch-hunting were few and relatively insignificant. The heartland of persecution lay in the Rhine Valley down through Switzerland, and west through northern France to Flanders. Lowland Scotland also saw major outbreaks of the witch craze, as did Essex in England.

In most of these episodes, the diabolical Sabbat was the main focus of prosecutions and paranoia. The remarkably consistent descriptions of the Sabbat given by the accused convinced many people that a satanic witch cult really did exist. Yet it did not. The Sabbat was an idea that was spread throughout Europe by means of anti-witchcraft propaganda, including pamphlets, handbooks and witch-hunters' guides. The lurid descriptions of the Sabbat gripped the imagination of the aristocratic and literate public – which was by its very nature superstitious and suspicious anyway – and the idea that the Sabbat really existed spread throughout Europe. The chilling methods of extracting confessions advocated in these hysterical publications were then imposed on the vulnerable victims of the witch craze.

This German woodcut of 1493 shows an episode of the persecution of Jews. Jews, as a distrusted minority, were vulnerable to accusations of witchcraft.

A FANTASY TAKES SHAPE

The myth of the diabolical Sabbat did not have its roots in popular culture – in fact, it was quite the opposite. In the medieval imagination the witch was a solitary person, not necessarily connected with the devil, who used magic to perform *maleficia*, magical acts harmful to others. The myth of the Sabbat, in contrast, held that the witch was a member of a secret cult. This idea grew from many different sources over centuries.

It is an ancient human fear that secret groups of people could exist within society who are so alienated from normal values that they might indulge in hideous rituals such as eating children. When fear for the stability of society is at its greatest, people whose values appear to differ from mainstream society are apt to be accused of these very crimes. In the Roman world it was the Christians who were accused of secretly practising abominable rites of human sacrifice. Later, in the medieval Christian world, those accused of secret obscene rites were Christian heretics and Jews. In the eleventh century, heretics were accused not merely of holding different beliefs from orthodox Christians, but of worshipping the devil.

In 1022 a group of aristocratic heretics living in Orléans, France, was accused of indulging in wildly promiscuous orgies and killing the resulting babies in order to make a magical ointment. In reality, these people did hold some sort of mystic interpretation of salvation and revelation, but their true beliefs became lost among all the wild accusations against them. Centuries later this same horrific stereotype would form part of the prevailing image of witches, who were supposed to use an ointment made from boiled babies to enable them to fly.

Most early allegations of devil worship stemmed more from ruthless political ambition than from any widespread or deeply held belief in

Witches were women out of control. As in this German picture from 1510, male writers on witchcraft conjured up images of naked witches in frenzied performance of evil magic.

The witches' Sabbat was fertile ground for the imagination. Originally witches were supposed to kill babies, but this nineteenth-century artist substituted the sacrifice of young women.

diabolical covens. Cases like the heretics of Orléans in 1022 were rare, and that accusation was actually based on more mundane political rivalries between two aristocratic factions.

Even in later times satanic conspiracies were not normally laid at the door of Christian dissenters, although heretics could be persecuted and executed if necessary, on the grounds of their beliefs alone. The church authorities' inability to stamp out dissent led to a growing feeling that heretics had to be part of a well-organized underground network, which aped and mocked the authorities. Such a network did not exist in the way some senior churchmen believed, but the persistence of heresy created the belief in a widespread, organized anti-Christian force within society. This fear helped to create the myth of the witch cult.

Another witch stereotype which persisted throughout the era was the belief that magicians could summon demons. As far as the Christian authorities were concerned, any demon must be a devil, and perhaps even the Prince of Darkness himself. Demons, devils and Satan himself were not usually distinguished from each other, and it is not clear whether a devil was meant to be Satan, or just one of his underlings. The idea that humans could summon the devil, coupled with the ancient accusations of sexual license and cannibalistic rituals, completed the stereotype of the diabolical cult of witches. Like the accusations of ritual cannibalism, this was more widely believed by the educated and wealthy than by poor peasants. Even the clergy in Rome were not immune – fears developed in the Papal court that high–

ranking clerics were engaging in ritual magic to advance their careers and harm their enemies within the court.

A DEADLY POLITICAL WEAPON

In 1320 Pope John XXII instructed the Inquisition to take action against practitioners of ritual magic. The fear of such magic had already been used as a tool to destroy political enemies. In a bizarre incident, the king of France, Philip the Fair, accused Pope Boniface VIII (1294–1303) of being helped by demonic spirits. Even after the Pope died, the king pursued and exaggerated his original accusations. Stories spread that the Pope had locked himself in his rooms with his familiar demons, demanding that they kill his enemies.

The Pope had made numerous enemies in his career, and there were many who were willing to tell lies about him now he was dead. It was claimed that he had been seen sacrificing a cock to a devil. On another occasion Boniface was supposed to have been found worshipping an idol, which he claimed was 'no painting, but the evil majesty.' The Pope's enemies knew very well that these charges were nonsense, but they pursued them until the Pope's successor, Clement V, gave in to the French king's real political demands. Thereafter, the charges against Boniface VIII were quietly dropped.

Political trials of this type were conducted at regular intervals in the late Middle Ages and gave rise to widespread rumours about sects of devil worshippers existing in Europe. Despite their horrific nature, such accusations remained a marginal part of the political scene of the elite classes, and there was no sign yet of the later accusations of devil-worshipping witch cults at the village level. The medieval church authorities

Devils haunted the medieval imagination and, as in this thirteenth-century illumination, were thought to be always about to pounce on a moment's distraction from faith in God.

The hideous tortures faced by those accused of witchcraft illustrated Jules Michelet's 1862 history of witchcraft. He thought, wrongly, that witchcraft was a form of social protest.

simply did not have the resources to mount widespread prosecutions of village practitioners of magic.

LET THE WITCH-HUNTS BEGIN

The Swiss canton of Valais was the scene of the first major witch-hunt and mass trial in 1428, when as many as 200 people were said to have been burned as witches. This sudden escalation in the scale of witchcraft prosecutions was down to a simple change in the judicial procedure at a local level. Secular judges, magistrates and bishops had begun to adopt the Inquisition's method of obtaining confessions: torture. Once someone had been accused of witchcraft, torture was used to obtain a confession and to discover the accused's fellow witches. By this time the belief had become ingrained that witches did not act alone but were organized in covens which attended the diabolical Sabbat. Therefore, the accused must undoubtedly have accomplices. Some people caught up in this first witch-hunt resisted confession until they died under torture, but many others confessed and in turn accused others. It was this combination of torture and belief in the Sabbat that created the mass witch trials.

THE 'NIGHT WITCH' AND THE HEART OF STRAW

Those who governed society were responsible for two important elements in the witch trials – the conspiracy notion of the Sabbat and the widespread use of torture. But another important element of the stereotypical witch rose from a folk tale from Western Europe. This was the story of the 'night witch', who had existed in people's imaginations since ancient times. In Italy she was called a strix (striges in the plural). Striges were supposed to fly about at night and kill and eat defenceless people. A similar myth existed in Germany, where for most of the Middle Ages the clergy tried to stamp out the belief.

Women in particular were thought to be likely to believe in the striges, and even to believe that they were capable of such supernatural activity. An eleventh-century penitential book described a priest asking a woman in confession if she believed that 'in the silence of the quiet night, when you have settled down in bed, and your husband lies in your bosom, you are able, while still in your body, to go out through the closed doors and travel through the spaces of the world'. Once out of her body, the strix was supposed to 'kill people who have been baptized and redeemed by Christ's

blood' and to 'cook and devour their flesh'. After eating the heart of her victim, the strix placed straw in the cavity. She then magically reanimated the victim, who bizarrely lived as normal for some time afterwards, but would then suddenly waste away and die.

This belief was not taken very seriously before the fifteenth century. The medieval punishment for believing oneself to be a strix was a relatively lenient 50-day fast on bread and water. However, by the fifteenth century, beliefs had changed and punishment had become stricter: those with the same beliefs were burned alive as witches. Indeed, the mythology of the strix appeared in the Valais witch-hunt. The 'witches' confessed to killing and eating children in the course of their nocturnal spiritual wanderings. The witches gathered at meetings presided over by the devil, who appeared in the form of a black animal and magically transported his followers from village to village or mountain to mountain. He gave them an ointment to smear on chairs, which could then be used to fly.

The flying night witch was an ancient terror that persisted into modern times. In Italy and Germany these striges, women who left their bodies in spirit form, were believed to steal and eat people's hearts at night, and to abduct babies.

FEAR OF ANYONE DIFFERENT

Central to these fantastic accusations was fear of an anti-Christian organization that met in secret to defy the authority of the church. In the area of the first witch-hunts, there were the Waldensian heretics, whose beliefs were similar to those of the early Protestants. The Waldensians had eluded the Inquisition for centuries in the mountainous areas of the Alps near France and Italy. The persistence of this secretive group of religious dissenters seemed unnatural to the authorities. The obvious explanation was that the devil was protecting the Waldensians, and that far than being just heretics, they posed a mortal threat to Christian society.

In the early witch trials in the Alpine regions, the terms for 'witch' and 'Waldensian' became interchangeable. These were the beliefs and fears that allowed the witch-hunts to begin and flourish. But despite the witch-hunts, the Waldensians survived.

A MORE TOLERANT ATTITUDE

Witches were not persecuted in every part of Europe. The beliefs in the Sabbat and the night witches, and the use of torture to impose preconceived ideas about witches, were rejected by the Inquisition in most areas where that infamous institution held authority. In Spain, Portugal and much of Italy, local magical beliefs were not usually linked with devil worship. In these areas there were some outbreaks of witch-hunting, but on a limited scale. The Inquisition authorities certainly took it upon themselves to suppress magical beliefs, but not to the extent of torturing and burning people as witches.

THE HAMMER OF WITCHES: A WITCH-HUNTER'S GUIDE

The first great innovation of the modern age was the printing press, which appeared in Europe in the middle of the fifteenth century. Not only could knowledge, news and learning be spread far and wide, but the dangerous fantasy of the Sabbat witch cult could likewise be spread. In those parts of Europe where the witch-hunts took firm hold, the stereotype of the witches' Sabbat was broadcast through certain sections of the ruling classes in books and pamphlets.

One of the earliest works on witches was a relatively cautious treatise by the German Dominican friar Johann Nider in 1435–37 (the Dominicans were an order of

Many of the earliest mass witch-hunts appeared in fifteenth-century Switzerland, where the heretics known as Waldensians had survived for centuries. These dissenters were now accused of being witches.

preaching friars, and the Inquisition was largely made up of men from this order). In his treatise, Nider accepted as fact a story that a peasant woman, interviewed by a friar, had admitted to being a witch. The woman was supposed to have flown at night with the pagan goddess Diana. The Dominican who interviewed her was initially doubtful, so she offered him a demonstration. Placing herself in a basket, and rubbing her body with an ointment, she became unconscious, and the two clerical witnesses present were unable to rouse her from the trance. When she awoke, she claimed to have been with Diana, and the two clerics could not convince her that she had never left the room.

It is unlikely that Nider's story contained any element of truth. He had only heard it from one of his teachers, who was not even the Dominican featured in the story. Tales of old women smearing themselves with psychotropic ointments and flying in their sleep recurred a number of times after Nider, but rarely in a form that can be trusted. Such stories are similar to what are now described as 'urban legends'. Like those tall tales, which are propagated by E-mail, this one spread around the literate world via the new technology of the printing press, and examples can be found in Italian, Spanish and Dutch literature of the sixteenth century.

Johann Nider regarded witches as heretics, and was the first writer to present them not as isolated individuals but as an organized group. And while he believed that certain men and women truly considered themselves to be witches, he did not believe in the reality of their evil magic. Later writers did not have the benefit of his scepticism.

One of history's most infamous works on witchcraft was written in 1456 by two Dominican Inquisitors, Heinrich Kramer and Jacob Sprenger. Their *Malleus Maleficarum*, or *The Hammer of Witches,* issued a horrific warning to the ruling classes that the heresy of witches was real, widespread and murderous in intent. They believed that almost every village in Europe was infected with a diabolical sect of witches, and that women in particular were prone to renounce Christianity and become worshippers of Satan.

Kramer and Sprenger were obsessed with the menace of female witches, and were convinced that across Europe most midwives were in fact witches who, far from aiding childbirth, were killing babies and their mothers. Most of the ideas contained in *The Hammer of Witches* were already current in many circles, and they described in detail the Sabbat and the magical powers attributed to witches. It was the two Dominicans' particular horror of female witches that most sets their work apart from the many other books on the

They believed that almost every village in Europe was infected with a diabolical sect of witches, and that women in particular were prone to renounce Christianity and become worshippers of Satan.

witch cult that were popular at the time. According to their views, nearly all women were witches, or were at least in grave danger of being seduced by the devil.

From the point of view of today's society, the extent to which the book's authors distrust and despise women is astonishing. They caution readers about women's appetite for power and the dangers of allowing them the slightest authority, warning that 'if you hand over the whole management of the house to her but reserve some minute detail to your own judgment, she will think you are displaying a great want of faith in her, and will stir up strife; and unless you quickly take counsel, she will prepare a poison for you, and consult seers and soothsayers and will become a witch'.

A PACT WITH THE DEVIL

According to *The Hammer of Witches,* a witch would make a formal pact with the devil in which she would

MALLEVS
MALEFICARVM,
MALEFICAS ET EARVM
hæresim frameâ conterens,
EX VARIIS AVCTORIBVS COMPILATVS,
& in quatuor Tomos iustè distributus,
QVORVM DVO PRIORES VANAS DÆMONVM verfutias, prastigiofas eorum delufiones, fuperstitiofas Strigimagarum caremonias, horrendos etiam cum illis congreffus; exactam denique tam pestifera secta disquisitionem, & punitionem complectuntur. Tertius praxim Exorcistarum ad Dæmonum, & Strigimagarum maleficia de Christi fidelibus pellenda; Quartus verò Artem Doctrinalem, Benedictionalem, & Exorcismalem continent.
TOMVS PRIMVS.
Indices Auctorum, capitum, rerùmque non desunt.
Editio nouiffima, infinitis penè mendis expurgata; cuique acceffit Fuga Dæmonum & Complementum artis exorcisticæ.
Vir fiue mulier, in quibus Pythonicus, vel diuinationis fuerit fpiritus, morte moriatur Leuitici cap. 10.

LVGDVNI,
Sumptibus CLAVDII BOVRGEAT, fub figno Mercurij Galli.

M. DC. LXIX.
CVM PRIVILEGIO REGIS.

'truly and actually bind herself to the devil'. Many later witch trials took this suggestion seriously. In making such assertions, Kramer and Sprenger were coming perilously close to heresy; therefore, it was most important that they present witches as acting of their own free will in signing such a damning pact.

In orthodox Christianity the devil has no power except that of illusion, and can harm no one against God's will. For the devil to have supremacy over witches and the ability to empower them to harm others in their own right was close to the 'dualist' heresy. In this belief God and the devil are equally

A 1669 edition of the famous witch-hunters' manual The Hammer of Witches. *Originally written in 1456, the book remained influential late into the seventeenth century.*

powerful. So to avoid being accused of dualism, Kramer and Sprenger emphasized that Satan persuaded witches to his will, and that this occurred with God's permission. By signing the pact, the witch was exercising her own free will, consciously denying God, and was therefore the worst of all heretics.

The Hammer of Witches is a potent example of the demonization of popular magic by the educated classes, principally the clerics, whether Protestant or Catholic, in the sixteenth and seventeenth centuries. Although magic had been frowned upon by the church for centuries, it had turned a blind eye to the fact that almost the entire population of Europe sought magical assistance of one sort or another for their problems and continued to do so. But when certain clerics and other educated men began to connect harmless village magic with satanic influence on daily life, magic of any kind became, for some, a sign of witchcraft being practised. 'White' witches, or the cunning folk, were condemned for secretly causing disease and then healing it to make the devil's power seem even greater. Once the authorities regarded the common magic of villagers as being tainted with the influence of the devil, it could easily be believed in turn that the network of witches across Europe was huge, and could include up to a third of the population.

THE INFLUENCE OF *THE HAMMER* IN DISPUTE

Although *The Hammer of Witches* was well-known in its time, the real extent of its influence is disputed. According to some sources, *The Hammer*'s damnatory views on witchcraft shaped the accusations that were made and the witch-hunts that took place in southern Germany, the very heartland of witchcraft hysteria. This could be true, since the publication was particularly popular in sixteenth-century Germany. Yet the work was rarely mentioned in the witch trials or in church sermons, nor was it available in every courtroom, as has been claimed. Furthermore, one of Kramer and Sprenger's principal obsessions – that witches caused impotence and therefore strife and unhappiness within marriage – rarely merited a mention in many of the witch trials. So although the book was undoubtedly influential, it was not the single dominant influence on the witch-hunts that it was once thought to be.

The Hammer's rampant hatred of women was also blamed for the fact that it was the female sex which was predominantly accused of witchcraft. Almost all the victims of the witch-hunts were female, and in some German episodes the proportion of women to men executed as witches was nearly nine to one. The misogyny of *The Hammer of Witches* has led to the misrepresentation of the witch-hunts as a war – consciously or unconsciously – against women. But this is a misunderstanding. Certainly clerics and many male figures of authority held an exceedingly low opinion of women's susceptibility to sin and believed that they were far more likely to become witches than men. Women were considered to be more vulnerable to temptation by the devil, and older women were accused of possessing an insatiable lust, which they satisfied by using magic to ensnare young lovers. While hatred and fear of women undoubtedly coloured most of the witch-hunts, the real enemy was an imaginary diabolical sect, which just happened to be mostly made up of women.

A witch signs a pact with a motley assortment of devils, unaware of the small devil behind her, chaining her foot to show the loss of her soul, in this German engraving of 1687.

In most early modern illustrations of an imaginary witches' Sabbat, both women and men are depicted enacting the diabolical rites. The witch cult was conceived to be a parallel 'evil' society, where all of society's norms were reversed, and it was a mirror image of the Christian authorities. In such a society women would naturally be imagined as prominent, since in reality they were largely excluded from positions of public authority.

PROTESTS AGAINST WITCH HYSTERIA

The idea of God allowing witches to kill and consume Christians, especially innocent babies, was a matter of concerned debate in the surviving writings on witchcraft, since it implied that the devil had the power to create suffering that God himself would not allow. In some Italian villages, folklore tried to

a witch's best friend?

The traditional depiction of a witch includes her demonic familiar, which today is usually a black cat. But this is a fairly recent image. The writers of The Hammer of Witches *made no mention of witches' familiars, although at the Sabbat witches supposedly copulated with a demon specifically assigned to them. As the witch-hunts developed in the sixteenth century, animals became more and more associated with witches' magic. To begin with, the devil himself appeared at the Sabbat in the form of a large black animal, such as a bull or a dog. The witches sometimes used an animal to fly to the Sabbat, so by analogy any black animal could be a demon transformed into a form that could carry a witch.*

When it became generally accepted that most witches did indeed have a demonic familiar, the familiar could be any animal that lived closely with the person accused of witchcraft. Since many people kept cats at that time, a cat was often thought to be an accused person's familiar, though it did not have to be black. In the absence of a convenient pet, a toad or even an insect could represent the familiar.

Witches were also thought to be able to transform themselves into animals. This was significant, since it was said that witches could enter houses by magical or undetected ways. Because they were small in size, cats were ideal for this purpose. In one sixteenth-century French witch trial, the accused women admitted under torture to transforming themselves into cats, and their confessions contained implausible and farcical escapades about entering and escaping from neighbours' houses.

Despite some examples of connections between witches and cats, the standard image of a witch and her black cat was far from being a common element in the early modern picture of witches. It was only in the later folk tales about witches, following the great witch-hunts, that the witch became firmly linked with a black cat. In nineteenth-century Germany it was said that 'a cat of 20 years turns witch, and a witch of a hundred years turns cat again'.

The black cat is firmly associated with witches in the modern fairy tale image of the witch, but in the age of the witch-hunts there were many other animals, black or not, who were imagined to be witches' familiars.

offer the simple explanation that witches could only kill the unbaptized; therefore, newborn babies were the most vulnerable. But this magical view of baptism as a talisman against evil was dismissed by the clerical writers on witchcraft, and most people continued to believe that witches could kill anyone, if they so desired.

It was even suggested that God allowed witches to kill innocent babies because it would prevent them from sinning when they grew older. But the more usual explanation avoided the fate of innocents and argued that God allowed the devil and his witches to commit evil in order to test the faithful and punish the wicked. Satan needed human accomplices because he was a spiritual phenomenon and could not, on his own, cause the material harm that witches achieved. This reasoning meant that the witches' pact with the devil was even more important than the Sabbat, for the pact was proof of conscious human complicity with the devil.

Most people must have found the explanation credible, since even the critics of *The Hammer of Witches* – who dismissed as preposterous stories of witches flying, copulating with the devil and transforming themselves into animals – continued to believe in the reality of witchcraft.

According to the witch-hunters, God allowed the devil and his witches to commit evil in order to test the faithful and punish the wicked.

VOICES OF DISSENT

But not everyone was convinced that witches existed. Chief among the doubters in England was Reginald Scot, whose *Discoverie of Witchcraft* was printed in 1584. Scot divided witches into four categories. First were those who were accused of witchcraft out of malice and ignorance. Second were those who were deluded and mentally ill, who believed they were evil servants of the devil. Scot considered these people to be the most likely to make confessions and to be incapable of harming anyone. The remaining two groups Scot considered to be witches of a sort, but without supernatural powers.

The third group consisted of villagers who wished to harm their neighbours and their animals using poison. Scot considered poison to be a natural, rather than supernatural, agent of harm, but many of his contemporaries thought otherwise. Poison, the traditional weapon of the witch, was regarded as magical in origin, and it was commonly believed that witches obtained their poison from the devil at the Sabbat. While Scot may have intended to diffuse fear of witches, few would have been comforted.

The final group of 'witches' was made up of travelling magicians and 'conjurers' who convinced simple country folk of their magical powers to heal, find lost goods and predict the future. The only real danger these charlatans represented was to the finances of the impoverished peasants who were deceived by them.

Scot's arguments were taken up by many others over the next century, but whether or not his reasoning had much influence on the scale of witch-hunting in England is uncertain. Some commentators at the time were pessimistic. Robert Burton wrote in 1621 that 'many deny witches at all, or, if there be any, say they can do no harm'. Unfortunately, as Burton admitted, 'on the contrary are most lawyers, divines, physicians and philosophers'. In other words, those most likely to be involved in judging witch trials and have an influence on opinion were the most likely to believe in witches. Some who denied the reality of witches were even accused of atheism, a most serious charge at this time.

Scot may have had some effect, however, for the English witch trials were generally small events and only on one occasion – in Essex in 1645 – did they actually develop into a large-scale witch-hunt. The widespread belief of the diabolical Sabbat failed to take hold in England, and that belief was a prerequisite for the mass trials that took place elsewhere.

MERCY ON FOOLISH WOMEN

Another early critic of the witch-hunts, the German doctor Johann Weyer, author of *On the Illusions of Demons* in 1563, took the view that the devil had power to plague humanity but could not break the laws of nature. Rather, he

In this chaotic Sabbat, the witches in the foreground release evil spells, while in the background devils drive a column of the damned to hell, while others perform a riotous dance.

took pleasure in deceiving foolish old women into believing that they were witches. Weyer felt that these women were not guilty of any serious offence and only needed better Christian instruction. He regarded it as profoundly unjust that while educated male magicians who claimed to be able to summon demons escaped serious punishment, deluded but harmless old women were executed by the hundreds. Weyer also was suspicious about the use of torture to extract confessions. The accused, he said, were 'constantly dragged out to suffer awful torture until they would gladly exchange this most bitter existence for death'. They confessed 'whatever crimes were suggested to them rather than be thrust back into their hideous dungeons amid ever recurring torture'.

There were many among the clergy, too, who spoke out against beliefs in the danger of witchcraft. Although they believed witchcraft existed, they did not think that the devil could cause physical harm. In 1562 a hailstorm devastated the crops in a large rural area near the German city of Stuttgart.

Eleanor Cobham, the Duchess of Gloucester, did public penance in 1441 for using magic in an attempt to further her husband's political ambitions. A century later she would have faced far worse punishment as a witch.

In most of Europe the punishment for witchcraft was to be burned at the stake, but the practice in England and Scotland, and subsequently America, was to hang those found guilty.

The hailstorm was so ferocious that people said it looked as if a battle had been fought over the fields. As ever, people were quick to blame witchcraft for the disaster, but two court preachers from Stuttgart, Matthaeus Alber and Wilhelm Bidembach, spoke out forcefully against this notion, declaring that all things that happened were the will of God.

The two preachers argued that the devil was only capable of persuading deluded people to 'work their magic by cooking and shaking their odds and ends together in their hail pot' (the 'hail pot' was supposed to be a sort of magical cauldron). Once the hailstorm arrived, 'then these poor bedazzled people think they caused it'. The devil's only power in this situation was an ability to predict the coming hailstorm. It is unlikely that any of these 'bedazzled' people would have boasted about causing a hailstorm, but suspicious types in the villages were only too quick to accuse vulnerable people of such a crime. The preachers went so far as to say that it would be better if a thousand witches escaped justice, as long as a single innocent person was not condemned.

THE WITCH-FINDERS HAVE THEIR SAY

There were many who responded to Weyer's and others' attacks on witchcraft theory, chief among them the witch-hunters themselves. One such figure, Nicholas Remy, Attorney General of Lorraine, France, was responsible for the execution of more than 900 witches in the late sixteenth century. In 1595 he published the *Demonolatriae* refuting Weyer's view that all witches were harmless but deluded and sick old women. According to Remy, too many people of all kinds had been condemned as witches for Weyer to be right.

Remy was correct only in the sense that by no means all those condemned as witches were old women. He pressed on with a series of arguments as 'evidence' of the existence of witchcraft, all of which did not stand up to close scrutiny. Because so many witches had been found guilty, he maintained, witchcraft must be a reality and the evidence against 'witches' must be treated as conclusive because the devil would attempt to deceive the godly.

If a 'witch' died under torture without having confessed to witchcraft, it was not taken as proof that the accused was not a witch. Someone who died under torture, having resisted confessing to witchcraft, would have been showing a heroic level of endurance in order to defend his or her innocence. To the witch-hunters, it merely showed that the devil had killed the accused to save himself from more pain, since the devil was thought to suffer along with his witches during torture.

In the early seventeenth century the French witch-hunter Pierre de Lancre was as obsessed with the threat posed to society by the French Protestants as he was with the threat from witchcraft. He considered the tolerant attitude towards Protestants at this time to be proof that society was on the verge of collapse. For that very reason, he wrote, the danger of witchcraft was even greater, for as society lost its moral and religious boundaries, more and more people would inevitably fall into the hands of the devil. The zealous de Lancre led a huge witch-hunt in the southern French Basque region, which resulted in the deaths of hundreds of people. Happily for the population of neighbouring Spain, de Lancre's activities were restricted to his own country. He took a dim view of Spain, a country that had no problem with witches, and considered the Spanish clergy to be either too lazy and corrupt to round up their witches, or worse, to be witches themselves.

> Someone who died under torture, having resisted confessing to witchcraft, would have been showing a heroic level of endurance in order to defend his or her innocence.

GUILTY UNTIL FOUND GUILTY

Remarkably, one of the most committed witch-hunters of the sixteenth century was King James I of England (1603–25), who was also King James VI of Scotland (1567–1625). When still solely king of Scotland, he initiated a witch-hunt directed against his sworn enemy, the Earl of Bothwell, accusing him of being allied with witches and trying to bring down his rule.

It is significant that the king did not pursue witchcraft trials so energetically later in England, where his rule seemed more secure and his political enemies easier to control. Even for so firm a believer in witches as James, the urge to hunt them was bound up with fears of political instability. Yet his beliefs in witchcraft were sincere. He wrote that witches were reluctant 'to confess without torture, which is witness to their guiltiness'. This chilling logic was shared by many of his contemporaries.

James was an enthusiastic advocate of the technique of 'swimming' witches. This involved tying the prisoner to an object such as a chair, or a specially made 'ducking stool', and throwing her into deep water. If she sank, she was not a witch, but if she floated, it was proof of her diabolical nature. Contrary to myth, a person subjected to this treatment was not left to drown, although they were in considerable danger nonetheless. Curiously, the same technique was used in Germany at the same time, but the results were judged the other way around. An innocent person floated, while the guilty sank.

King James estimated the number of female to male witches as 20:1, and expected each one to have a visible 'mark of the devil' somewhere on his or her body. This mark could be any spot on the body that was found to be insensitive to pain or did not bleed when pierced. A search for the devil's mark, amounting to a terrible torture in itself, was a common way of identifying witches throughout Europe. James believed that no evil could be committed in the course of the witch trials, because God would not let the innocent suffer.

Ultimately, though, it was not the writings of demonologists like King James, or earlier books like *The Hammer of Witches,* that caused the witch trials. The stories of the Sabbat and the powers of witches described by fanatical witch-hunters existed before their books. The literature of the witch-hunters was as much a consequence of the witch-hunts as a cause. Some of the great witch-hunts began before even *The Hammer of Witches* had become well-known.

WITCHES IN HIGH PLACES

While most of the victims of the sixteenth- and seventeenth-century witch-hunts were ordinary village women, this was not so in the first convulsions of witch hysteria. In some cases educated men of considerable social standing were accused by the Inquisition of being magicians and summoning demons.

In 1438 a French knight, Pierre Vallin of La Tour du Pin, was tried for witchcraft by the Archbishop of Vienne. Under torture, Vallin confessed to pledging his body and soul to the demon Belzebut 63 years earlier. He also admitted to riding on a stick to the Sabbat where children were eaten alive. Once the church officials had obtained his confession, Vallin was handed over to the secular authorities, who tortured him more to discover his accomplices at the Sabbat. The authorities were particularly interested in priests, nobles and rich men who might be involved in the 'diabolical conspiracy'. In the end Vallin gave up the names of more than 10 people, most of whom were men. Then he was executed.

Those who did not believe in the witches' Sabbat also might find themselves in danger. One French theologian, who preached against the reality of the Sabbat, William Adeline, was accused in 1453 of being in league with the devil. He was supposed to have made a pact with the devil in which he promised to deny the existence of the Sabbat. Under torture, he confessed to flying by broomstick to the Sabbat where the devil appeared in the form of a goat. Adeline further confessed to ritually kissing the devil under his

Torture was a regular part of legal systems across Europe. Judges determined to uncover diabolical conspiracy could torture subjects until they confessed to fantastical crimes.

tail and giving him his own baby daughter to kill. In later trials witches would normally also be made to confess to other crimes, such as killing cattle and people and causing storms. But Adeline was not accused of, and did not confess to, carrying out any other harmful magic besides his attendance at the Sabbat. He escaped a sentence of death owing to his connections with the masters of the influential University of Caen, who supported his case, but he died in prison four years later.

King James VI of Scotland faced a serious threat to his rule from the Earl of Bothwell. The king secured his power partly by accusing the earl of being in league with witches.

Adeline's case marks a crucial turning point in the trials involving the summoning of demons or devils (remember that there was no real distinction made between demons and devils). Unlike earlier trials of magicians accused of summoning demons, in Adeline's case the balance of power between demon and human had changed. Normally demons were thought to be subservient to the magician; now the devil himself was in control of the witch. This pattern, where the devil dominated witches, made the idea of a conspiracy of witches more terrifying. It was no longer a case of ambitious individuals manipulating demons for their own benefit, but of the devil controlling humans for his wider diabolical purposes.

THE WRETCHED CITIZENS OF ARRAS

One of history's most relentless and brutal witch-hunts occurred in the northern French city of Arras in 1459. A hermit had been accused and convicted of witchcraft, and was tortured to reveal the names of the others who had attended a Sabbat with him. All sorts of people would visit hermits to gain their blessing, as they were believed to be holy men, and so among those whose names he gave were a prostitute from the nearby city of Douai and a painter and poet from Arras. The elderly poet was well known in Arras for his pious verses in praise of the Virgin Mary, but both he and the prostitute were charged with practising witchcraft.

At this point the affair came under the jurisdiction of two particularly fanatical believers in the witches' Sabbat, the Inquisitors Bishop Jean of Beirut and Jacques de Boys, a senior Dominican official. The poet and the prostitute were tortured to yield the names of other local witches, who in turn revealed more names of those who had attended the Sabbat. The two Inquisitors believed that as many as a third of all nominal Christians were witches – they even believed it possible that bishops and cardinals were secret witches. Anyone who voiced objections to the increasing scale of the accusations and burnings

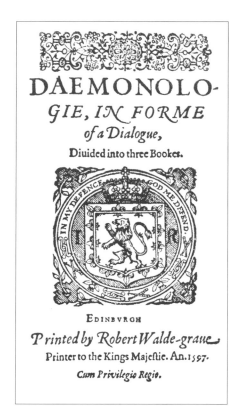

DAEMONOLO-
GIE, IN FORME
of a Dialogue,
Diuided into three Bookes.

EDINBVRGH
Printed by Robert Walde-graue
Printer to the Kings Majeſtie. An.1597.
Cum Privilegio Regio.

King James's anti-witch tract, Daemonologie, *introduced many of the ideas of European witch-hunters into Britain. James advocated the 'swimming' of witches to test their guilt.*

was in turn accused of being a witch due to the very fact of objecting. At least the two Inquisitors could not be accused of targeting only the impoverished practitioners of everyday magic, for they were equally interested in hunting down Satan's wealthy followers.

During the witch-hunt of Arras, the townspeople were gripped with fear. No one knew if they might be the next to be accused. Many people voluntarily admitted to being a witch in the early stages of the hunt because they were assured that if they confessed quickly, their sentence would simply be to make a short holy pilgrimage. As they were led towards the flames, these unfortunates cried out that they had been deceived and had never really attended the Sabbat. Their cries fell on deaf ears. The trials reached such intensity that the city's economy began to suffer, and trade broke down.

Eventually the trials came to the attention of the Duke of Burgundy, who ordered an assembly of clergy to discuss the reality of the Sabbat. No firm conclusion was reached by the duke's gathering of learned theologians, so the duke ordered his herald to attend the examinations of the accused witches and the trials abruptly ceased. The city Inquisitors refused to carry on with the trials despite the urgings of Bishop Jean and Jacques de Boys. The pair wished to continue the trials, even though it was clear that even they no longer believed in the Sabbat.

The traumatized citizens of Arras did not let the matter rest there. The sons of one of the rich victims of the witch-hunt pursued an appeal to the highest judicial body in France, the parlement of Paris. At this, Jacques de Boys went mad and died a year later. After a legal process lasting 30 years, the parlement finally issued a decree declaring that all the victims of the witch-hunt had been innocent and fined those involved in the persecution who were still alive.

After such an outcome to the first high-profile witch-hunt, it might be expected that belief in the Sabbat and enthusiasm for the persecution of witches would have been dealt a severe blow. After all, even the two main protagonists were broken and disillusioned by the experience. But this was not the case, for the greatest witch-hunts were yet to come, and would continue for another two centuries.

During the witch-hunts, witches were imagined as flying to the Sabbat on ordinary objects like shovels or broomsticks, but nineteenth-century artists designed more exotic vehicles.

HYSTERIA IN ROTTENBURG

The early witch-hunts reached their climax in southwest Germany in the 1560s and 1570s: 21 mass trials took place in the first decade and 50 in the

second. Not until 1650 did the panic begin to subside. At least one trial took place every year up to this date, and most of the accused were executed in large groups. The reason for the trials was usually some natural disaster, such as crop failure or plague.

The city of Rottenburg experienced intense witch-hunts beginning in 1578, when 16 women were executed after fears that they were causing storms that would ruin the crops. As it happened, the harvest was particularly good, but by then the 'witches' who were supposed to have caused the storms were dead.

This turn of events did not halt the rising witch panic, and two years later an additional nine witches were executed. The men among them who were executed were often guilty of other capital crimes, such as theft or murder, to which charges of witchcraft were added. The accused women were more likely to have been victims of their neighbours' suspicion, which arose from petty quarrels. Once an accusation had been made, and investigated through torture, random friends and enemies of the accused would subsequently be accused. In almost every year from 1578 until 1585, large groups of women were executed until magistrates halted the witch-hunts, declaring that if they carried on, there would soon be no women left in Rottenburg.

This pause in the witch-hunts lasted for only four years, and in 1589 five more women – rumoured to have caused harm – were executed for making a pact with Satan. The trials that continued through May to July 1596 were sensational, with 35 witches executed. Professors at the University of Tübingen complained that many of their students deserted their lectures to watch the burnings.

In the early stages of the hunts those accused of being witches were mostly poor women. But as the panic continued – it seems that despite its numerous executions Rottenburg was still riddled with witches – the accusations became broader in scope. Charges of witchcraft were brought against members of the nobility, to the extent that the Protestant noblewoman Agatha von Sontheim zu Nellingsheim was accused in 1590. Agatha's family members were powerful enough to save her from prosecution, but in return they had to pay 10,000 gulden and restore their lands to Catholicism. Other members of the ruling classes were less fortunate, however; members of the city government and their wives were tried and executed as witches.

EVERYONE A SUSPECT

As the number and frequency of accusations and executions increased, more and more people became embroiled, and the normal bonds of social trust broke down. Anyone could be accused and executed as a witch. Finally a high-ranking city official, Hans Georg Hallmayer, was accused of having sexual relations with the devil, who had taken the form of a hospital nurse. Hallmayer had been a leader of the witch-hunts, and was reported to have ordered the execution of 170 witches in his time in office.

Once accusations of witchcraft were made against members of the government, the trials could no longer continue. If those who were responsible for putting witches on trial were also witches, then it was inevitable that the legal machinery of the witch-hunts would have to be questioned. From this point, witch trials were held less frequently and fewer witches were accused. After 30 years of terror, the witch-hunt of Rottenburg ended in 1613 when a group of women accused of witchcraft was released. They were saved when the court took legal advice from a respected lawyer, Jacob Halbritter of the University of Tübingen, who argued that the evidence was insufficient to bring formal charges of witchcraft.

NO RHYME OR REASON

The witch scare was over for Rottenburg, and did not reappear. But other places had not learned Rottenburg's lesson, and similar events occurred in many cities and regions throughout Europe for much of the rest of the seventeenth century.

It has proved almost impossible for historians to explain why some areas were free of witch trials for many years and then suddenly major hunts began. Catholic and Protestant areas were equally at risk from the witch-hunters. And poor mountain villages and prosperous cities were little different in their vulnerability to witch panics. In almost every community, the basis for a witch-hunt already existed in the underlying fear of witchcraft and in the authorities who believed in the Sabbat. A mass witch-hunt could be sparked by practically any event that caused tension and suspicion in a community.

RELIGION, WAR AND WITCH-HUNTING

Sixteenth-century Germany was intensely divided by religion, and conflicts between Catholics and Protestants were the underlying cause for a number

A mass witch-hunt could be sparked by practically any event that caused tension and suspicion in a community.

of witch-hunts. In Wiesensteig, religious controversy arose in 1555 when Protestant preachers were invited to the town by popular demand. Count Ulrich von Helfenstein was the leading supporter of Protestant reform in the area, and this led him into conflict with the Bishop of Augsburg. Under intense pressure from his Catholic wife, the count was brought back into the fold of Catholicism. The town was now bitterly divided between Catholics and Protestants. In circumstances such as these, whereby a society had become destabilized due to uncertainty and religious anxiety, a witch panic was almost inevitable.

Count Ulrich's own personal religious dilemmas may have been the motivating force behind his enthusiasm for witch-hunting. Where the conflicting pressures of Catholicism and Protestantism could not be resolved,

Witches had to prepare a magical salve to smear on their broomsticks in order to fly. This was often provided by a devil, although witches were thought to know the recipe themselves.

179

Counter-magic — How ordinary people defended themselves against witches

While the authorities were occasionally moved to round up large numbers of people and try them for being devil-worshipping witches, witchcraft of a more everyday kind was a constant concern for many villagers across Europe. Ordinary people rarely wished to involve the courts in their affairs. They had their own means, including magic, of protecting themselves from witches.

Many people were quite blunt in their approach. A farmer from Lorraine suspected one Catherine la Rondelatte of casting evil spells on his animals. He found her and beat her, saying, 'Witch, I have come to kill you since you have caused the deaths of my horses and cattle, now you too will die at my hands.' She complained to the authorities and the farmer was ordered to pay her compensation. He also paid her a small sum after she promised she would no longer cause his animals magical harm. This was a relatively mild case of witch-beating.

In other instances the accused were killed, and the murderers were sometimes pardoned by the authorities who considered it reasonable and acceptable to slaughter a suspected witch. But this was not always so. In 1677 in Yorkshire, England, three men were hanged for killing a suspected witch.

Another way to remove a witch's curse was to force the witch to remove it by using magic to control her. Just as a witch's magic often worked by her using something connected with her intended victim, people could use something connected to the witch to break her spell. One method was to burn some thatch taken from the suspected witch's roof. The destruction of something belonging to the witch was thought to make her come in search of her 'attackers', therefore forcing her to go to the victim's home. Once she was there, threats of violence could make her reverse the curse.

Acts of violence against witches had magical connotations. It was thought that a witch's curse could be undone by scratching her to draw blood. In 1579 a stableman in Windsor, England, was advised by a cunning man that his sickness had been caused by witchcraft, and he was even given the witch's name. The cunning man told him, 'If you can meet her, and all to scratch her so that you can draw blood of her, you shall presently mend.' Court records in England contain numerous cases of suspected witches being dragged from their homes and clawed and pricked with pins and knives until enough blood was spilled to break the spell.

A demonic pact illustrated in the psalter of Ingeborg of Denmark, from about 1210. She herself was accused of bewitching her husband, King Philip Augustus of France, on their wedding night.

ridding his territory of witches may have seemed to be a way to break the deadlock and bring some assured spiritual purity to his lands. In 1562 the count ordered the arrest of a number of women, blaming them for a hailstorm that had devastated the region's vineyards. The arrests found much support in the surrounding areas, and Naogeorgus, the pastor of the nearby town of Esslingen, began preaching about the threat of witchcraft. Some urged caution, however, and the city council of Esslingen warned its preachers against stirring up the population.

Esslingen was fortunate in having a cautious city council. In Wiesensteig, Count Ulrich executed six women shortly after the initial arrests. He then announced that the Wiesensteig witches had witnessed some townspeople from Esslingen at the witches' Sabbat. In many places such an accusation would have led to a witch scare spreading from its original centre into the surrounding countryside. The town council of Esslingen remained firm, however, and released the three people accused of witchcraft. Count Ulrich was enraged by the council's lenience, but could not interfere. In Wiesensteig, where he controlled the judicial system, he ordered 63 executions in a matter of four months.

Both Wiesensteig and Esslingen were Protestant towns at this stage, but the reforming religious leaders of each town had differing views on witchcraft accusations. The nearby University of Tübingen was a moderating influence on witchcraft hysteria, and the leaders of Esslingen were also influenced by the sermons of the preachers Alber and Bidembach in Stuttgart. Their sermons were printed in Esslingen to counter the inflammatory preaching of the town's Protestant pastor, Naogeorgus. In Wiesensteig, however, the lead in inflammatory preaching against witchcraft was taken by the unorthodox Lutheran pastor Leonhard Culman, and the authorities there did not bring in any moderating influence.

It was not just eccentric Protestant leaders who were liable to provoke witch-hunts. By 1583 the town of Wiesensteig was fully Catholic again, and another witch-hunt began, resulting in 25 more victims. The town endured at least one more large witch-hunt in the early seventeenth century. Whether Catholic or Protestant, the religious leaders took to witch-hunting with great enthusiasm.

Germany's religious troubles continued in the seventeenth century, and between 1618 and 1648 it suffered from the (initially) religious wars known as the Thirty Years' War. The fear and uncertainty brought about by war easily

The fear and uncertainty brought about by war easily became yet another catalyst for witchcraft panics.

became another catalyst for witchcraft panics. It was not just the traumatized civilian populations who suffered from witch panics. Mobile populations, such as armies, also witnessed the events.

At this time, large numbers of women trailed behind the armies, and were known as camp followers. While these women were often useful and even essential to the army, military leaders frequently resented their presence and the women were often accused of witchcraft. In 1643 the Bavarian army responded to these accusations by deciding to test every officer's and soldier's wife for witchcraft. The women were tested by the swimming trial, in which those who failed to float were denounced as witches. Many were executed.

THE TERROR OF THE WITCHCRAFT TRIALS

In southwest Germany, during the period from 1561 to 1670, an astonishing 3,200 people were executed as witches. Only the use of torture to secure confessions could have led to such a torrent of accusations and executions. In one small territory containing 700 peasants, 43 women and 11 men were burned between 1586 and 1588. In 1631 another area came close to being decimated by a series of witch trials. Oppenau in Württemberg had a

Most misfortunes could be attributed to the malign actions of witches. In Germany bad hailstorms, causing severe damage to crops, were the spark that ignited some of the worst witch-hunts.

population of just 650. In the space of nine months, 50 people had been executed and an additional 170 awaited trial. Fortunately, at this point the judges involved began to doubt the legality of the trials and called a halt to the proceedings.

Some of the worst witch-hunts occurred in lands ruled by the church – both Lutheran and Catholic. Between 1587 and 1593 the Archbishop Elector of Trier sponsored a witch-hunt that claimed 368 people from 22 villages. Two villages were left with only one surviving woman each. Bishop Philipp Adolf von Ehrenberg executed 900 people in the 1620s, including his own nephew, 19 Catholic priests and several young children. At Bonn, the Archbishop Elector of Cologne ordered the execution for witchcraft of his own chancellor, the chancellor's wife and his secretary's wife.

The horrific scale of some of Germany's witch-hunts might give the impression that an especially virulent fanaticism existed in Germany. But this was not the case. There were zealous witch-hunters elsewhere who were just as relentless in their pursuit of suspected witches. And, significantly, much of Germany actually escaped any significant witch persecution. German theologians and preachers had a strong and vocal tradition of criticizing the paranoia concerning witches, and they preached frequently against the belief that witches could cause thunderstorms to ruin crops.

It was the unique political circumstances that prevailed in parts of Germany that made the scale of persecution possible. Germany was divided into a vast number of small states of varying size and complexity. In these circumstances, an isolated territory could be controlled by people with an intense belief in the threat of witchcraft. The largest territories avoided the more spectacular mass trials, but so did the smallest. Those tiny territories that were controlled by insignificant noblemen in southwest Germany were the most free of witch trials, since these backwaters tended to be stable. It was the medium-size territories, the imperial cities and church lands that suffered the most. The almost total independence of these territories – answerable to no outside authority – allowed witch panics to explode and quickly spiral out of control.

SANITY IS RESTORED

By the middle of the seventeenth century, the authorities were starting to suppress witch-hunts. In 1672 the council of Altdorf in Schwaben banned all accusations of witchcraft. When a trial began in the Rhine territory of

> Two villages were left with only one surviving woman each.

Kappel, all of the accused were released and the local preacher was told to instruct the children in his care not to believe in the threat of witches. Gradually it came about that people who accused others of witchcraft were in more danger of legal censure than those they had accused.

At the height of witchcraft hysteria, anyone accused of practising petty magic and being involved in a diabolical witch cult would have been subjected to a horrific witch trial. But by the end of the seventeenth century, anyone charged with being superstitious received only the mildest of punishments. The authorities had reverted to the attitudes of the late Middle Ages, whereby magic was regarded as an offence against the Christian faith, not a great danger to society at large. Poisoning, once indelibly linked with witchcraft and the actions of evil spirits, now began to be viewed simply as another kind of murder, committed by natural, not supernatural, means.

By the end of the seventeenth century, anyone charged with being superstitious received only the mildest of punishments.

ENGLAND'S LIGHTER TOUCH

Fear of witches was rife in England in the sixteenth and seventeenth centuries. In 1542 the English Parliament made it a felony, punishable by death, to conjure spirits or practise witchcraft, and additional severe Acts of Parliament followed during the next 60 years. But the persecution of witches in England differed from that in Germany and other countries that experienced massive and intense witch-hunts. England held many more trials of individual witches, and these trials rarely spiralled out of control to the point where tens or hundreds of people might be accused and tried for witchcraft.

The crucial difference between England and elsewhere was the idea of the Sabbat. In the great witch trials, the accused person was tortured to give up the names of other witches attending the Sabbat. They in turn were tortured to reveal further people supposedly involved. The idea that witches congregated at these occult meetings originated in Continental Europe and spread slowly in England. There was no mention of the Sabbat before 1612 in any English witchcraft trial, and there were few subsequent references. Without the idea of the Sabbat, a mass witch trial was unlikely to happen, since the accused witch remained only a solitary person suspected of practising black magic. Furthermore, torture was rarely used in England, except in cases of treason, so confessions and accusations were not tortured out of people, as they were in the Continental European mass trials.

Although England conducted many witch trials, only one major witch-hunt took place, in Essex, between 1645 and 1647. In Essex and surrounding

Despite vicious tortures, many of those accused of witchcraft refused to confess. Witch-hunters saw this only as proof that they must be protected by the devil to withstand torture.

counties over the course of those two years, about 200 people were executed for witchcraft and for making a pact with the devil. This one incident was entirely out of proportion to the normal run of witch trials in England. Between 1558 and 1736 in the counties around London, only another 200 people were convicted under the witchcraft statutes, and not all of those faced the death penalty. Many witchcraft trials that appear in court records are in fact the result of people suing for slander after having been accused of being a witch.

Witch-hunting in Essex simmered on until 1620, when the trials stopped. No more than 25 years later, the panic erupted again from 1645–47. Other parts of England saw sizeable panics, too. In Lancashire, 21 people were tried as witches in 1612, and 20 in 1633. The greatest number of witchcraft trials occurred during the 1580s and 1590s during the rule of Elizabeth I. These two decades were a period of intense anxiety, with economic depression and fears of political upheaval affecting the entire population. Well over half of all the known executions for witchcraft were carried out during these two decades. Yet even at the height of the witch panic, only 40 percent of those charged with witchcraft were found guilty. Sometimes the judges were displeased with the outcome of the trials. Justice Bromley, in a trial of Lancashire witches in 1612, told those who were acquitted that he believed they were just as guilty as those who were condemned.

Unlike the wild accusations common in Continental Europe, witchcraft in England was commonly thought of as just the practice of magic intended to harm. Among ordinary people it was never transformed into the idea of a diabolical sect. Nonetheless, plenty of magistrates and lawyers were well versed in Continental European ideas about the witch cult, and these men spread the fear of witchcraft. Chief Justice Anderson warned in 1602 that witches 'abound in all places' and without tough measures they would 'in short time overrun the whole land'. Bishop Hall wrote in 1650 that witches used to be rare but 'now hundreds are discovered in one shire'.

THE LEGAL PROFESSION AND WITCHCRAFT

Certain legal figures of high regard persecuted witches with a seemingly perverse enthusiasm. In 1616 two judges in Leicester pursued convictions with such determination, and on such flimsy evidence, that even the witch-hunt-loving King James I censured them. Other officials cast doubt on witchcraft accusations even at the height of the craze. In 1633 one observer

The sufferings of Christian martyrs have a long history in art and literature, but the sincere Christians tortured and executed as witches by Christian authorities have rarely been martyrs.

Legal figures of high regard persecuted witches with a seemingly perverse enthusiasm.

the evil eye and the devil's powder

During the witch trials in Germany, the authorities were primarily concerned with whether or not someone had attended a diabolical Sabbat. Peasants and poor townspeople, on the other hand, did not pay much attention to the Sabbat as the source of witches' magical powers. They believed that magical powers were inherent, and that a particular person might even have been born a witch, rather than having been initiated into a secret demonic cult.

From this belief arose a fear of the 'evil eye'. With the evil eye, a witch could cause an emanation of evil spirits through a sheer act of will, just by looking at her victim. It was almost as if witches were the carriers of an infectious disease, and coming into any sort of contact with them put a person in danger of becoming gravely ill. Witches, if they wished, could also 'breathe over' a person, thereby causing illness. This evil 'looking' and 'breathing' could be accompanied by a touch, and there are cases in which people claimed to have come under an evil spell simply by touching the hand of a witch by accident.

Educated notions about the Sabbat eventually began to infiltrate popular ideas about witchcraft. Witches had always been thought to cast their evil spells using special powders and poisons made of toad venom, stillborn babies, and consecrated wafers stolen from churches. But as more and more

ordinary people began to hear lurid tales about the Sabbat, they started to describe the powders as gifts of the devil, obtained during the witches' dance, the Sabbat. These powders became an alternative source of healing, and for many people an ambivalent source of power, which could be either harmful or helpful.

The powders were said to have been of various colours: red, black or white, for example. A French witch, Claudatte Parmentier, claimed in her confession that the black powder was used to kill people, the red to kill animals, and the white to heal. It seems, however, that she became confused during her interrogation because she later claimed to have healed a man using the red powder. She had probably been pressured into inventing details about 'devil's powder' while under interrogation, and then became confused and forgot her own system of classification.

Witches were seen by most ordinary people as solitary women and men, rather than as part of a demonic conspiracy. Witches' powers were thought to be a natural, if malign, talent.

remarked that if it were not for the cautious and merciful attitudes of the judges, many more harmless old women would have been executed.

As the seventeenth century progressed, judges became increasingly unconvinced about charges of witchcraft. The Lord Chief Justice Sir John Holt (1689–1710) presided over 11 consecutive trials in which each 'witch' was found innocent. It was said at the time that his questions and directions to the jury revealed that he believed 'nothing of witchery at all'.

THE END OF AN ERA

The last person in England to be hanged for witchcraft was Alice Molland at Exeter in 1685. In 1736 Parliament repealed previous witchcraft legislation. It made accusations of witchcraft illegal, and also punished the claim to be able to work magic with a year's imprisonment.

Witchcraft had been downgraded to the status of a trivial and vulgar act of fraud, rather than a threat to society. But while educated opinion had dismissed witchcraft, it remained a genuine fear at village level. After it was no longer possible to take witches to court, individual acts of violence were carried out against witches. Villagers became vigilantes and forcibly 'swum' witches to prove their guilt in 11 known cases between 1665 and 1735. Some of these incidents led to the death of the accused person.

The monstrous nature of witches is seen in their familiar animals. A pig was not an animal that could be ridden, but this diabolical pig could carry three witches to the Sabbat.

Witches could be tried by means of the 'ducking stool'. This was a form of torture where the suspected witch was tied to a chair and half-drowned until she confessed to witchcraft.

AMERICAN WITCHES: THE SALEM TRIALS

The beliefs that led to the witchcraft trials in Europe in the sixteenth and seventeenth centuries naturally found their way across the Atlantic as Europeans began to settle America. Just as in England, there were frequent accusations of witchcraft between neighbours in small towns. The authorities did not often believe such accusations, and most accused people were acquitted. Often enough, however, people were convicted of witchcraft and hanged for the offence. There was only one spectacular witch trial in the American colonies, the famous episode at Salem, Massachusetts, in 1692. More people were executed for witchcraft in this one incident than in the whole previous history of New England.

The notion that witches conspired at the Sabbat does not appear in New England trials before the events at Salem. As in most of the European cases, this idea allowed an almost routine accusation of witchcraft to be swiftly followed by mass persecution. The Salem witch-hunts ended with 156 people imprisoned on charges of witchcraft, 19 people hanged, one person tortured to death, and four more victims who died in prison.

The Salem witch trials have captured the imagination of the American people ever since they occurred. Every generation has put forward its own explanations for the tragedy, and inevitably many myths have become part of traditional accounts of the events.

The story at Salem begins with two girls, Betty Paris and Abigail Williams, who were the first to become ill and blame witchcraft for their apparent suffering. For no apparent reason, the girls had convulsions and fell into fits of screaming in what seemed an inhuman fashion.

The first myth begins here. In many accounts since the nineteenth century, the girls were supposed to have become obsessed with witches, demons and voodoo through listening to the stories of Tituba, a slave of Betty's father. She is usually said to have come from Barbados. Tituba, along with Sarah Osborne and Sarah Good, was one of the three original women to be accused of witchcraft. These tales of dark magic were supposed to have encouraged the girls to fake their hysterical state. But in none of the original accounts was it suggested that Tituba told the girls any horror stories whatsoever. At her trial she confessed to witchcraft and used her own folklore to detail her own and others' magical deeds, but she was not the only one of the accused to do so. The traditional narrative of Salem gives this woman the role of an unwitting catalyst for events, but it is clear that she was innocent.

When Betty Paris and Abigail Williams first fell ill, every effort was made by the local doctor to discover the nature of their illness and to cure it. When all his efforts failed, Betty's father, the local church minister, turned to prayer and sought the advice of the other local clergymen. Finally it was decided that the girls must be under some sort of magic spell, and they were pressured to reveal the names of their tormentors. While these two girls were the first to suffer from witchcraft, they were soon joined by two others, 12-year-old Ann Putman and Elizabeth Hubbard, who was probably 17.

(continued on page 194)

Matthew Hopkins, the 'Witch Finder-General' of Essex, England, was supposed to have been executed as a witch himself. In fact he is known to have died of consumption in 1647.

the Witch finder-General Reaps What He Sows?

Essex in 1645–47 experienced England's worst witch-hunt, orchestrated by the self-styled 'Witch Finder-General' Matthew Hopkins.

In the July 1645 trial in Chelmsford, England, 36 women were tried for witchcraft, and of these 19 were executed, nine died of diseases contracted in jail, six were still in prison in 1648, and only one escaped punishment. By the end of the witch-hunts in 1647, 200 people had been executed.

England at this time was in a state of civil war between King Charles I and Parliament, and in many places the normal practices of government had broken down. These circumstances allowed fanatics like Hopkins and his supporters to exercise their reign of terror over a whole region.

At the beginning of the witch-hunt, Hopkins found supporters across the county willing to come forward with accusations that their neighbours were witches. As many as 92 people from all levels of local society gave evidence in the July 1645 trial in Chelmsford. Hopkins was a firm believer in the existence of devil-worshipping witches, and he manipulated the testimonies of these people to indicate that the accused were not just witches but part of a diabolical conspiracy. He claimed to have found pacts with the devil that had been signed by the accused. These pacts had frequently appeared in witch trials in Europe but had been almost unknown in England before Hopkins.

In Essex before 1645, witches were tried not merely for being witches but also for causing harm to someone through magic. Hopkins's trials were different. Many of the 'witches' were accused only of being seen entertaining diabolical spirits, including an ox-headed greyhound and a legless dog.

Hopkins was also responsible for accusations that witches ritually married the devil and had sexual intercourse with him. The witches themselves provided many of these details, accusing each other of fantastic acts of magic at their weekly Friday meetings.

These incredible accusations and confessions were obtained by torture, which had not been used in earlier trials. Hopkins made sure that accused witches were kept awake for many nights in a row, and they were forced to walk back and forth continually until their feet were blistered.

As the trials and witch-hunts became more ferocious, support for Hopkins began to wane and opposition to his reign of terror became more confident. A vicar in Huntingdonshire wrote a pamphlet condemning the witch-hunt in Essex, declaring that 'every old woman with a wrinkled face, a furred brow, a hairy lip, a gobber tooth, a squint eye, a squeaking voice or a scalding tongue…having a dog or a cat by her side, is not only suspected but pronounced for a witch'.

Long after Hopkins's activities had passed into history, a legend arose that

During Hopkins's witch trials, women were forced to confess to having demonic familiars. The names of these demons, such as Vinegar Tom and Griezzell Greedigut, were names of mischievous fairies in local folklore traditions.

the witch-hunts had come to an end when the great witch finder himself was grabbed by a mob and 'swum' as a witch – a method Hopkins himself had used to murderous effect.

According to the legend Hopkins sank but survived to be hanged as a witch by the mob. Such a death might have been seen as a kind of poetic justice in view of the hundreds of innocent victims of Hopkins's witch-hunt. However, all the reliable evidence shows that Hopkins in fact died of consumption in 1647.

The Salem trials began to break down in confusion when the supposedly bewitched young women of Salem began to accuse more and more respectable and influential men of the state.

The girls claimed that witches had appeared to them in spirit form, had stuck pins in them, and cursed them with a convulsive illness. The evidence in the trials depended on this 'spectral evidence', visions that only the girls had seen, so no one else could prove or disprove their claim.

Shortly before the events at Salem there had been a well-known case in which a Boston woman had been hanged for bewitching four children who had 'taken dumb, their mouths stopped, their throats choked, their limbs wracked and tormented so as might move a heart of stone'. The Salem children suffered from the same symptoms as the Boston children. At the time this connection was taken as proof that the charges of witchcraft were genuine, since why else would children from two different places suffer in identical ways? The Boston story was known to everyone in Salem and probably influenced their opinions and reactions to events. Even though the witchcraft trials in Europe were drawing to a close, stories from European trials were also well-known in New England, and many people were prepared to believe the allegations of diabolical witchcraft.

The three women originally accused of witchcraft at Salem were all marginal and despised members of the Salem community. Sarah Good was a local beggar who cursed those who ran into her. She was the ideal candidate for a witch, the sort of solitary old woman who was so frequently accused of witchcraft throughout Europe and America.

Tituba, a slave and subject to the habitual racism of the white community, was also an outsider. She has sometimes been described as black and sometimes as half Native American, but it seems that she was in fact fully Native American in origin. The third victim, Sarah Osborne, was a much richer woman than the other two but had damned herself in the eyes of the Puritan community by living with a man for a year before marrying him.

The first of the three women to be interrogated on March 1, 1692, was Sarah Good, who attempted to deflect blame from herself by accusing Sarah Osborne of afflicting the children by magic. This in fact sealed her own fate. She was the only one of the original three to hang for witchcraft. Sarah Osborne died in prison. Tituba confessed to witchcraft and also accused the other two women, claiming that there were many others in the village who were devoted to Satan. She was the only survivor of the three women and was released from prison at the end of the scare.

Once the accusations had been made by Sarah Good and Tituba, the situation escalated. The afflicted girls were elevated to the status of oracles, rooting out the secret evil in the community. They continued their probably feigned convulsions and hysterical outbursts, and began to accuse more and more people, many of whom were respected and pious people. They even accused children such as Dorcas Good, the five-year-old daughter of one of the original accused women.

By the spring of 1692, the hysteria had spread outside Salem to Andover. The Salem magistrates were replaced by colonial officials in a new hearing that was an attempt to halt the torrent of accusations and confessions. However, the new judges were just as easily convinced of the afflicted girls' sincerity and of the role of witchcraft. Those who were accused most often confessed to save themselves from being hanged. Those who refused to admit any guilt were executed.

A transcript of the deposition of Ann Putnam. The trials had a lasting effect upon U.S. law. 'Spectral evidence', which by definition only one person could see, would no longer be acceptable as testimony.

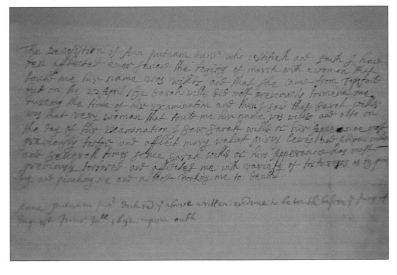

An evocative statue of Salem's founder, Roger Conant, stands outside the Salem Witch Museum, where the history of the witch-hunt is presented in macabre detail.

The accusations became even more fantastic in their scale, and at one point Lady Phips, the wife of Governor William Phips, was named as a witch. Finally the Salem girls accused Samuel Willard, who was president of Harvard University and pastor of the First Church of Boston.

At this, the credulity of the magistrates snapped and they told the girls they were mistaken. From this point on, the authorities began to doubt whether there was any truth in the whole business. The accusers then argued that the devil could have appeared to the girls in the form of innocent people. This idea that Satan had been involved meant that the girls could be absolved of all blame, because they had simply been mistaken in their accusations.

Finally the governor stepped in, calling a new hearing in which the visions of the Salem girls were not admitted as evidence. Fifty-two people were tried once again, and only three were found guilty of witchcraft. Even these three were reprieved by the governor, who released all those remaining in prison and issued a general pardon for all those who had been accused. The Salem witch-hunt was over, but opinion was still divided about whether the original accusations had been fraudulent. It took time before a consensus appeared that there had been no witches in Salem, and that it was not the devil who had afflicted the girls. Whether the girls were total frauds, or were afflicted with a psychological or physical illness, may never be resolved, and opinion differs widely to this day.

THE END OF THE WITCH TRIALS

The members of the ruling classes that were most likely to prosecute witches and undertake mass trials were the lower- and middle-ranking clergy and local magistrates and judges. Higher authorities were most likely to be suspicious of the witch-hunts, if only because they were dismayed by the chaos that could be unleashed by a mass witch panic.

Many of the witch-hunters became disillusioned with torture as a method of obtaining evidence. Someone who was remembered as a merciless witch-hunter, Benedict Carpzov, actually campaigned to remove torture from the instruments of trials. The Jesuit priest Friedrich von Spee acted as confessor to witches about to be executed, and became the most important

seventeenth-century opponent of witch trials and the use of torture. He claimed that none of those he interviewed had committed any of the evils to which they had confessed. His warnings, and his condemnation of the use of torture, had great influence, and through his and others' objections the witch-hunts came to an end.

Although the witch-hunts remain among the most horrific events of European history, one good emerged from all the misery: torture ceased to be a normal part of the judicial process.

Tituba, the slave of the Paris family, shown here terrifying girls with horror tales, became part of the mythology of Salem. This standard part of the account has no basis in reality.

Witches in their Own Words

I f you consider the history of the persecution of witches in Europe and America, you may receive the impression that witchcraft was a delusion invented by fearful people and searched out by fanatics with tragic results. Yet not only were there many ordinary village people who believed that they could perform useful magic, but there also were a few who in fact believed that they were witches and even confessed to witchcraft without undue pressure. Others became convinced that they must have been witches during the course of their arrest and trial. Those who confessed to being witches brought to their false confessions many elements of their own folklore and their imaginations. These stories are far from trivial, for beneath the fantasies we can see the pressures under which people lived and the circumstances in which witchcraft seemed like a credible threat.

The magic performed by female witches was always strongly identified with instruments of women's work, but used in a way contrary to the usefulness of obedient labour. The old witch pictured here is using her distaff, normally used to spin wool or flax, to conjure up a thunderstorm.

FANTASIES OF THE DEVIL'S SABBAT

Those who believed in the reality of the witches' Sabbat imagined a meeting full of wild abandon to the basest desires the imagination could create. Witches were supposed to be consumed with unbridled lust, so that they would copulate with devils, often in the form of animals. In a time when food was rarely plentiful for the poor, wondrous feasts were imagined as a temptation for men and women alike to swear allegiance to the devil.

When 'witches' were questioned about their participation in the Sabbat, however, a very different picture emerged. Suspected witches relayed imagined details of the Sabbat, but the details they provided were not entirely what their interrogators expected. In 1596, a Frenchwoman from Lorraine, Barbe Mallebarbe, when asked if the devil had been kind to her, replied sarcastically, 'Ho, what gentleness, seeing that when he commanded us to cause harm and we did not want to obey his wishes, he would beat us thoroughly.' The experience of being arrested for witchcraft did not encourage suspects to imagine forbidden delights at the imaginary Sabbat. They imagined misery and mistreatment, which was exactly what they were experiencing in reality.

AN IMAGINED EVIL

The devil presides over this 1808 French illustration of the Sabbat. Witches feast on children, they dance for the devil, and boil children's limbs in a pot to perform their magic.

Barbe Mallebarbe's story illustrates particularly well the experience of being accused of witchcraft. She was about 60 years old when she was arrested. Her husband, Jean, was older and crippled, and none of their children had survived to adulthood. The two had been day labourers all their lives, so as they grew older it was increasingly difficult for them to survive. To make ends meet, they had to sell the small amount of land they owned. With only a house and a small garden left, they became dependent on the charity of their neighbours, and ill feeling towards them began to grow. Barbe was accused of

witchcraft, and she fled the town, returning a few months later hoping that feelings would have died down. Unfortunately, she was wrong, and she was arrested on suspicion of witchcraft as soon as she returned.

Barbe gave up all hope of survival when she was arrested, and her only concern was to avoid torture. She even tried unsuccessfully to hang herself in prison. At her first confession, she stated that she had been seduced by 'Master Percy', as the devil was called in this part of France, and had been promised 'money in abundance'. The devil also gave her two sacks of magical powder which she was supposed to use to harm people. But she claimed to have dumped the powder in a stream, and that she had not used it to harm anyone. At this point, despite her fear of torture, she was unwilling to admit to having done anyone any harm through witchcraft.

The judges did not believe Barbe's avowals of innocence of wrongdoing, as many of the villagers claimed that she had harmed them with witchcraft.

The rack, depicted in a nineteenth-century wood engraving. Most of the tortures visited upon suspected witches used much less complicated procedures, but were no less painful.

Barbe now faced torture and was at one point put on the rack. Her confession became more detailed and extensive. She said that she had been a witch for 20 years and that she had been killing cows and men through the use of witchcraft over all that time.

In her confessions, Barbe exacted a kind of imaginary revenge on the people who had mistreated her in the past. One woman, Claudon Basle, had called her an 'old bigot and witch' some years before. Barbe remembered this incident and claimed that Claudon's death 18 months after their quarrel was due to her witchcraft. Barbe said she had poured the infamous devil's powder down Claudon's neck after their quarrel, causing her to die as the result of a lingering and debilitating illness.

BARBE AND MASTER PERCY

Pressured to admit to more victims, Barbe tried to put the judges off, relating a story of a time when she resisted the devil's instructions. She had met a village official on the road by chance and asked him for charity. He refused, calling her an old witch, so the devil whispered in her ear and told her to kill him. Barbe remembered that the man had often been very kind and generous to her in the past, and so she refused to carry out the devil's instructions. The devil tried to force her to obey him by thrashing her, but however often he beat her, she resisted his will.

The judges continued to demand more confessions from Barbe, and after a demonstration of the tortures they would inflict, she came up with a series of admissions. She became more imaginative after this point and found different ways that the devil could communicate with her. In one incident, she said she had heard crows calling her and telling her to kill those who had refused to give her charity. She also claimed that the devil had transformed her into a cat so that she could strangle a woman whose husband had accused her of creating a fog through witchcraft. When she was unable, quite naturally, to strangle the woman when she was in the form of a cat, she instead terrorized the woman by speaking to her in her cat form and then attacking her with cat claws.

Once the judges were satisfied that Barbe had confessed all her evil deeds, they wanted her to reveal all the other witches in the area. They began to concentrate on the Sabbat, asking the names of others she had seen there. Barbe was still trying to limit the degree to which she was an evil witch and described herself as resisting other witches' plans at the Sabbat. A man had

Once the judges were satisfied that Barbe had confessed all her evil deeds, they wanted her to reveal all the other witches in the area.

The fairy tale image of witches familiar to us have their origins in illustrations such as this one from an early twentieth-century romanticized story of a genuine case of 1580.

been executed as a witch in a village nearby a short time before, and so she happily identified him as one of the witches she had met at the Sabbat. She portrayed him as something of a ringleader of the witches, making plans to destroy the crops. Barbe claimed to have objected to this act of evil because

Three witches are burned at the stake in the Harz Mountains in 1555 in this German engraving. Normally, those executed in this way were strangled before the flames were lit.

of the misery and starvation it would inflict on the poor. For her sympathy, the devil beat her soundly.

The judges were not interested in a witch that had already been caught and executed, so they pressured Barbe to provide the names of other witches who had attended the Sabbat with her. Finally she named two other elderly women who used to go begging with her, Claudon la Romaine and Chesnon la Triffatte. On August 6, 1596, Barbe Mallebarbe was executed by strangulation and her body was burned at the stake, which was the usual means of executing heretics and witches. The other two women were executed a month later.

This case illustrates the tragic story of many of those accused of witchcraft. Three poverty-stricken women were executed because the villagers had become resentful of the demands for charity that the old women had to make in order to survive. This is an extraordinary and horrifying outcome of what may seem like a petty cause. It also would never have occurred if the judges had not believed so strongly in witchcraft and the existence of the Sabbat. Yet there also is a deeper psychological cause.

WITCHES OR BAD NEIGHBOURS?

Village life in the sixteenth century demanded a degree of dependence among the villagers that today would be considered extraordinary, even by those who live in small towns. The almost claustrophobic way of life exerted tremendous pressure on people to keep their passions carefully hidden. There were few, if any, outlets for pent-up emotions, and people lived with a great deal less privacy and solitude than we do in the Western world today. The picture of a witch in village societies of the sixteenth and seventeenth centuries was that of a bad neighbour – someone who was routinely rude, quarrelsome, resentful of others and mean-spirited.

In these circumstances, hidden anger and resentments could build up to a dangerous degree. In the language of modern psychiatrists this would be commonly known as 'projection', where individuals unconsciously project their deeper fears and desires onto others, expecting from them what they most dread or wish. This state of mind can easily reach hysterical proportions, and it clearly did so in the case of Barbe's neighbours. The fears and

This nineteenth-century artist depicted the witches' dance at the Sabbat as a wild pagan ceremony, presided over by a horned devil with a hooded witch-priest at his feet.

aggression of the villagers became projected upon a poor woman whose constant demands were irritating and, no doubt, made many feel guilty. It was an easy thing for her neighbours to believe that she was aggressive and violent in some hidden way. In a society that believed in witchcraft, this meant that she must indeed have been a witch. In another twist, the hostility that Barbe experienced from her neighbours was enough to convince her that their fears had a foundation and she was in fact a witch.

SEDUCED BY THE DEVIL

The judges and prosecutors of witches were relentless in their questioning, seeking to discover the diabolical delights the witches had enjoyed while at the Sabbat. The 'witches' themselves must have been aware of the kinds of confessions their tormentors were expecting, but the details they gave of their experiences at the Sabbat confounded expectations. The men and women accused of witchcraft were unable to imagine Satan's living up to the promises he made to tempt them. The food the devil provided always tasted of ashes or excrement; the music at his celebrations was loud, discordant and painful to hear. The women often reported being violently raped by the devil.

One woman presented her induction as a witch as being entirely against her will. Catherine la Rondelatte, a relatively young widow with no children, was interrogated in 1608. She described walking back from visiting her sister one day, consumed with loneliness and frustration. Although she wished to remarry, her relatives were against this and without their support she could not. As she was walking, the devil suddenly appeared in the form of a man and said to her, 'Poor woman, you are very thoughtful.' From the man's obviously evil presence, Catherine immediately knew that the man was the devil and crossed herself, calling on Saint Nicholas to protect her. This did her no good as the devil threw her down, raped her and 'at the same time pinched [her] roughly on the forehead'. This pinch was the act that gave her the mark of a witch, sealing her fate as a servant of Hell. According to Catherine, Satan then said, 'You are mine. Have no regret; I will make you a lady and give you great wealth.' She was then forced to renounce God and her baptism.

This representation of the Sabbat from 1687 shows many of its main themes. Witches kiss a goat-devil, while a witch prepares an evil spell in her cauldron.

THE WITCHES' DANCE

Although common wisdom had it that witches went to the Sabbat to indulge in wild dancing, cannibalism and promiscuous sex, few actually described the demonic festivities in this way. The Sabbat was sometimes described as a parody of a village festival, with folk dancing done backwards. Instead of a festival to bless the crops and encourage the fertility of the fields, the witches created hail and caterpillars to destroy their village's crops, while eating foul food such as rotten or diseased meat, bread mixed with ashes, or food that tasted and smelled of excrement.

One Frenchwoman, Claudon Bregeat, gave a very gloomy account of her experience of the Sabbat. Some incompetent musicians played 'the flute on some wooden sticks like whistles, while nobody said a word'. Everyone was also very careful to avoid being identified by

207

the other witches, so they wore masks or headdresses pulled over their faces. Since witches would be forced to name the others who attended the Sabbat, this was a sensible precaution to take. In the real world, it also meant that Claudon did not have to accuse anyone else of witchcraft.

It was usually the poor with little social standing who were accused of witchcraft. Perhaps surprisingly, this did not mean that their role in the imaginary Sabbat was full of the power and authority they did not possess in the real world. The opposite was usually the case. These 'witches' imagined themselves as being just as powerless at the Sabbat as they were in everyday life. One woman, Didielle Simmonel, complained that the devil always chose male witches to be the 'mayor' and 'dean' of the Sabbat. While the male witches flew off to carry out the exciting business of causing hailstorms and ruining the crops, 'she and the other women remained on the spot, and did the cooking while they waited for the men to return for the banquet'. Male witches related a similar sense of inferiority. Nicolas Raimbault, a poor herdsman, complained that the head witches 'seemed to him to be gentlemen – being more cherished and favoured than the small'. The gentlemen witches also made all the decisions, choosing to destroy crops that would cause the most hardship to the poor, while the oats grown to feed the horses of the rich remained untouched.

English witches drew upon the village stories of demons and spirits to describe the behaviour of their familiars.

WITCHES AND THEIR FAMILIARS

The Sabbat very rarely made an appearance in the confessions of English witches, and they rarely made a formal compact with the devil in human form. Instead, English witches had demonic familiars, who played the role of the devil. Devils appeared in the form of animals, often a cat or dog, but sometimes a toad, wasp or butterfly. The relationship between the witch and her familiar was very personal, and the familiar often fed on the witch's blood.

In 1566, Elizabeth Francis admitted that her grandmother had introduced her to witchcraft through a spotted white cat called Satan, which she fed milk and bread. The cat spoke to her 'in a strange and hollow voice'. She asked her familiar to make her rich, and, in return for some of her blood, the cat brought 18 sheep into her pasture. It seems, however, that these sheep were merely an illusion, since after some time they all 'did wear away, she knew not how'.

Elizabeth turned to her familiar once again when she wished to marry a certain wealthy man. The devil cat advised her that she would have to allow the man to sleep with her before marriage. Predictably, however, he did not marry her after 'abusing' her, so Elizabeth sought the help of her familiar yet another time. In Elizabeth's imagination, it was the devil who first ruined the man's property and then killed him merely by touch at her request. Yet the promises of the devil never seemed to work out satisfactorily for these 'witches'; Elizabeth, for instance, never became rich and gained only an imaginary revenge over the man who had mistreated her.

Just as those accused of being part of the Sabbat in Continental Europe turned to folklore to supply the details of their witchcraft, English witches also drew upon the village stories of demons and spirits to describe the behaviour of their familiars. Still, some of the names the witches gave to their familiars sound more like the names a lonely person might give to their pets. Mary Hockett, a victim of Matthew Hopkins's Essex witch-hunt of 1645–47, was accused of entertaining three devils in the form of mice, whom she called 'Littleman', 'Prettyman' and 'Daynty'. Another woman named her mouse familiar 'Prickeares'.

WITCHES AND ELVES

Those accused of witchcraft did not simply create their fantasies to keep their prosecutors happy. Many clearly identified strongly with these imaginings, which gave them a sort of morbid satisfaction during the dreadful experience of being accused as a witch. These 'witches' drew on the full range of folklore at their disposal and often revealed aspects of witchcraft beliefs that would otherwise be lost to history. In the case of elves in witchcraft confessions, it seems that these supernatural creatures acted as a replacement for the devil and his Sabbat in English and Scottish trials.

In Scotland and England, a great many people believed in the existence of elves or fairies, and these creatures became associated with witches very easily in people's minds. Far from being the noble creatures of Tolkien's *Lord of the Rings*, or whimsical fluttering creatures like Peter Pan's Tinkerbell, elves and fairies were usually considered to be malevolent and dangerous spirits, and they came in many different sizes, from tiny to gigantic. Elves were thought to cause disease, and many of the cunning folk directed their magical remedies against fairies and elves.

Although the devil's Sabbat rarely appeared in English witch trials, it did have its equivalent in the elves' imagined magical feasts and dances in the wilderness. Witches often referred to elves as the 'good people' or the 'good neighbours', but this did not imply that elves were thought of as friendly.

the witch's cauldron: myths of cannibalism

Cannibalism is an ancient fear among people across the world. The idea that humans, who are used to eating almost any other creature they want, might become the eaten is seen as a nightmarish reversal of the normal order of nature. European folklore provides many monsters whose chief delight is to consume human flesh. Ogres abound in mythology, including the monster Grendel of Anglo-Saxon mythology, who could kill entire troops of armoured and hardy warriors. In Russian myth, the witch Baba Yaga travelled in a mobile nightmare hut. Her magic made the hut hop along on a gigantic chicken leg in her search for children to cook in her cauldron.

The witch's cauldron was known in stories across Europe as the instrument in which they cooked their magical ointments. The essential ingredient in all their magical recipes was the boiled flesh of children, or sometimes unbaptized babies. A classic example is the German tale of Hansel and Gretel, the two children left in the woods by their wicked stepmother. Hansel and Gretel found themselves at a house made of bread, cake and sugar candy, made by a witch to trap starving children. Like many witches of German folktales, this one had red eyes and was very short-sighted. She intended to cook and eat the children, but was foiled by Gretel, who kicked the witch into her own oven. Variants of this story, where

children escape from the clutches of witches, have been known across Europe and Asia for many centuries.

Witches are universally imagined as antisocial people who delight in acts that normal people abhor. Perhaps the worst imaginable act of evil in any society is the killing and eating of children. Hence, wherever people believe in witches, they are usually imagined to consume the flesh of children. Fortunately, even those who believed in the power of the black arts never turned these horrors into reality.

Hansel and Gretel are enticed into the cottage made of bread and sugar candy by a near-sighted, red-eyed witch of the kind that commonly appeared in the fairy tales collected by the Grimm brothers in nineteenth-century Germany.

Rather, they were considered so dangerous that it was unwise to insult them or show them any ill will. The fairy spirit 'Robin Goodfellow', for example, was very often a figure of fear and dread.

Witches were natural allies of elves and fairies, since they were both malevolent workers of magic. Isabel Gowdie, a Scottish witch, confessed that she had gone to the 'Downie Hills', where the elves were supposed to live. In this mythical place, she 'got meat from the Queen of the Faerie, more than I could eat'. In contrast to the devil, all of whose promises of food and delight turned to misery and disgust, the elves provided witches with a pleasant experience. Isabel Gowdie described the Queen of the Elves as 'brightly clothed in white linens, and in white and brown'. Equally, the King of 'Faerie', in the land of the elves, was 'well favoured and broad faced'. Another Scottish witch, Andrew Marr from Aberdeen, confessed in 1597 to meeting the Queen of the Elves in the company of the devil. Again, the beautiful Queen of the Elves put on a splendid banquet for him and played pleasant music and danced. Marr even enjoyed pleasant sexual relations with the Queen. His was an exceptional fantasy – witches almost never enjoyed the demonic entertainments offered to them.

The ogre who eats babies is now merely a children's tale, but the ogre who eats human flesh was an adult terror found in folktales across Europe throughout the centuries.

A FLYING SOLUTION

In the northeast Italian region of Friuli, it was once believed that there were people – the benandanti – who flew in spirit at night to fight witches. This belief is best illustrated through the story of two men, Paolo Gasparutto and Battista Moduco, who were the first to be arrested for their belief in the battles between the benandanti and the witches. Yet many others in Friuli shared their belief, and similar beliefs had probably been widespread in central Europe in earlier times. This extraordinary story emerged almost by accident in March 1575, when an Inquisitor named Fra Felice heard a confusing report from a parish priest concerning a man who cured people who had been bewitched and was rumoured to go about at night with witches and goblins.

The man who allegedly flew at night with supernatural spirits was an ordinary peasant called Paolo Gasparutto, and when he was summoned to appear before the Inquisition, who suspected him to be a witch, he happily explained that he was not a witch, but rather a benandante. This was a regional term that the Inquisitors did not understand, but which they translated as 'vagabond'. At first, Gasparutto explained himself freely, saying, 'I am a benandante because I go with the others to fight four times a year.' His adventures always took place at night: 'I go invisibly in spirit and the body remains behind. We go forth in the service of Christ, and against the witches of the devil.' Over the next 50 years, the Inquisition found many other people in this area of Italy who believed themselves to be benandanti, and all these people, men and women alike, told very similar tales of their battles with witches.

This strange piece of folklore was a kind of magic associated with ensuring the fertility of the fields. The ember days, when the benandanti said they went out to fight, were three days in each season dedicated to certain saints and regarded as turning points from one season to the next. As Gasparutto said, 'In the fighting that we do, one time we fight over the wheat and all the other grains, another time over the livestock, and at other times over the vineyards. And so, on four occasions we fight over all the fruits of the earth and for those things won by the benandanti that year there is abundance.' In the fight, the witches were armed with stalks of sorghum, a type of cereal. Any symbolic significance the sorghum had is lost to us now. The benandanti were armed with stalks of fennel. Fennel was thought to have magical healing properties, and it was particularly valued as an antidote to witchcraft. Fennel was supposed to be as powerful against witches as legend says that garlic is against vampires.

It was not just the harvest that the benandanti were protecting. Witches were also known to prey upon children, and the benandanti claimed to be able to recognize any child who was under attack from witches. The

The interior of a church in Friuli, Italy. Even in such a heavily urbanized and Catholic country, the strange beliefs of the benandanti existed alongside orthodox beliefs. The benandanti believed that they had a sacred duty to do battle in spirit form with witches.

benandanti could cure a child made ill by the witches simply by weighing him or her on three successive Thursdays. Their notion was that the child was being drained of his flesh by the witch's invisible attack, which usually happened on a Thursday. The benandanti would take the scales with them in their dream fights with the witches, and their captain would attack the particular witch with the scales used to weigh the child. If the benandante's assault upon the witch was successful, the child would return to health, and the witch would die.

JOINING THE FLYING ARMY

Fra Felice, the Inquisitor, asked the self-styled warrior against witches what made him join these benandanti. Paolo Gasparutto replied that at night in his house, about midnight, 'an angel appeared before me, all made of gold, like on those altars, and he called me, and my spirit went out'. Gasparutto realized at this point that he was in trouble with the Inquisition, and he hoped that by stressing the Christian nature of his belief he would escape any punishment. Unfortunately, this only made things worse, as the Inquisitor ceased to have any more doubts that the angel was clearly a devil tempting the peasant into evil ways.

The Inquisitor asked Gasparutto, 'What were you promised? Women, food, dancing?' He employed this type of leading question hoping that the man would reveal himself to be a witch. Gasparutto denied that he had been promised anything by the angel, but said that the witches at these meetings 'do dance and leap about'. The Inquisitor was convinced by this point that Paolo Gasparutto was a witch and attended the diabolical Sabbat, the very opposite of what Gasparutto was claiming.

The Inquisitor began to suggest things to the poor peasant in order to make his account square with the idea of the diabolical Sabbat. One of the standard elements in the Inquisition's concept of the Sabbat was the throne of the devil at the centre of the witches' celebrations. The Inquisitor questioned Gasparutto closely about the devil's throne and whether the 'angel' had led the benandanti to bow down before it and kiss the devil. Exasperated, Gasparutto exploded, 'But he is not of our company, God forbid that we should get involved with that false enemy! It is the witches that have the beautiful thrones.'

Both Gasparutto and Moduco tried to make the meetings of the benandanti sound as martial as possible. They both described their company as being led by a 'captain', who was evidently human. Moduco related how they would salute their leader as if they were soldiers. Becoming a benandante was similar to being called up for military service. Upon reaching maturity, 20 years old in Moduco's case, the two men were called up to serve and were permitted to retire from the benandanti after a term of service of perhaps 10 or 20 years.

Fennel was thought to have magical healing properties, and it was particularly valued as an antidote to witchcraft.

Spells and Superstitions: the Magic of the Caul

Occasionally across Europe, but most prominently in northern Italy, it was believed that those born with the amniotic membrane, or caul, covering their head were connected with supernatural powers. The caul was an object endowed with magical powers to many of the people of Friuli, and those born with it would keep it as an amulet throughout their lives. Among other things, it was supposed to protect soldiers from being wounded. Even educated people valued the power of their cauls; it was said, for example, that a lawyer's caul could help him win cases.

Battista Moduco, one of the first men to be arrested as a benandante by the Italian Inquisition, claimed that his mother had given him his caul. She taught him that he was destined to be a benandante and to fight the witches in spirit form to defend the harvest. According to Moduco, after he lost his caul, he was no longer called out to fight the witches, since its loss meant that he had also lost his magical powers.

There were others who believed that someone born with the caul was destined to become a witch. The caul was seen as capable of giving witches the ability to separate their souls from their bodies and to fly at night to do evil. As with most things to do with magic, possessing a caul could lead to either good or evil.

Despite the huge advances in arts and sciences being made in cities such as Florence, Italy's rural population retained its ancient superstitions throughout the Renaissance period.

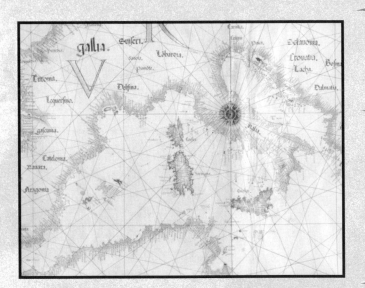

Moduco and Gasparutto believed that they were fighting for the fertility of the fields against the supernatural enemies of society. The two men were eventually imprisoned for six months and made to renounce their 'heresy' in public, where they were forced to admit that the benandanti gatherings were really the meetings of witches. It is quite clear from the record of their trials, however, that Gasparutto and Moduco did not cease to believe in the importance and goodness of their experiences as benandanti.

THE LEAVING OF THE SOUL

When the soul left the body of a benandante, the body was not merely in a state of deep sleep, but it was almost lifeless, as if in a coma. Gasparutto told the Inquisitor that it was his spirit which went forth 'and if by chance while we are out someone should come with a light and look for a long time at the body, the spirit would never re-enter it until there was no one left to see it that night, and if the body, seeming to be dead, should be buried, the spirit would have to wander around the world until the hour fixed for that body to die'.

The fennel plant was believed to have magical healing properties, and the benandanti dreamed that they armed themselves with stalks of fennel in their night battles with witches.

Both witches and benandanti believed that their bodies were very vulnerable in this state. One woman who thought herself a witch, Margherita of San Rocco, said that if her body was turned face downwards while she was at the Sabbat, then her soul and body would die. If she had been out and about in the shape of a cat and her spirit 'did not return before dawn at cock's crow, we would not change back into human form, and the body would stay dead and the spirit remain a cat'.

Sometimes the spirit was thought to look like a mouse as it entered and left the body. One witch interrogated in Lucca in 1589 declared: 'Forty years or more ago, I knew a witch called Gianna, and once when she fell asleep I saw a mouse come out of her mouth. It was her spirit and I did not know where it was going.' Gasparutto, the benandante, was also convinced that his soul left his mouth in the form of a mouse.

THE END OF THE BENANDANTI

The beliefs of the benandanti, the enemies of the witches of Friuli, were not confined to the few men who were first arrested, but were shared by a number of people questioned by the Inquisition. These beliefs appear in many cases in Friuli between 1575 and 1620. Additionally, some sixteenth-century Italian wise-women accused of being witches seem to have shared some of the mythology of the benandanti. One woman, Anna la Rossa, who practised magical cures for a range of illnesses, also claimed to be able to 'see' the dead and to bring messages back to the living.

Under interrogation by the Inquisition, Anna la Rossa said that she fell into deep trances in which her spirit would go where the witches gathered, and there she learned all the magical secrets she practised. If she revealed these secrets, she would be beaten with sorghum sticks, just as the benandanti said they would be if they revealed too much about their night battles. La Rossa was most fortunate to escape being prosecuted as a witch, since the local Inquisitors found her stories baffling and were unable to convince themselves that she was simply a witch.

The Inquisitors believed wholeheartedly, however, in the Sabbat, as it was described in the books circulating around Europe. Over the course of many trials and investigations, the Inquisition did manage to suppress beliefs concerning the benandanti. Gradually, the Inquisition convinced people that the benandanti were either witches or that their tales of the night battles were pure fantasy. Parish priests condemned the benandanti as ruffians who undermined families and were only out to make money from their false claims that they could cure bewitchment. Under this kind of pressure, this unusual fertility folklore disappeared.

LEGENDS OF THE WEREWOLF

In the Baltic country of Livonia, there was a belief regarding werewolves that was curiously similar to those of the benandanti in Italy. In Livonia, the equivalent of the benandanti were self-confessed werewolves. They claimed to turn into animals during their dreams and to go out in spirit form to fight the witches. This was in contrast to other parts of Europe where werewolves were thought to exist, but where these supernatural creatures were believed to be evil and supremely dangerous.

In 1692, judges interviewed an 80-year-old Livonian man named Theis. He claimed that he had once fought with a dead man called Skeistan, who

was a witch. Theis discovered Skeistan stealing seed grain and carrying it down to Hell. He gathered the other werewolves and went down into Hell to fight with Skeistan, who was armed with a broom handle wrapped in the tail of a horse. The significance of the broom remains a mystery, unless it was simply there as the traditional prop for a witch. The werewolves were armed with long iron rods.

The werewolves' invasion of Hell was not a single incident, but a regular ritual. Three times a year, on certain Christian holy days at Christmas and in May, the werewolves walked to a place 'beyond the sea' where they could reach Hell. Here they fought the devil and his witches. It was believed that if the werewolves failed in this ritual, the harvest would be lost.

Water torture, shown in this 1560 engraving, where the victim was forced to drink unbearable amounts of water, was one of the means by which suspected witches were forced to confess.

The Livonian judges were astonished by the old man's stories. They had never heard of the battle between the werewolves and the witches, and they kept trying to get Theis to admit that the werewolves were really servants of the devil. Theis was adamant that the werewolves hated the devil and were instead servants of God. He called the werewolves the 'hounds of God'. When a werewolf died, he was buried like anyone else, but his soul was assured of entrance into Heaven, according to the old man.

Theis also believed that there were companies of Russian and German werewolves who journeyed to their own Hells. Apparently in Theis's mind each country had its own distinct Hell. The judges sentenced the old man to 10 lashes for his beliefs. Theis was just the first to be found with these beliefs in Livonia. But, as with the mythology of the benandanti, once the judges had discovered its existence, they made strenuous efforts to stamp out what they saw as a dangerous heresy. As a consequence, belief in witch-fighting werewolves gradually died out.

THE WILD HUNT: THE ORIGIN OF FLYING WITCHES

The unusual beliefs of the benandanti related to other beliefs held across Europe in which supernatural spirits flew about in night revels. These spirits were sometimes called the 'wild hunt'. As was the case with the benandanti, the authorities saw these spirits only in terms of their theory of the witches' Sabbat or as diabolical illusions. Beliefs in the wild hunt or the 'furious horde' first appeared in the ninth century. A German bishop found that 'there are

Werewolves were a common supernatural terror throughout much of Europe, but in Baltic countries some believed that werewolves were good creatures who fought the witches.

wicked women who believe and openly avow that in the hours of the night they ride on certain animals, together with Diana, the goddess of the pagans, with a numberless multitude of women; and in the silence of the dead of night cross many lands; and obey Diana's orders as though she were their mistress, and on particular nights are summoned to her service'. While the ninth-century bishop did not believe these tales, there were many women throughout the centuries that followed who did believe that they trailed some sort of female spirit during these night flights.

In the following centuries, there were occasionally other mentions of the wild hunt, led sometimes by Diana, or by a German goddess figure called Holda. Holda was originally a pagan goddess associated with the winter solstice, and she was

most active during the winter when she was preparing the earth for the return of fruitfulness. Nineteenth-century German folklore held that snowflakes were feathers from her bed. Holda was a motherly figure, looking after homesteads, as well as a terrifying one, leading the wild hunt during storms. When angered, especially by children, she appeared as a witch-like creature – a hag with huge teeth and a long nose.

The followers of the 'furious horde' of airborne spirits could be joined by the spirits of mortal men and women, if they had the ability to separate their souls from their bodies during the night. Since Holda could be a witch-like creature, it is easy to see how the mortal women who claimed to follow her at night were also seen as witches. At the beginning of the sixteenth century in Germany, there were stories of women who, during the ember days, would fall into a trance at night that made them impervious to minor cuts or

(continued on page 224)

The idea that witches flew to the Sabbat has its origins in beliefs that hosts of usually female spirits, the wild hunt, flew through the night sky at certain times of the year.

221

Images of witches: women on broomsticks

In one of our most traditional images of the witch, one or more black-clad crones are shown flying past the moon on broomsticks and cackling with evil delight. Pictures like those opposite, from the illustrations of nineteenth-century children's stories, were not how most people imagined witches during those earlier centuries when they were most feared. Only one witchcraft trial in England in the period of the persecution craze even mentioned the broomstick as a witch's magical instrument. Images of witches before the nineteenth century were much more varied than the fairy-tale cliché, and broomsticks were only one of many props that became associated with witches' activities.

The everyday witch of village folklore was not the fairy-tale kind of supernatural figure, but merely a neighbour suspected of using magic to cause harm to crops, animals and people. Witchcraft accusations springing from ordinary village life rarely recall fantastic stories of witches flying or transforming into animals. The flying witch only became a dominant theme when churchmen and members of the local governing class became obsessed with the idea of the witches' Sabbat, where witches were supposed to gather to worship the devil.

These secret Sabbats were often imagined to take place on distant mountaintops, and the witches needed to possess some kind of magic to reach them.

Some of those accused of witchcraft, and tortured to produce a confession, said that the devil had carried them to the Sabbat. Others claimed they had ridden there on pigs, cows, dogs or other animals. Ordinary household implements, such as shovels and, of course, broomsticks, could also have been used. Many also confessed to having a magical ointment that they rubbed over themselves in order to fly. It is clear that broomsticks were only one of the many ways in which witches could fly to the Sabbat.

It was children's tales of the last two centuries that made the image of witches flying on broomsticks universal, as in this 1907 drawing by Arthur Rackham.

European beliefs in various kinds of spirits which flew through the sky at certain times of the year were suppressed in the 1700s and merged with ideas of the witches' Sabbat.

scalding. In this trance state, they joined the followers of 'Fraw Fenus' (the goddess Venus), and upon waking they described being in a strange sort of Heaven, where there were feasts and riches. This Fraw Fenus was evidently a variant name for the goddess of the myths associated with Holda.

Apart from those mortal women who went on these spiritual journeys, the main followers of the 'furious horde' were the souls of the dead, particularly those who had died young or by violent means. Furthermore, it was not only female spirits that led the 'furious horde'. One medieval French peasant claimed to have seen the wild hunt led by King Arthur, with his legendary knights as his followers.

THE ORIGINS OF HALLOWEEN

The wild hunt did more than simply fly through the air. In some places it was feared because its members were thought to pass through walls and barred doors, invading houses and eating and drinking the family's supplies. Sometimes the rapacious appetite of the wild hunt could actually bring good fortune to a household. In thirteenth-century France, the horde of ghosts was led by Dame Abundia or Satia, and if she and her followers found offerings of food and drink laid out when they invaded a house, Dame Abundia, meaning 'abundance', would bless the house and ensure its prosperity. Only if there were no offerings would the horde cause harm. In Germany, Holda was similar in her dual nature, both vengeful and helpful. She was alleged to reward diligent work in the household with gifts placed at the window.

The myth of the wild hunt was known in Italy as the 'ladies of the night'. A fourteenth-century story tells of a bishop dining at a house with friends. After dinner, he was astonished to see the table reset. He was informed that this was done for the 'ladies who enter at night'. The bishop sat up to observe this spectacle and saw 'a multitude of demons in the form of men and women', whom he then exorcised. The figures admitted to being demons and departed quite tamely. This story was written to convince people that, if they believed in the ladies of the night and left offerings for them, they were letting their house be invaded by evil spirits, rather than the possibly friendly spirits associated with the ladies of the night.

The myth of the ladies of the night has survived in Sicily to the present day, where they are also known as the 'ladies from outside', 'ladies of the home' or the 'beautiful ladies'. Those who claim to have seen them describe tall and beautiful women with long, shining hair. They appear at night, especially on Thursdays and, if provided with food, drink, music and dancing, they will bless a household. Disrespectful behaviour to the ladies can bring illness and poverty upon a home, although the ladies are quick to forgive if they are treated properly at their next visit. Unlike the wild hunt of earlier centuries, in Sicily there is no confusion between these female spirits and witches, who are seen as human and entirely evil.

Another survival of the wild hunt myth, although few are aware of the connection, is the modern ritual of Halloween. The day after Halloween (which means All Hallows' Eve) is All Saints' Day or All Hallows' Day, a Christian festival which honours all the saints in Heaven. The folklore of the common people of Europe believed that on All Hallows' Eve the horde of the dead would walk freely upon the earth, just as the wild hunt did. People feared that the wild hunt would invade their homes and cause mischief, if not serious harm.

In many places in the early modern period, there were various times of the year when young people, particularly young men, would march around a town or village imitating the wild hunt and other mythological forces. The young men would create a disruption that was only marginally more controlled than that which the army of the dead might cause. This was meant to mark the importance of the dead in the yearly cycle of growth and decay. The custom also was intended to appease the roving spirits of the dead. The origins of Halloween have been long forgotten, and it is now associated with evil spirits and monsters in all their forms. Inevitably, witches are now strongly associated with Halloween, despite the fact that there was originally no connection between them and All Hallows' Eve.

THE WILD HUNT AND WITCHCRAFT

It is unlikely that many of the women who believed they followed the wild hunt thought they were witches, especially once the fear of witches had begun to spread in scale and intensity in the fifteenth and sixteenth centuries. Once the clergy and magistrates began to suppress the whole range of popular beliefs concerning magic and the world of the spirits, beliefs in the wild hunt were condemned as diabolical illusions.

Over the years, elements of wild hunt mythology became associated with witchcraft. All witches were supposed to have a 'devil's mark', a place on their body which was insensitive to pain. This notion was influenced by the story

(*continued on page 228*)

Witches' visions of flight: flying high on drugs or imagination?

Some of the women accused of witchcraft confessed they had used a magical ointment which enabled them to fly to the devil's Sabbat. We can dismiss the idea that witches met at these diabolical festivals, whether through flying or via more normal means, as part of the witch-hunters' fantasy. However, there were many women and men who genuinely thought that their souls could leave their bodies to fly about as witches when they were in a trance state. This belief also applied to followers of night goddesses, benandanti and werewolves, the foes of the witches. Were these stories pure imagination or could they have been induced by the witches' fabled 'ointments'? These concoctions could have contained hallucinogenic substances that could have led people to have the kinds of fantastic dream experiences these people felt were real.

Some of the medicines used by 'white' witches did contain substances that could have induced trance states and hallucinations. Ergot, a poisonous fungus, can be used as a painkiller in small doses, and midwives used it for childbirth. In higher doses, it can cause convulsions and hallucinations. Some sixteenth-century Italian writers reported meeting old women who claimed to be witches that visited the Sabbat, and offered to demonstrate their power. According to these few stories, the women rubbed themselves with ointments, lay upon their beds and fell into a deep sleep from which they

could not be woken. When the witches did awake, they claimed in each case to have flown through the air and visited far away countries. They would not believe the observers who saw them simply lying in bed in a comatose state.

We cannot be sure how reliable these few stories are. Most of them are secondhand reports, and they may have been entirely fictional. In an effort to solve the problem, a few brave scholars have experimented with a surviving recipe for witches' ointments, which do contain possibly psychotropic substances. One of those who tried the witches' ointment merely experienced a headache, while another, well-known for arguing that the witches' Sabbat was real, predictably experienced the Sabbat himself. It seems impossible to prove or

Dancing and music are among the means by which the shamanic healers of Siberia drove themselves into a trance state so that they could join the realm of the spirits and effect magic. Many cultures have discovered that strong rhythms can bring on a hallucinogenic state.

A medicine-man of the Blackfeet people of North America, dressed in animal skins as he prepares to enter a trance.

disprove whether European witches used hallucinogenic drugs.

In any case, drugs of any kind may not be necessary in order to experience these dreams of flight and transformations. The visions experienced by witches and others who felt their souls flying from their bodies can be compared to those of shamans in many traditional cultures from Amazonian Indians to Asian Arctic peoples. Shamans report experiencing their souls leaving their bodies to fly with the spirits or transform into animals. There is a broad similarity between the experiences of European witches and these ecstatic experiences.

Some South American peoples use a very mild drug known as maté tea to accompany their trance states. This tea is no more a hallucinogenic drug than weak coffee, and it has no chemical ingredient that could cause visions. South American shamans, like those in many other cultures, achieve their trance states purely through the mental techniques they have learned from their elders. The visions they see are not caused by chemicals, but are informed by the stories of their culture and their unconscious imaginations.

It is possible that some European 'witches' did have some concoctions that could chemically induce a psychotropic trance, but many of those who freely described their fantastic experiences did not mention any ointment or other drug. The benandanti, who flew to battle witches during ritual times of the year, make no mention of ointments or potions at all. Their trance states were self-induced, with no chemical aids. In the end, as with shamans across the world, it was not drugs that were important in creating the fantasies of witches, but the folklore of their own culture.

A sixteenth-century engraving by Pieter Bruegel shows witches brewing the magical ointment to smear on themselves or their broomsticks so that they can fly to the Sabbat.

that the women who followed the wild hunt in spirit form left their bodies behind numb and resistant to pain. Also, the witches' Sabbat was often said to meet on a Thursday, the same day that the ladies of the night were commonly said to go out.

In some Italian witchcraft trials of the sixteenth century, women showed that they truly believed they flew at night with the wild hunt. By now, they had become convinced by the sermons of the clergy that those spirits were evil demons, rather than the ambiguous spirits of earlier times. These women still held on to their belief in the wild hunt, but concluded that they were evil witches. Domenica Barbarelli, a witch in the Italian town of Novi, was prosecuted by the Modenese Inquisition in 1532. She was entirely convinced that she was indeed a witch and had wanted to go to the 'games' of Diana, as she called the wild hunt. Her family tried to stop her by watching over her as she slept, but upon waking she declared that her spirit had secretly escaped. She also claimed that while at the games, she committed many of the evil deeds usually expected of witches. She danced with devils and profaned the holy cross.

DELUSIONS OF SELF-CONFESSED WITCHES

It is difficult to imagine why anyone would really believe themselves to be a witch and be capable of committing horrible acts of cannibalism and murder while asleep. It seems especially bizarre to confess, without duress, to such dreams at a time when stories of witchcraft would not be dismissed as absurd fantasies and might well lead to imprisonment, if not execution. An obvious explanation is that these people, mostly women, could have been mentally ill. While there is some truth to that, there are other explanations.

For centuries, many diseases such as epilepsy, as well as symptoms of mental illness, had been attributed to demons invading the patient's mind. Epileptics in the sixteenth century were particularly in danger of being accused of witchcraft, since their seizures were seen as evidence of diabolical activity. However, there were far too many people accused of witchcraft for epilepsy to be an explanation for more than a handful of witchcraft cases.

While today we would consider people unbalanced who claimed to experience night flights with hosts of supernatural beings, in the sixteenth century they might have been seen as entirely normal. The stories of flying with the wild hunt of Diana or Holda were an intrinsic part of the folklore of many communities,

A Swedish woman is plunged into the river to determine whether she is a witch. In this kind of ordeal by water many accused would drown, only thereby proving themselves innocent.

the Salem witches: demonic possession?

The convulsions and hysterical outbursts of the girls of Salem, Massachusetts, in the seventeenth century baffled their community, and no explanation for their illnesses could be imagined except witchcraft. In our scientifically minded age, it is attractive to conclude that the girls' 'demonic possession' had a chemical cause, and it has often been argued that they were suffering from ergot poisoning.

Ergot is a fungus that attacks cereal crops, particularly rye, and was a common cause of illness during or after cold, wet weather, which encourages the growth of the fungus. Eating cereal foods infected with ergot can cause two types of illness. The first can cause gangrene, and its symptoms include a painful burning sensation. The other form of the disease causes convulsions, hallucinations and sensations of tingling, choking and biting. The hallucinogenic symptoms are caused by a chemical in ergot that is related to the artificial drug LSD, although it is considerably weaker than its synthetic cousin.

The symptoms of the Salem girls were similar to those of ergot poisoning, but there are numerous reasons why it is unlikely that this was the cause of their 'possession'. Convulsive ergotism normally occurs in people who have a poor diet, but the New England community was well fed. If ergotism had struck, it would have been the gangrenous form of the disease, and if crops were diseased it would have affected entire households. But only a few people in

Salem showed symptoms, and never a whole family. Finally, the hallucinations caused by ergot are far too mild to have sustained the constant and detailed visions related by the Salem girls.

In fact, the girls, and also some women as the affair grew, do not seem to have been unwell at all. The visions and convulsions in Salem were likely to have been caused by a mixture of psychological factors and sheer fraud. As the witch-hunt grew in intensity, others joined them and made new accusations, probably to share in the notoriety and attention the girls were receiving. Soon, however, so many people were being accused of witchcraft that it became safer to be among the accusers than risk being the accused.

At one point in the Salem trials the possessed girls claimed to see yellow birds flying around the head of the accused. The spectral birds were assumed to have a demonic origin.

and people could develop this folklore into a personal fantasy that could seem real without fear of being called mentally ill. The world of dreams was considered to have a more serious spiritual reality at this time than it does for us today.

The fantasies of the men and women who believed themselves to be benandanti, or fighters of witches, do not seem to have been caused by mental imbalance either. None of those interviewed by the Inquisition show any visible signs of disturbance apart from their extraordinary accounts of the night battles. The men and women who believed they were benandanti would probably have gained a sense of peace from their belief that they fought evil forces in their sleep. In a world where the harvest was uncertain, and disaster could easily come upon villagers and their community each year, the fantasy that their dreams could ensure prosperity must have helped them allay anxieties caused by a difficult and precarious existence.

These people were not mad at all, but instead felt that they had been called from birth to defend their community and its prosperity. This 'calling' was often indicated by a physical sign of their 'uncanny' nature, their birth caul, which they kept with them at all times in the form of an amulet. It was given to them by their mothers, who probably also taught them the folklore of the battles for the fertility of the fields. The fantasies of the benandanti were a cultural tradition, rather than a sign of individual madness.

ECHOES OF ALIEN ABDUCTION

Neither insanity nor conditions such as epilepsy entirely explain why some women claimed to be witches who performed acts of evil. The answer lies in the ordinary pressures of life from which everybody seeks to escape from time to time. Some men and women would draw upon the folklore of ecstatic spiritual experiences to express their rage and resentment at the often stifling bonds of family and community, especially in the conditions of poverty from which self-confessed witches normally came.

If these people lived today, they might well claim to have been abducted by aliens, rather than being witches. This fantasy offers a similar release from the stresses of ordinary existence, even if it is into another kind of horror. Self-confessed witches must have felt a similar horror at their imagined experiences of the witches' Sabbat as people do today who claim to have been the subject of gruesome alien experiments. While the folklore has changed between the sixteenth and twenty-first centuries, the two kinds of stories emerge from

> If these people lived today, they might well claim to have been abducted by aliens, rather than being witches.

similar social problems. Overall, however, it is not the problems of the individual that lead to belief in witchcraft. It is the belief in magic along with the fear that neighbours will seek to do harm through this magic.

WITCHCRAFT ACROSS THE WORLD

People in nearly all cultures have believed in witches, and some common themes can be seen across the world. Perhaps one surprising aspect of witchcraft beliefs is that people usually accuse their neighbours of witchcraft because of tensions within close-knit communities. The more people depend upon each other's goodwill, the more they can become fearful that those close to them secretly want to harm them. These fears are often consciously suppressed but can break out into accusations of witchcraft. This was probably the cause behind many accusations in villages in Europe. In modern Nigeria, accusations of witchcraft are usually directed at close friends and family. Those we know the best can be the source of the greatest tension. The same pattern was also once found among the Navajo Indians in the United States.

WITCHES AND JEALOUS NEIGHBOURS: NAVAJO WITCHCRAFT

In common with the European witchcraft tradition, Navajo witches were

A modern Native American medicine man, named Rolling Thunder. In the past some indigenous American cultures feared witchcraft as much as Europeans and turned to such men for aid.

said to use shocking ingredients to achieve their black magic. Witches made their magic poison from the flesh of corpses. Bones from the back of the head, for example, could be ground into a powder and given to victims while they were asleep. Also like European witches, Navajo witches were active at night and were said to turn themselves into wolves or foxes. However, unlike in Europe, most Navajo witches were supposed to be men.

According to accounts of Navajo witchcraft in the first half of the twentieth century, people became witches in order to gain vengeance, wealth or simply because they were jealous of other people. Those said to be victims of Navajo witchcraft were often the richest men in the community. Victims suffered from fainting, lockjaw and a black and swollen tongue. Cursed by witchcraft, they simply withered away, and all the usual Navajo techniques of ceremonial magic were thought to be useless against the poisons administered by the witch. The danger of becoming a victim of jealous witchcraft was a powerful incentive for rich individuals to be generous to their neighbours and to avoid showing off their wealth in a way that would make others jealous.

The Navajo believed that witchcraft is passed along in the family. Individuals might learn the 'witchery way' from a parent, grandparent or even a spouse, but they might also keep their witchcraft secret from everyone they knew.

As in Europe, the secrecy surrounding witchcraft meant that people could become extremely paranoid about witches' activities. Any of your friends, family or neighbours could be a witch, undermining and subverting the life of your family and community. Witches are by definition antisocial creatures, and their acts always reverse the normal customs and beliefs of their host society. Navajo witches, for instance, would supposedly copulate with the corpses of dead women and practise cannibalism.

Senior Apolonio, a Huichol Indian shaman, is pictured here in 1998 performing a religious ritual in the desert of Wirikuta, Mexico.

SECRET RITES OF NAVAJO WITCHES

The deeds of Navajo witches are eerily similar to those of European witches. This is no surprise; the most extreme antisocial actions that anyone in any society can imagine are likely to be similar, no matter where they live. European witches profaned Christianity, while Navajo witches profaned the sacred ceremonies of Navajo religion. Their magic was imagined as being much the same as good magic, but with crucial parts of the ceremony reversed or profaned. Like European witches, they gathered in secret meetings. At these meetings, the witches were supposed to have sat naked in a circle, wearing only masks and beads. According to the accusers, around the circle were piled mounds of the flesh of corpses and human heads. Traditional Navajo healing magic makes use of complex 'paintings' drawn in the sand and ritual chanting of long songs. Witches were imagined as doing the same, only in a 'bad' fashion, with the paintings representing the intended victim of a curse. During the 'bad singings', the witches would spit, urinate and defecate upon the paintings.

Navajo sorcerers were also thought to exist, practising evil magic. Navajo sorcerers were thought of as being quite separate from Navajo witches, but they performed similar evil deeds to witches in European culture. Sorcery

There is great variety in the world's shaman religions, yet in almost all societies there is also the fear of witches. A main role for the shaman is to cure people of bewitchment.

was carried out against animals, crops, property and people. Insects such as grasshoppers and caterpillars could be sent by a sorcerer to destroy crops. Like European witches, sorcerers would employ secret spells, sometimes normal 'good prayers' said backwards. Sorcerers also had a particular 'power' that assisted their evil magic; this power could be the earth, the sun, lightning, darkness or an animal such as a bear or snake.

One of the few evil spells that are fairly well-known was intended to kill pregnant women. An evil charm was supposed to be placed inside the belly of a horned toad, and a spell recited over the animal. The victim would die four days later. It is again no surprise that the Navajo should imagine that pregnant women were particularly vulnerable to evil forces. Pregnancy is a very vulnerable time, and many societies explain the dangers of pregnancy and childbirth in terms of evil forces acting against women in that condition.

Shamans in traditional cultures carried tremendous prestige, unlike their equivalents in Europe, the cunning folk, whose social status was eclipsed by the authority of the church.

PROTECTION FROM WITCHCRAFT AMONG THE NAVAJO

Like the ordinary people of Europe, the Navajo protected themselves against evil magic with their own magic, and there were good practitioners of this

235

art. As with the wise-women and cunning men of Europe, there was some ambiguity in the practice of good magic. In order to protect oneself against witchcraft, a Navajo magic singer had to know some of the practices and spells involved in witchcraft. 'Know thy enemy' might have been the motto of the good magic singer, but some knowledge of witchcraft could put a singer in danger of being suspected as a potential witch himself. The vulnerability of magic singers to accusations of witchcraft created certain customs to prove their reliability. Before giving medicine to a patient, the magic singer would taste it himself to show that it was not poisonous.

The best way to cure a disease caused by witchcraft was to force the witch to help, as was also the case in Europe. A witch's confession was thought to be a step towards the cure – the confession would lift the evil spell. A suspected witch would be subjected to a form of torture, being brought to a meeting and not allowed to eat, drink or relieve himself until he confessed to being a witch. In the distant past, some suspected witches were killed, but by the middle of the twentieth century fears of witchcraft had died down, and Navajo communities took steps to prevent witchcraft accusations leading to violence.

By the mid-twentieth century, stories of Navajo witchcraft had become rumours about communities in far-off places. Witchcraft was becoming more of a myth than a present fear, and it was something that happened in other places. This was perhaps in part a reaction to the explosion of Navajo witchcraft accusations in the late nineteenth century. Navajo communities were divided about whether to continue the wars against the United States or to make permanent peace. Some chiefs used accusations of witchcraft to silence those who wanted to continue fighting. Apart from this period, Navajo witchcraft beliefs never led to the kinds of great witch-hunts that ravaged Europe in the sixteenth and seventeenth centuries.

AZANDE WITCHCRAFT

The Azande of Nigeria have complex beliefs about magic, and they think that witchcraft is hereditary, passed on in families through a special invisible substance located in the belly. This substance, said to be a 'round, hairy ball with teeth', can be seen only by those with knowledge of magical arts, during an autopsy. It is quite common for an Azande to acknowledge the possibility that he or she could be a witch without realizing it, and could have harmed relatives unwittingly.

> Before giving medicine to a patient, the magic singer would taste it himself to show that it was not poisonous.

When the anthropologist E. Evans-Pritchard stayed with the Azande in the 1920s, he posed the delicate question of whether certain people were witches or thieves to those he knew well enough. When he asked a friend whether he was a thief, he would receive an angry and indignant denial. However, if he asked whether he was a witch, a calmer, more thoughtful answer was sometimes given: 'If there is witchcraft in my belly I know nothing of it. I am no witch because people have not seen witchcraft in the bellies of our kin.'

When a friend is sick, an Azande man might visit him, and it is considered polite to take ritual steps to counteract any inadvertent witchcraft. Taking a gulp of water, the visitor swills it around his mouth and sprays it on the ground, saying, 'O Mbori [God], this man who is sick, if it is I who am killing him with my witchcraft, let him recover.' When a man goes into battle, his wife will perform a similar ritual at a local ghost shrine, saying, 'May nothing happen to him. May my witchcraft cool towards him. O fellow-wives, may nothing happen to our husband. Be cool towards him.' In both of these situations, the men and women do not seriously believe that they are witches, but they must be open to the chance that they are and take appropriate actions to counter the possibility.

Nigeria in the 1970s saw one of the worst modern outbreaks of witch-hunting. The cause of the outbreak lay less in superstition than in the frustrations of a poor but educated class.

WITCH-HUNTING IN MODERN NIGERIA

Witchcraft beliefs and an underlying fear of witches can exist in a society without causing much damage or disruption, until suddenly the fear of witches becomes an epidemic of witch hysteria. The spark for an outbreak of witch persecution is often the instability caused by a civil war or the breakdown of normal government. This was the case in Europe in the sixteenth and seventeenth centuries, and it has also happened in some developing African countries in recent decades. Nigeria has suffered from

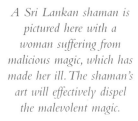

A Sri Lankan shaman is pictured here with a woman suffering from malicious magic, which has made her ill. The shaman's art will effectively dispel the malevolent magic.

periodic witch-hunts, with a major outbreak of witch-hunting in the Cross River state in 1978. The organizers of the witch-hunt were educated but poor Nigerians led by Edem Edet Akpan.

Akpan would send messages to villages that he and his witch-hunters would be questioning the entire village to search out witches. The villagers would be duly rounded up and individuals picked out and tortured until they confessed to witchcraft. The randomness of the terror inflicted by the witch-hunters is reminiscent of the horrors of the witch hysteria in Europe. Far from being a sign of backwardness, the witch-hunt in Nigeria was the product of the country's economic and educational development. The Ibibio people of this part of Nigeria have become particularly well educated, but the number of appropriate job opportunities has not kept up with the numbers of educated young people. Young men turned to witchcraft as an explanation for their lack of success, and older men and women were the most likely to be accused of witchcraft.

Many of the villagers rounded up by Akpan's band of witch-hunters confessed to being witches immediately, in order to avoid being tortured. Those who refused to confess were forced to kneel with their hands tied behind them while pepper or red ants were sprayed over their bodies and into their eyes and noses. This was enough torment to force most people to make up answers to all the questions asked of them. They were asked to name all the people they had killed through witchcraft and whose money and property they had cursed. Many 'witches' were beaten to death or their houses burned down in retaliation for their supposed crimes.

A third question asked of the Nigerian 'witches' was their rank in 'witchcraft society'. Similarly to the Europeans who believed in the fantasy of the witch cult in Europe, the Ibibio believe that all witches form part of a secret society, with its own leaders and ranks of followers. The witches meet at night and practise cannibalism, just as European witches were supposed to do. However, many of the witches are thought to be unaware of their witchcraft, even while attending the witches' meetings. Since they are thought to be in a dream state while at any such meeting, they do not remember their activities when they wake up, safe in their beds and unaware of their nightly adventures.

Some Ibibio women were openly witches and claimed to attend the witches' meetings. These women said that they did not participate in the ceremonial acts of cannibalism and were only 'white' witches. Their powers were only used to defend their families against the 'black' witches, although they did admit that they also became witches for the power and status it gave them. It might be dangerous to claim to be a witch, but it could also bring benefits, if your neighbours are afraid to offend you.

The randomness of the terror inflicted by the Nigerian witch-hunters is reminiscent of the horrors of the witch hysteria in Europe.

WOMEN WHO BELIEVE THEY ARE WITCHES

It is one thing to believe yourself to be a 'white' witch and quite another to believe that you fly about at night, eating the flesh of the recently dead. Some women of the Shona people in Zimbabwe really did appear to believe that they were cannibalistic witches. Like Europeans and other peoples across Africa and South America, the Shona have tales of the 'night witch', a woman who strips naked to fly at night on hyenas, owls or crocodiles. The witch flies to find newly buried corpses to feast on, although it is also believed that the

The role of the magician in traditional African magic includes elements of necromancy. Here the magician Thenyemba of Gaugwi, Botswana, appeases the spirit ancestors of a patient.

witches kill children in order to eat them. This is a familiar story, but there are Shona women who have freely claimed to commit these acts.

Two women in Zimbabwe in the late 1950s made these claims to the bemused British colonial authorities. One woman called Muhlava said that she had formed a friendship with another woman named Chirunga, who introduced her to witchcraft. 'We go about at night bewitching people,' she said. The pair also claimed to have inducted another woman into witchcraft. This woman, Dawu, was still young and living with her parents. They took her out to the fields one day and made a small cut on Dawu's hips, rubbing in some white magic medicine: 'I explained to Dawu that this meant she was now a witch. I explained that we should go about at night bewitching people.'

One night the three witches gathered to teach their new recruit how to

practise witchcraft. Chirunga and Dawu came to Muhlava's home, 'riding hyenas at night. We all went to my husband's hut. They came with me in order to bewitch my husband Chidava'. In this strange fantasy, the witches poured sweet beer mixed with 'bewitching medicine' into the husband's mouth and then sprinkled more of this medicine onto the poor man's body. Three days later he died: 'A little later my two friends, Dawu and Chirunga, came at night on hyenas and we all went to the place where the body was buried. We exhumed …my husband, we skinned the body, we cut a piece of meat and took it to my hut.' Once back at Muhlava's hut, 'we cooked the meat and ate it, it was good'.

The colonial authorities were not willing to believe any of Muhlava's stories and actually had her husband's body exhumed and examined. There was no evidence that his body had been interfered with or that he had died of anything but natural causes. It is quite clear that the stories came from the imagination of Muhlava (and Chirunga, who also willingly confessed to the same actions). One of Muhlava's statements is revealing: 'I cannot explain the reason for this witchcraft, it only comes to us in a dream.' Later, Muhlava and Chirunga, again riding hyenas, decided to abduct a baby: 'We wanted to bewitch the child – I cannot tell the reason because it only came to us as if we were dreaming.' Like the benandanti of Italy who fought witches in their sleep, these women had created a dream experience out of the folklore of their culture.

Even if the witchcraft of these two Shona women was wholly imaginary, it was clearly believed by some members of their community. Muhlava also claimed that after the three witches had finished with her husband's body, they decided to bewitch his brother: 'We went into the village and we found him sleeping. We each of us laid hands on him. The next morning Meke was ill.' However, a village elder came to them the next day and said that 'we should not bewitch the man Meke so we relented and Meke lived'. The three women had evidently allowed others to know that they were witches. As a result, if someone fell ill, they were suspected of causing the sickness.

Muhlava and Chirunga could not have been in a normal state of mind at the time that they believed themselves to committing these acts of evil magic. Nonetheless, they were not at all insane. They had been found capable of giving evidence in a trial, where their revelations appeared quite to everyone's surprise, for the trial had nothing to do with witchcraft. Perhaps Muhlava's fantasies of witchcraft were caused by a strange reaction to her husband's death and a desire to shock her community. The idea of eating the flesh of corpses is just as shocking to the Shona as it would be to us, and it is considered to be an act of deadly evil. Whatever the personal explanation for these women's fantasies may have been, the history of witchcraft in this case shows that people are capable of believing the most bizarre stories from folklore and even believing themselves to be agents of evil within their own communities. It was not just Shona women who believed that they were evil witches. It is clear that European women sometimes believed similar things about themselves.

The history of witchcraft shows that people are capable of believing themselves to be agents of evil within their own communities.

WITCHES AND THE IMAGINATION

The confessions of men and women accused of witchcraft in Europe in the sixteenth and seventeenth centuries reveal a rich tapestry of personal imagination – usually of the nightmarish kind – and depict village folklore and the mundane reality of quarrels and tensions in village life. All societies that believe in witchcraft are liable to break out in violent episodes of witch-hunting, given the right circumstances. The witch-hunts of Europe in the sixteenth and seventeenth centuries were exceptional in their ferocity and the pain and agony they inflicted upon so many innocent people.

These witch-hunts could only occur through the coincidence of a number of changes in society and culture. Village life had always been stressful, and there had always been enough tensions to lead to accusations of witchcraft, but society was undergoing major upheaval in the sixteenth and seventeenth centuries. In England, the old collective bonds of village life were

Salem was only the most spectacular outbreak of witch-hunting in America. At the time there were many other cases of individual men and women being accused and executed as witches.

breaking down and society was becoming much more market driven. The need to support the weaker and more vulnerable members of the community was increasingly resented by the more prosperous farmers. The guilt of denying charity to a poor, elderly widow probably led many a farmer to accuse her of being a witch, transferring his guilt onto another's shoulders.

There are many similarities between the folklore of witchcraft in Europe and the stories found in other cultures in the world, from the United States to Africa. The witch-hunters of the past undoubtedly concluded that witches had to be real since the stories told of them revealed so many connections. In reality witchcraft beliefs are similar across the world simply because, at the end of the day, human fears are fundamentally the same in any culture or at any time. Even the dark side of the human imagination demonstrates our unity.

tHe decLiNe aNd rise of magic

By the eighteenth century, magic and witchcraft were very much discredited beliefs among the educated population of Europe and America. The growing urban and industrial populations regarded the universe as controlled by rational and mechanical forces that could be explained by reason and mathematics without any need to resort to magical influences. Belief in witchcraft could not be sustained in this climate, and the governing elites suppressed any accusations of witchcraft in rural areas.

Yet even after the horrific witch trials of the sixteenth and seventeenth centuries, belief in the existence of witches did not entirely die out among people in the countryside. Of course, the likes of doctors, lawyers and other middle-class, educated people were very unlikely to hold on to such ideas. Nevertheless, anthropologists have found that, even in the twentieth century, people in some rural areas in Europe still blame misfortune on witchcraft, although this is admitted only in private. Unlike the witchcraft beliefs of the sixteenth and seventeenth centuries, however, the devil has vanished from the picture. Yet beliefs in acts of malevolent magic remain, tied very much to village jealousies and quarrels, and with them, imaginary power struggles between individuals, families and the community.

QUACKS REPLACE THE CUNNING FOLK
Despite some lingering belief in witchcraft, for the majority of people during the eighteenth century, science and medicine were replacing traditional magic practices to help in the problems of everyday life. The cunning folk,

After the seventeenth century, magic was slowly eclipsed in the day-to-day lives of most people by the rise of scientific medicine. With the decline of wizards and cunning folk, a new character appeared, the quack doctor, whose remedies were at best little better than magic, even though they claimed a scientific basis.

who were always on the margins of respectable village society, began to lose what respect they still had, and went into a slow decline as a regular facet of life in the countryside. Although it was a long time before modern medicine became particularly effective, people began to put more trust in educated doctors than the traditionally uneducated wise-women and cunning men.

Still, 'scientific' medicine was not always any more reliable or respectable than the remedies of the cunning folk. There were many 'quack doctors' throughout Europe and North America who travelled around offering supposed miracle cures that were at best harmless, at worst fatal. Kelly Booker, a man in nineteenth-century East Anglia, England, prescribed a powder to a woman suffering from an unsightly skin ailment. Unfortunately, the powder contained poison and the woman died less than a day after drinking it dissolved in water.

Poor people could rarely afford to consult trained doctors or veterinarians for help with their own or their animals' illnesses, and there remained men in the countryside known as 'handymen' who claimed to be able to treat all types of diseases in people or animals. Some of these handymen had pretensions of practising respectable forms of medicine, while others were still wedded to the old magical techniques and would regularly prescribe herbal concoctions handed down to them over generations.

Sometimes the quack doctors and the old-fashioned cunning folk became one and the same. One such person was a handyman named James Murrell, who earned a living in Hadleigh in Essex, England, from 1812 until his death in 1860. He was said to be the seventh son of a seventh son, and he was known to cast spells and exorcise demons from his patients. He was known as the Cunning Man of Hadleigh, and men and women like him persisted in some parts of the countryside in Europe and North America into the twentieth century.

SPIRITUALISM AND THE PERSISTENCE OF THE ESOTERIC ARTS

Even as the age of reason, science and industry was reaching its height in the nineteenth century, many people still found it difficult to shake off the idea that magic was a reality and the world was full of spirits, ghosts, angels and demons. Since the nineteenth century, a striking number of otherwise sensible people have shown an interest in contacting the spirits of the dead. So a new kind of magic practitioner appeared on the scene as a result, the medium. There had always been some people who claimed to be able to speak with the dead, and necromancy is among the oldest of magical practices. Modern-day mediums have simply carried on this tradition, but they lost the other roles such people would have had. Contacting the dead was once simply a source of magical power or a means of discovering information hidden to the living, and many in the seventeenth century would have included this kind of magic with their techniques of healing magic. With the general decline in belief in magic, the medium has become simply an exploiter of people's grief at the loss of a family member or loved one.

'Spiritualism' and other esoteric forms of pseudo-knowledge had some surprising advocates at the turn of the nineteenth and twentieth centuries. One of these was the Irish poet W. B. Yeats (1865–1939), an icon of modern literature who was obsessed with magic, or the occult, as it came to be known. Although Yeats's obsessions were seen as slightly ridiculous at the time, his explorations into the world of magic and spiritualism did not do him any great harm.

Just as beliefs in witchcraft have not entirely died out in parts of rural Europe, the magical and esoteric traditions of the Renaissance magicians and philosophers have not lost all of their appeal among educated people. In the past few decades, there has been much scholarly research into the alchemical and magical traditions of the Renaissance. There are still some people, however, whose interest in those traditions comes not simply from historical curiosity, but from a persistent hope or belief that there may have been something in it after all.

Forms of magic made a comeback in the nineteenth century, when some educated people became attracted by mediums and their claims to be able to contact the souls of the dead.

White witches perform one of their ceremonies at the Long Man of Wilmington, a mysterious ancient figure marked out in stones on a hillside in southern England. There are now many groups of people who claim to practice pagan magic and religion.

REASON COMES UNDER SUSPICION

Magic has never quite gone away, even though for most of the nineteenth and twentieth centuries few people would admit to believing in magic for fear of being thought superstitious or silly. Magic has been seen as a source of entertainment and acknowledged as trickery and illusion, rather than being the crucial aid and potential terror of the past. However, the history of the twentieth century has shaken many people's faith in reason and technology as a force for progressive good. Some iconic events have hastened our disillusion. For example, the Nazis' attempt to wipe out Europe's Jewish population using technology and the industrial process has cast a dark shadow over the 'rational' nature of Western society. Of equal horror was the use of the atomic bomb against Japan, and the events of September 11th, 2001, when terrorists subverted the benign technology of the passenger airliner and the skyscraper to bring about the deaths of thousands of innocent civilians.

The power of technology and industrial and corporate organizations now seems to overshadow the individual's ability to control his or her life. Technology and reason once promised liberation from the anxious and uncertain struggle for survival that humanity has lived with for all its history. For many people today, we seem to be enslaved by technology and progress, rather than liberated by it. And it is not just the great horrors of the twentieth century that have shaken many people's faith in reason and technology. The almost frenetic, stressful lifestyle of many of the Western world's urban dwellers gives many people a yearning for some way of controlling the course of their lives. Magic, or magical ways of thinking, are coming back into fashion in the Western world, precisely because many people want to find some way that they can determine or alter their circumstances themselves.

New Age witches

In Britain in particular, the twentieth century saw a revival, or rather a reinvention, of witchcraft with the foundation of many 'Wiccan' covens. These self-confessed witches claimed to be practising an ancient religion, one that combined magic with the worship of a god and goddess, which the Wiccans assert is descended from the pagan fertility and nature worship of ancient Britain. But there is no evidence or record of this so-called ancient pagan religion. What the Wiccans have really done is to invent something new that contains only echoes of the cults and beliefs that existed in ancient times. This new religion has little to do with ancient paganism, and it also has no real connection to the witchcraft of earlier centuries.

The Wiccans naturally claim to practise only 'white' magic, and no one has any doubt that they are, by and large, well-meaning and sincere in their beliefs. The 'spells' and other magic practices of the Wiccans are an eclectic combination of many bits of old folklore, a few scraps of mythology, some borrowings from the writings of Renaissance magicians, and more practices of their own invention. Anyone is entitled to create a religion if he or she wishes, but Wicca has nothing to do with historical witchcraft.

As far as the belief systems of the villagers went, witches were never thought to be organized into covens. It was the paranoid witch-hunters of the organized and authoritarian Christian church who imagined witches as an alternative alliance, plotting to undermine and corrupt Christian society.

The covens of the modern Wicca are extremely varied in their practices and beliefs, and there is no overall organization. Some wear robes during their ceremonies, while others practise their magic naked. The idea that magic has to be done in a state of undress is certainly a modern idea. None of the wise-women or cunning men of sixteenth- and seventeenth-century Europe would have thought nudity necessary.

Charismatic people who gathered followers around them founded individual Wiccan covens. Dr. Gerald Gardener, who claimed to have been initiated into witchcraft by a hereditary witch – that is, someone who

Dr. Gerald Gardener established a coven of Wiccan witches in the 1940s. His group and others seek to recreate a witchcraft that they believe was once a benign nature religion.

claimed to be descended from witches – founded one such group in the 1940s. Such claims are impossible to prove or disprove, but any real continuity is very unlikely. Dr. Gardener wrote many books on the subject of witchcraft and founded a museum on the Isle of Man devoted to his ideas about witchcraft. Most of the Wiccan groups seem to include both men and women, although there are some that are exclusively female.

Many other groups claim to be witches of one kind or another. They follow a supposed nature-based religion, sometimes centred on the British Stone Age monument of Stonehenge, or the ancient British Druid religion, about which little is recorded. Although numerous fanciful beliefs have grown up around Stonehenge and pagan religions, few, if any, have any basis in historical fact.

MAGIC AND FICTION

Magic ceased to be an everyday reality for members of Western society in the eighteenth century. So now it is very easy for people to create their own systems of magic and mythology out of fairy tales and folklore. The beliefs of modern 'pagans' and 'witches' are really concoctions of various disconnected pieces of mythology and folklore, melded by their followers' imaginations.

Even non-believers have turned to magic to entertain people with stories of witches and magic that have little or no basis in the folklore of the past. The classic story and film *The Wizard of Oz* utilizes the now traditional image of the evil witch. In this story, however, the witches are forces of nature. There are two evil witches – one of the west and one of the east – and two good witches – one of the north and one of the south. Despite the fact that in the past witches were never imagined in such a way, the story has nevertheless become part of our own folklore of witches.

There is currently a boom in the production of television and film stories featuring witches and magic, with witches and the supernatural appearing as part of the struggles of teenagers in everything from television series such as

Buffy the Vampire Slayer to films such as *Practical Magic* and *The Craft*. Only a few decades ago, witches were most usually imagined as old crones. Stories that are part of this new breed, however, all possess the common thread of young women who can become witches and whose powers can be used for good, as well as for evil or harm. This does not mean that ambivalence about the powers of witches is no longer a feature – a common theme in these new stories is the unwise use of magic by young women, whose powers often turn out to be of dubious value. Stories with magic as their theme can reflect wider social concerns, and today it seems that the issues and difficulties young women face are the focus for concern. Fiction has long been a way of exploring problems that a society does not wish to face more openly.

THE ENDURING MAGIC OF STORY

As this book is being written, many across the world are enjoying the new films about the boy wizard Harry Potter and of J. R. R. Tolkien's epic story *The Lord of the Rings*. Both stories, in different ways, provide a world of magic in which the ordinary and mundane problems of everyday life are not merely forgotten, but transformed into a heroic landscape. In this world, the ordinary boy or the sleepy village hobbit can draw upon his innermost resources of heroism and triumph over evil to save his world and himself.

Stories such as these are as old as human history. The legends of King Arthur and his knights in medieval Europe, for instance, or of Odysseus in ancient Greece, provided sorely needed magic and romance for hard-pressed people trying to live in a difficult and often cruel world. Today, we need these stories every bit as much as humans always have, as a source of entertainment and comfort, rather than reality. We have learned the difference between magic and reality, and, however much we yearn for a return of magic, we would be wise to remember that it has always been an illusion, springing from our hopes and fears. It has never represented the reality of the world around us.

Witchcraft is no longer a reality for most people but the fascination remains, as can be seen in many stories and films, such as The Lord of the Rings: The Fellowship of the Ring, *which continually reinvent mythologies of magic.*

BIBLIOGRAPHY

Ankarloo, Bengt and Clark, Stuart (series eds.) *The Athalone History of Witchcraft and Magic in Europe Vol. 2.* University of Pennsylvania Press, Philadelphia, 1999.

Anon. (ed. and trans. Christine Fell) *Egil's Saga.* Dent, London, 1975.

Augustine (trans. Rev. E. B. Pusey) *The Confessions of Saint Augustine.* Dent, London, 1904.

Bede (trans. Leo Sherley-Price) *A History of the English Church and People.* Penguin, London 1955.

Briggs, Robin *Witches and Neighbours.* HarperCollins, London, 1996.

Cohn, Norman *Europe's Inner Demons.* Heinemann, London, 1975.

Dukes, Eugene D. *Magic and Witchcraft in the Dark Ages.* University Press of America, Maryland, 1996.

Evans-Pritchard, E. E. *Witchcraft, Oracles and Magic among the Azande.* Clarendon Press, Oxford, 1976.

Flint, Valerie I. J. *The Rise of Magic in Early Medieval Europe.* Clarendon Press, Oxford, 1991.

Gantz, T. *Early Greek Myth.* Johns Hopkins University Press, Baltimore, 1993.

Ginzburg, Carlo (trans. John and Anne Tedeschi) *The Night Battles: Witchcraft and Agrarian Cults in the Sixteenth and Seventeenth Centuries.* Routledge & Kegan Paul, London, 1983.

Ginzburg, Carlo (trans. Raymond Rosenthal) *Ecstasies: Deciphering the Witches' Sabbath.* Hutchinson Radius, London, 1990.

Hoffer, Peter Charles *The Devil's Disciples: Makers of the Salem Witchcraft Trials.* Johns Hopkins University Press, Baltimore, 1996.

Homer (ed. and trans. E.V. Rieu) *The Odyssey.* Penguin, London, 1945.

Horace (ed. and trans. P. Michael Brown) *The Satires.* Aris & Phillips, Warminster, 1993.

Jeffers, Ann *Magic and Divination in Ancient Palestine and Syria.* E. J. Brill, New York, 1996.

Kieckhefer, Richard *Magic in the Middle Ages.* Cambridge University Press, Cambridge, 1989.

Kirk, J. S. *The Nature of Greek Myths.* Penguin, London, 1974.

Kluckhorn, Clyde *Navaho Witchcraft.* Peabody Museum of American Archaeology and Ethnology, Cambridge, Massachusetts, 1944.

Macfarlane, Alan *Witchcraft in Tudor and Stuart England.* Routledge & Kegan Paul, London, 1970.

Malory, Sir Thomas (ed. Lumiansky, R. M.) *Le Morte D'Arthur.* Scribner, New York, 1982.

Marwick, Max (ed.) *Witchcraft and Sorcery.* Penguin, London, 1970.

Pinch, Geraldine *Magic in Ancient Egypt.* British Museum Press, London, 1994.

Quaife, G. R. *Godly Zeal and Furious Rage: The Witch in Early Modern Europe.* Croom Helm, London, 1987.

Rosenthal, Bernard *Salem Story: Reading the Witch Trials of 1692.* Cambridge University Press, Cambridge, 1993.

Sophocles (ed. and trans. E. F. Watling) *The Theban Plays.* Penguin, London, 1947.

Storms, Godfrid *Anglo-Saxon Magic.* Martinus Nijhoff, The Hague, 1948.

Thomas, Keith *Religion and the Decline of Magic.* Weidenfeld and Nicolson, London, 1971.

Walker, D. P. *Spiritual and Demonic Magic: From Ficino to Campanella.* Studies of the Warburg Institute, London, 1958.

Weisman, Richard *Witchcraft, Magic and Religion in Seventeenth Century Massachusetts.* University of Massachusetts Press, Amherst, Massachusetts, 1984.

Wilson, Stephen *The Magical Universe: Everyday Ritual and Magic in Pre-Modern Europe.* Hambledon and London, London, 2000.

INDEX

Note: Page numbers in *italics* refer to illustrations